MW01505181

Educational Leadership, Culture, and Success in High-Need Schools

A Volume in:
International Research on School Leadership

Series Editors:
Ross Notman
David Gurr
Elizabeth Murakami

International Research on School Leadership

Series Editors:

Ross Notman
University of Otago, New Zealand

David Gurr
University of Melbourne, Australia

Elizabeth Murakami
University of North Texas

Educational Leadership, Culture, and Success in High-Need Schools

Edited by

Elizabeth Murakami
David Gurr
Ross Notman

INFORMATION AGE PUBLISHING, INC.
Charlotte, NC • www.infoagepub.com

Library of Congress Cataloging-in-Publication Data

The CIP data for this book can be found on the LIbrary of Congress website (loc.gov).

Paperback: 978-1-64113-501-6
Hardcover: 978-1-64113-502-3
eBook: 978-1-64113-503-0

Printed in the United States of America

CONTENTS

Preface.. vii
Bruce Barnett

**Educational Leadership, Culture and Success in High-Need
Schools: Introduction from the Editors** xi
Elizabeth Murakami, Ross Notman, and David Gurr

PART I
CONTEXTUALLY-RESPONSIVE LEADERSHIP

1. **Principals in High-Performing, High-Poverty, Minority-
    Serving Schools in Texas** 3
    Elizabeth Murakami, and W. Sean Kearney

2. **Successful School Leadership That is Culturally Sensitive but
    not Context Constrained** 25
    David Gurr, Lawrie Drysdale, Fiona Longmuir, & Kieran McCrohan

3. **Principals' Work in High-Need Schools: Findings from Rio
    de Janeiro** 45
    Ana Cristina Prado de Oliveira and Cynthia Paes de Carvalho

PART II

LEADERSHIP FOR LEARNING

4. School Leadership for Social Justice and STEM: Findings from a High Need Secondary School in Belize........................... 65
Lorenda Chisolm, Noemi Waight and Stephen Jacobson

5. Leadership Practices for Equity and Excellence: An Exploratory Narrative of Two Principals of High-Need Elementary Schools in California................................. 85
Betty Alford

6. Creating a Culture for Learning in a High-Need Inner-City USA School: The Unique Leadership Challenges 103
Mette L. Baran and Glady Van Harpen

PART III

SUCCESSFUL EDUCATIONAL LEADERSHIP PRACTICE

7. Leadership in High-Needs/High Performing Schools: Success Stories from an Urban School District 131
Jami Royal Berry, Sheryl Cowart Moss, and Peryenthia Gore

8. Sustaining a Culture of Academic Success at a High-Needs Elementary School 149
Nathern S. Okilwa and Bruce Barnett

9. School Leadership Practices in Early Childhood Education: Three Case Studies from New Zealand 169
Ross Notman and Stephen Jacobson

Epilogue: Making World Connections: Educational Leadership in High-need Schools................................. 185
David Gurr, Elizabeth Murakami, and Ross Notman

Biographies.. 195

PREFACE

Bruce Barnett

This book is the fruition of research studies conducted by members of the International Leadership Development Network (ISLDN), which was established in 2010 as a joint initiative between the British Educational Leadership, Management, and Administration Society (BELMAS) and the University Council for Educational Administration (UCEA). Stimulated by the success of the International Successful School Principalship Project (ISSPP) and the International Study of the Preparation of Principals (ISPP), UCEA and BELMAS members participated in a series of discussions as to what might be researched under the banner of the ISLDN. Two areas of study have emerged: one group focuses on leadership in high-need schools, and the other examines leadership for social justice. This book captures studies conducted by research team members examining leadership in high-need schools.

The high-need schools project has evolved through various phases of work. Initially, our efforts focused on identifying what constitutes a high-need school context, which has been summarized in the introduction to this book. Our conceptualization relied on studies of turnaround school leaders who are striving to improve academically low-performing schools. The next phase of our work consisted of conducting a series of case studies in different cultural contexts. Using a set of common interview protocol questions, we pilot tested these interviews in several locations around the globe, including Australia, China, Malaysia, Nepal, Sweden,

Educational Leadership, Culture, and Success in High-Need Schools, pages vii–ix.
Copyright © 2019 by Information Age Publishing
All rights of reproduction in any form reserved.

and the United States. Revisions were made to the original protocol based on the feedback of principals, teachers, staff and governing body members, and parents who were interviewed. Based on these revisions, team members began conducting multi-perspective qualitative case studies across countries and within different school types. The cases explore a range of male and female principals primarily leading public-, state-, or government-supported schools in each country in different levels of education (early childhood centers, primary, secondary, special) and in different geographic locations (urban, suburban, rural, isolated).

The protocol obtains information from school leaders, senior staff, governing body members, teachers, parents, and students (if appropriate). Based on the researcher's discretion, additional interviews, focus groups, observations, and/or other data collection methods may be included. In addition to interview data, relevant documents are collected, such as school mission and vision statements, school development plans, school prospectuses, school review reports, professional development plans, newsletters, examples of media coverage, and other documents focusing on student learning.

This edited volume is the first book capturing information from various cultural contexts using our revised protocol. In particular, the chapters examine a diverse sample of high-need school leaders serving 19 schools across five countries (Australia, Belize, Brazil, New Zealand, and the United States). The cases examine rural, suburban, and urban settings; range from elementary to middle to high schools; and are located in government/public and charter schools. The principals also reflect tremendous diversity based on ethnicity, gender, and years of experience.

Overall, these chapters combine a rich blend of conceptual frameworks and leadership practices aimed at addressing the social and academic needs of their students, many of whom come from communities where families lack social and economic opportunities. The authors not only employ a host of existing conceptualizations (e.g., social justice, critical theory, school climate and culture, ethics) underlying the work of principals in high-need schools, but also create their own constructs based on their findings (e.g., advocacy leadership, hyper vigilance, intentionality). These conceptualizations complement the four elements (school culture and context, leadership for school improvement, expectations and unique contributions, and outcomes/impact/success) in the conceptual framework outlined by the editors in the introduction to the book.

The real contribution of this book, however, are the cases of the various high-need school leaders that capture their values, actions, and expectations for student success. On the one hand, the findings reveal how principals and leadership teams read the internal learning environment and shape the conditions for student learning. Numerous examples demonstrate how leaders intentionally develop relationships between themselves and their teachers, set direction for the school, develop the talents of teachers, redesign organizational structures and policies, establish culturally-responsive instructional practices, establish high expectations for student success, nurture a collective responsibility for student learning, and use data to inform their decisions. Rather than focusing exclusively on academic outcomes, these school leaders understand the importance of developing students' character, values, and career opportunities. On the other hand, the cases examine how high-need school leaders deal with the external environment, particularly working with parents and community members, many of whom have had negative educational experiences and are skeptical of schools. Excellent examples of authentic support for families are provided, including how to develop welcoming environments, provide assistance for young parents, and engage parents in meaningful school activities. Overall, these chapters capture school leaders' tireless advocacy for students' learning in extremely challenging social and economic conditions.

Although each chapter stands alone as an example of how leaders influence school culture for student success, the breadth of cases from different cultural contexts highlights nuances in how leaders read their internal and external environments and create contextually-relevant responses. These leaders clearly have inspired students, teachers, and parents in their school settings. We hope you, too, will be inspired by their deeds and words.

—Bruce Barnett
ISLDN Co-Director

EDUCATIONAL LEADERSHIP, CULTURE AND SUCCESS IN HIGH-NEED SCHOOLS

Introduction from the Editors

Elizabeth Murakami, Ross Notman, and David Gurr

This volume in the series *International Research on School Leadership* promotes the continuous conversation about educational leadership around the world as a means to generate a deeper and a more holistic understanding of their contribution, especially in high-need contexts in contemporary times. In this introductory chapter we present the purpose and significance of this volume in exploring school leadership as influencing the culture and school success, especially in challenging contexts of high-need schools.

As part of a global network entitled International School Leadership Development Network (ISLDN), scholars from different countries participate in this volume, generating a common understanding of leadership qualities critical to high-need schools, focusing on three areas: learning, leadership, and context. This network began while scholars from different countries networked during conventions. The University Council for Educational Administration (UCEA) , an organization that continuously supports global conversations about school lead-

Educational Leadership, Culture, and Success in High-Need Schools, pages xi–xix.
Copyright © 2019 by Information Age Publishing
All rights of reproduction in any form reserved.

ership through a center for the study of international school leadership, supported this initiative with the creation of a new role of Associate Director of International Affairs, around 2008. Opportunities to consolidate research networks with the British Educational Leadership, Management and Administration Society (BELMAS) on the quality and effectiveness of leadership and management further encouraged the activities of the group, and in the establishment of the ISLDN network. Scholars who are part of this network also migrated from other important research networks such as the International Successful School Prinicpalship Project (ISSPP), generating a productive cross-fertilization of ideas and conceptual advances in the field. Some chapters in this volume show how the research of these different networks overlap.

The ISLDN carries two major strands: One group of scholars focuses on social justice issues in educational leadership, and the other on high-need schools. The two groups meet jointly and separately during working meetings at UCEA and BELMAS, in addition to carrying separate retreats specific to the advancement of each topic. These meetings are focused on the development of common objectives and protocols, and in the reporting of results. The High-Needs Schools group is composed with more than 50 members in different universities around the world. The group finalized their research protocols in 2015, and we are proud to share this volume featuring the first results from this effort. Subsequent volumes and journal issues are concurrently planned to further inform the findings from this group as the research evolves.

RATIONALE FOR THIS VOLUME: SCHOOL LEADERSHIP AND THE IMPROVEMENT OF SCHOOLS

There has been a concern related to the improvement of schools in the past decades, especially when focusing on improving the quality of education. In educational leadership, the impact of school principals in the improvement of schools has been a concern among scholars. For example, in an early longitudinal study around the turn of the century, Hallinger and Heck (1999) summarized findings from studies around the world seeking to explain how school principalship impacts school effectiveness. These scholars observed that school leaders influenced the purpose, the structure of schools, the social networks and people. They also highlighted the importance of considering the context of school leadership, especially when comparing leadership across countries.

Other leadership studies valued curriculum and instruction as instrumental in changing schools, especially with a focus on poor communities (Heck, Larson, & Marcoulides, 1990; Leithwood & Montgomery, 1982). In studies observing poor urban areas where high-need schools can be found, instructional leaders were often perceived as assertive, strong, and directive (Bennett & Murakami, 2016; Hallinger, 2011; Leithwood & Montgomery, 1982). Hallinger (2011) perceived three important dimensions in the instructional leadership construct: The focus on the school mission and goals; the management of instruction; and the promotion of a positive school learning climate. When analyzing the limitations of instructional leadership, it was important to recognize that instruction is not the only focus principals carry in their positions. Hallinger (2003) also reflected on the effects of contextual variables, which would cause principals to adjust priorities accordingly, with more measurable results in smaller schools, and often, in elementary schools. In low-poverty schools, principals were more effective in demonstrating a clearer and uniform mission, especially when articulated collectively by all school stakeholders.

Hallinger (2003) further argued that a transformative characteristic in educational leadership impact schools. He perceived instructional leaders as culture builders, goal-oriented, and presenting a stronger focus on the school mission. He observed that transformational leadership models in education may have emerged out of dissatisfaction when instructional or traditional models of leadership positioned the principal at the center of instructional improvement—especially by means of power and authority. Leithwood and Jantzi (2000) added that transformational leadership provided a way to articulate collaborative and participatory ideas when innovating schools' improvement. Shared knowledge is at the center of transformational leadership, where the principal sets and models high expectations. These principals are perceived as motivating stakeholders in developing individual capacity. This trend was theorized by Hallinger (2003) as second-order change, where the leader creates conditions that link personal goals with organizational goals in order to effect first-order change—subsequently impacting school improvement. Measurable outcomes of transformational leadership have been shared in research through teacher or student engagement (Leithwood & Jantzi, 2000). However, there are perceived difficulties in isolating engagement when measuring principal leadership, as many variables can prevent engagement, such as school context, lack of resources, events affecting school climate, or student absenteeism, to name a few.

To date, the debate is not so much about instructional or transformational leadership, but rather that both are important, and that these need to be supplemented with other views of leadership (e.g. Day & Leithwood, 2007; Day & Sammons, 2013; Gurr, 2015; Pashiardis & Brauckmann, 2018). Indeed, contemporary views of transformational leadership incorporate instructional leadership, such as Leithwood's more recent view that includes setting directions, developing people, redesigning the organization, improving the instructional program and related practices (see Leithwood & Sun, 2012).

Scholars in educational leadership also recognized that principal leadership must be analyzed within the contexts in which schools exist (Dimmock & Walker, 2000; Hallinger, 2003, 2018). Halllinger (2003) attests that "the context of the school is a source of constraints, resources, and opportunities that the principal must understand and address in order to lead" (p. 346). In an expanded version of his instructional leadership view, he identified six contexts that influence schools: three contexts have a general influence on the school (economic, political and socio-cultural), and three contexts have direct influence on school leadership (community, personal and institutional) (Hallinger, 2018). Examples of contextual variables include aspects such as the school's structure and culture, size, fiscal investments, the type of local support and community participation, students' background, teachers' preparation, conditions and support, as well as the mutual investment of all stakeholders, including the principal, towards education.

There is evidence that in challenging contexts, the role of school leadership is even more important in influencing school success (Leithwood & Patrician, 2015; Leithwood & Riehl, 2003; Leithwood & Steinbach, 2003). Often cited, but often poorly attributed, it was in Leithwood, Louis, Anderson and Wahlstrom's (2004) report that the following claim was first stated: "Of all the factors that contribute to what students learn at school, present evidence led us to the conclusion that leadership is second in strength only to classroom instruction" (p. 70). Six years later, in the final report of this study, the claim was reaffirmed (Louis, Leithwood, Wahlstrom, & Anderson, 2010). Whilst this is a very important and influential claim, there is an equally important second part to the claim that is often ignored: That 'effective leadership has the greatest impact in those circumstances (e.g., schools "in trouble") in which it is most needed' (Leithwood, Louis, Anderson & Wahlstrom, 2004, p. 70). As such, the scholars in this volume are dedicated to the improvement of high-need contexts.

High-need schools in challenging contexts in this volume include not only socioeconomic issues influencing the performance of students. Such contexts include multiple factors impacting leaders, teachers, students, and their families, in schools situated in high-need areas. The selection of high-need schools and their context followed identifiers such as:

- Schools with a high percentage of individuals from families with incomes below the poverty line;
- School with a high percentage of teachers a different content area from their credential or preparation;
- Schools with a high turnover of teachers and/or leaders;
- Schools with a high percentage of non-native language speakers;
- Schools with a high percentage of historically/socially excluded or under-represented groups;
- Schools with a high percentage of indigenous groups;
- Schools with a high percentage of students with learning differences;
- Schools with a lack of basic physical infrastructure, and/or a high-need based on such events like a natural or manmade disaster

In addition, from an economic viewpoint, we perceive the importance to consider the critical connection between poverty and education. Tilak (2002) argued that "education poverty and income poverty mutually reinforce each other," and "poverty of education is a principal factor responsible for income poverty; and income poverty, in turn, does not allow the people to overcome poverty of education" (p. 198). When considering a culture of success, leadership that focuses on impacting schools in these high-need areas can bring about lessons on how to create sustainable environments for student learning. Therefore, the chapters in this volume considered the following research questions:

- What fosters student learning in high-need schools around the world?
- How can principals and teachers enhance individual and organizational performance in this context?
- How do internal and external contexts impact the individuals and the school?

The studies are developed using qualitative case studies respecting different countries school systems, and how children are divided into primary, secondary, or specialized schools. Studies also combine cases of schools in urban, suburban, and isolated contexts.

CONCEPTUAL FRAMEWORK GUIDING THE OBSERVATION OF LEADERSHIP IN HIGH-NEEDS SCHOOLS

When successful, school performance reflects the organization's cohesiveness—by aligning beliefs, people, structures and contexts (Marcoulides & Heck, 1993). In fact, Marcoulides and Heck (1993) asserted that organizational culture consists of three interrelated dimensions: "a sociocultural system of the perceived functioning of the organization's strategies and practices, an organizational value system, and the collective beliefs of the individuals working within the organization" (p. 209). They went further to claim that the strong integration of these dimensions can lead to school effectiveness. However, schools exist within multiple contexts and within wider cultural influences. As such, the nexus between leadership, culture, and success is explored observe the complex impact of leadership in these sites. A conceptual framework for school improvement in the study of high-need schools include broad considerations related to (a) leadership for school improvement; (b) school background and context; (c) expectations and unique contributions; and (d) outcomes, impact, and success:

The influence of contexts and cultures may have a profound impact on school success. Gurr (2014), for example, attests that whilst context and culture do influence the practice of leadership, there is now a substantial body of research across diverse contexts and cultures that indicate core characteristics and practices of successful leaders that transcend context and culture. These core characteristics and practices center on the well-known areas of setting direction, developing staff, leading organizational change and improving teaching and learning as observed by a number of scholars (Gurr & Day, 2014; Leithwood & Sun, 2012; Louis, Leithwood, Wahlstrom & Anderson, 2010).

Conceptual framework for the study of school leadership in high-need schools.

OVERVIEW OF THIS VOLUME

The exploration of the intersection of leadership practices (principal and others), school culture, and school success across different high-need contexts and cultures make this volume unique. Chapters in this volume present original investigations or reanalysis of empirical research enhancing our understanding of the interrelationship between leadership, culture and success through descriptions of practice that can contribute to lessons in leadership for school improvement. One of the chapters also extends the school context to explore successful leadership practice in an early childhood environment before children transition to elementary schools. Core thematic areas are identified in the chapters, taking their genesis from a range of research and conceptual literature:

1. Contextually-responsive leadership
2. Leadership for learning in a social justice context
3. Successful educational leadership practice

The first three chapters are grouped under the theme of **contextually responsive leadership**. Murakami and Kearney explore the philosophies and practices of four public school principals in South Texas, USA, as part of their research agenda to examine school leadership in high-poverty, high-minority public schools. Gurr, Drysdale, Longmuir and McCrohan report on multi-level contexts of three underperforming schools in Melbourne, Australia, all of which face challenges related to school closure and pressure to succeed. The third chapter by de

Oliveira and de Carvalho shares Brazilian research findings of principals working in challenging circumstances in high-needs schools in Rio de Janiero.

The second theme focuses on **leadership for learning**, often against a backdrop of seeking social justice for students to aid their learning. Chisolm, Waight and Jacobson trace the social justice impetus that led to the establishment of a secondary school in Belize, Central America. Alford's narrative study identifies leadership practices in two high-needs elementary schools in Southern California, USA, including culturally responsive, school-wide instructional practices. Baran and Van Harpen conclude with an analysis of challenges facing the leader of a K–8 high-needs school in Midwestern USA which resulted in a successful turnaround through an improved culture of learning and character building.

In the final focus on **successful educational leadership practice**, Berry, & Cowart Moss describe success stories of leadership from an urban school district in Southeastern USA. Here, a leadership model is proposed that is formed around the concepts of contextualization, hyper-vigilance and intentionality. Okilwa and Barnett share research findings from a study of academic success at a high-needs elementary school in South Texas, USA. Finally, Notman and Jacobson provide a parallel lens on a different education sector with case studies on successful leadership practices among three early childhood centers in New Zealand.

Each chapter in this book concludes with reflective questions or a reflective narrative for the reader, in the hope that it will engender further thinking and action about how best to lead and support student learning across early childhood, elementary and secondary school sectors, particularly in areas of high-need. As Notman, Morrison and McNae (2017) contend in advancing the cause of social justice in our high-needs schools and centers:

> We talk about closing 'achievement' gaps for disparate groups of children, but there are also 'opportunity' gaps for us to consider filling. Leadership is not a place where we sit. It is about being and it is about doing. It is about making a difference for all students. (p. 11)

In the quest to improve high-need schools, and understand strategies for principals dedicated to a variety of contexts, we hope this volume inspires researchers, policy-makers, and practitioners to join us in the quest to improve the quality of education among worldwide communities.

REFERENCES

Bennett, J. V., & Murakami, E. (2016). Heroic leadership redefined in the United States border context: Case studies of successful principals in Arizona and Texas. *International Studies in Educational Administration, 41*(1), 5–24.

Day, C., & Leithwood, K. (Eds.) (2007). *Successful principal leadership in times of change: An international perspective*. Dordrecht, The Netherlands: Springer.

Day, C., & Sammons, P. (2013) *Successful leadership: A review of the international literature*. Reading, England: CfBT Education Trust.

Dimmock, C., & Walker, A. (2000). Developing comparative and international educational leadership and management: A cross-cultural model. *School Leadership & Management, 20*(2), 143–160.

Gurr, D. (2014). Successful school leadership across contexts and cultures. *Leading and Managing, 20*(2), 75–88.

Gurr, D. (2015). A model of successful school leadership from the International Successful School Principalship Project. *Societies, 5*(1), 136–150.

Gurr, D., & Day, C. (2014). Thinking about leading schools, in C. Day & D. Gurr (Eds.), *Leading schools successfully: Stories from the field* (pp. 194–208), London, UK: Routledge.

Hallinger, P. (2003). Leading educational change: Reflections on the practice of instructional and transformational leadership. *Cambridge Journal of Education, 33*(3), 329–352, Doi: 10.1080/0305764032000122005

Hallinger, P. (2011). A review of three decades of doctoral studies using the principal instructional management rating scale: A lens on methodological progress in educational leadership, *Educational Administration Quarterly, 47*(2), 271–306.

Hallinger, P. (2018). Bringing context out of the shadow. *Educational Management Administration & Leadership, 46*(1), 5–24.

Hallinger, P., & Heck, R. (1999). Can leadership enhance school effectiveness? In T. Bush, L. Bell, R. Bolam, R. Glatter, & P. Ribbins, (Eds.), *Educational management: Redefining theory, policy, and practice* (pp. 178–190). London, UK: Paul Chapman Publishing.

Heck, R., Larson, T., & Marcoulides, G. (1990). Principal instructional leadership and school achievement: Validation of a causal model. *Educational Administration Quarterly, 26,* 94–125.

Leithwood, K., & Jantzi, D. (2000). The effects of transformation leadership on student engagement with school. *Journal of Educational Administration, 38*(2), 112–129.

Leithwood, K., & Montgomery, D. (1982). The role of the elementary principal in program improvement. *Review of Educational Research, 52*(3), 309–339.

Leithwood, K., & Patrician, P. (2015) Changing the educational culture of the home to increase student success at school, *Societies, 5,* 664–685.

Leithwood, K. A., & Riehl, C. (2003). *What we know about successful school leadership.* Philadelphia, PA: Laboratory for Student Success, Temple University.

Leithwood, K., Louis, K. S., Anderson, S., & Wahlstrom, K. (2004). *How leadership influences student learning.* New York, NY: The Wallace Foundation.

Leithwood, K., & Steinbach, R. (2003) Successful leadership for especially challenging schools. In B. Davies & J. West-Burnham (Eds.), *Handbook of educational leadership and management* (pp. 25–43). London: Pearson Education.

Leithwood, K., & Sun, J. (2012). The nature and effects of transformational school leadership: A meta-analytic review of unpublished research. *Educational Administration Quarterly, 48*(3), 387–423.

Louis, K. S., Leithwood, K., Wahlstrom, K. L., & Anderson, S. E. (2010). *Learning from leadership: Investigating the links to improved student learning.* Minneapolis, MN: University of Minnesota.

Marcoulides, G. A., & Heck, R. H. (1993). Organizational culture and performance: Proposing and testing a model. *Organization Science 4*(2), 209–225.

Notman, R., Morrison, M., & McNae, R. (2017). Introduction: Leading for social justice and high-needs in education. In R. McNae, M. Morrison, & R. Notman (Eds.), *Educational leadership in Aotearoa New Zealand: Issues of context and social justice* (pp. 1–13), Wellington, NZ: NZCER Press.

Pashiardis, P., & Brauckmann, S. (2018): New public management in education: A call for the edupreneurial leader?, *Leadership and Policy in Schools.* Retrieved from: https://www.tandfonline.com/doi/abs/10.1080/15700763.2018.1475575.

Tilak, J. B. G. (2002). Education and poverty. *Journal of Human Development, 3*(2), 191–207.

PART I

CONTEXTUALLY-RESPONSIVE LEADERSHIP

CHAPTER 1

PRINCIPALS IN HIGH-PERFORMING, HIGH-POVERTY, MINORITY-SERVING SCHOOLS IN TEXAS

Elizabeth Murakami, and W. Sean Kearney

An increased awareness of the effects of poverty in the United States has motivated us as scholars to examine school leadership in high-poverty, high-minority public schools. This study examines the philosophies and practices of four public school principals in south central Texas. School leaders, whose schools are closing the achievement gap and experiencing high levels of academic success despite socioeconomic factors were observed. The research question asks: How do principals in high-performing high-poverty minority-serving schools in Texas enhance performance at the individual and organizational levels? The findings reflect the schools and the contextual characteristics of the principals' campuses, showing how the context impacted learning in their schools. In addition, we report on the principals' work experience and commitment, evidenced in their school's mission as well as high-need characteristics of the families, including the neighborhood, family income and schooling. Finally, we report on the principals' advocacy in relation to generating authentic spaces for learning, teacher investments, and the development of support needed for students and their families.

Educational Leadership, Culture, and Success in High-Need Schools, pages 3–23.

Keywords: School leadership, high-poverty schools, high-minority schools

I know every student by name and face. You call a child by their name, and they say, "You know who I am?' Yes I do know who you are…you are very important and it's my job to know you well!" (Principal Interview, April 14, 2016).

INTRODUCTION

Every school around the world is unique, and not every leadership strategy that works on one school will necessarily work on another school (Duke, 2006; Herman et al., 2008). In the USA, an increased awareness of the effects of poverty has motivated the country to examine changes in the way high-poverty, high-minority public schools, defined in this context as high-need schools, can be led. School leaders, whose schools are closing the achievement gap and experiencing high levels of academic success in high-need areas in Texas are observed here. This study examines the philosophies and practices of four public school principals in south central Texas, considering Anderson's (2009) framework of advocacy leadership in the promotion and success of students in high-need schools. The research question asks: How do principals in high-performing high-poverty minority-serving schools in Texas enhance performance at the individual and organizational levels?

RATIONALE FOR OBSERVING PRINCIPALS IN HIGH-POVERTY AND HIGH-MINORITY SCHOOLS IN THE U.S.

There are factors important to the observation of school principals in high- poverty, high-minority schools in the USA. For example, when the No Child Left Behind Act of 2001 (NCLB) was adopted, the law required that students be tested yearly (in reading and math between grades 3 through 8, and once in upper secondary schools). NCLB required that students demonstrate progress where all students were to reach a "proficient level" by 2014. However, by 2015, the results showed that none of the states in the USA had gotten "all 100 percent of its students over the proficiency bar" (Klein, 2015, para. 7).

Many of the struggling students can be found in areas of poverty. Oftentimes schools presenting persistent underperforming patterns are located in high-need areas (Herman et al., 2008), and are underfunded. Funding in USA schools vary, where federal, state, and local funding is determined depending on the state and neighborhood in which the school is located (Brown, 2015). In fact, Foskett and Lumby (2003) remind us that simply enrolling children in schools does not necessarily guarantee that they will receive a quality education.

To address underperforming schools, the Department of Education has created what has been named School Improvement Grants (SIG)–specifically to support schools with persistent low academic achievement (United States Department of

Education, 2016). While this support was put in place, a concurrent movement at the governmental level to shrink public investment, especially in public education can be found (Anderson, 2009; Apple, 2001; Hursh, 2007). In this environment, competitiveness and results guide decisions regarding "who" or "what" should (or should not) be funded. To advocate for schools, Anderson (2009) called our attention to "market and test-driven educational reform [as] draining schools of authentic teaching and leading practices and making schools more racially segregated and unequal" (p. 1). Nonetheless, federal expectations for academic performance are the same for affluent schools, or those in high need areas. Hence, principals are restricted in the way inequitable social policies, resources and opportunities are redistributed in schools challenged by "inequities in resources and opportunities in American society" (Anderson, 2009, p. 15).

REVIEW OF LITERATURE: IMPROVEMENT OF HIGH-NEED SCHOOLS

Recognizing the condition of public schools in the USA. as confronting issues of high- poverty, especially in minority-serving schools, is humbling. Even though a large number of public schools around the nation are preparing students well, there is increased awareness of the effects of poverty which in the case of USA defines what can be considered high-need schools. In these schools, the concern of improving low-performing schools includes federal efforts in the Department of Education related to turning around schools presenting persistent low achievement.

In 2015 more than 1,500 schools around the country developed improvement interventions with the support of federal School Improvement Grants (SIG) (U.S. Department of Education, 2016). The grants define schools in need of improvement as in need of turnaround. Different states have developed plans to apply changes in areas such as: data-based decision making, performance monitoring, professional development, community engagement, quality improvement of staff, learning time, and improving English Language Learning (ELL) interventions. In relation to preparing educational leaders, a higher number of sites invested in recruiting, preparing, or changing leaders' skills and practices (U.S. Department of Education, 2015).

Can school leaders develop skills and practices to specifically address high-need school improvement? Current research indicates that school leaders positively impacting schools intervene at different levels, using multiple strategies (Brookover & Lezotte, 1979; Duke, 2014; Duke & Jacobson, 2011; Medina, Martinez, Murakami, Rodriguez, & Hernandez, 2014; Reeves, 2003). Duke (2006) argued that the following areas were shared by school personnel as positively affecting student achievement: leadership, policy, programmatic changes, processes and procedures, staff, classroom practices, parents and community involvement, as well as facilities. Oftentimes, this multifaceted approach includes impacting a vision and culture in schools while working directly with teachers to improve instructional strategies.

In addition, participants in other studies provided data related to what contributed (or not) to the success of students in high-need contexts. Areas of concern included: (a) student achievement and behavior, (b) school programs and organization, (c) staffing, (d) school system concerns, and (e) parents and community (Duke, Tucker, Salmonowicz, & Levy, 2007). In addition, Gurr, Drysdale, Clarke, and Wildy (2014), added important aspects of resilience and professional focus in the work of leaders as equally relevant in impacting changes in these high need contexts. In the context of Texas, Medina et al. (2014) highlighted leadership aspects in defining high-need schools "as institutions where students come with issues, concerns, academic, economic, social, emotional, physical deficits that have not been met and have not been addressed" (p. 93). They recognized that schools in high-poverty areas required enhanced principal and teacher involvement, especially because these areas would not necessarily offer programs engaging families, and economically depressed areas would not often have community centers or health centers. They argued that high need areas require leadership that brings in "pride, high expectations, and positive motivation" (p. 94), while getting teachers prepared through training, and accountable by motivating students and families to engage in learning activities.

Presenting on what they defined as the toughest low-performing high school cases in Texas, Duke and Jacobson (2011) focused their research on school structures, indicating the importance of principals in developing multiple strategies, which included partially replacing faculty and staff, streamlining student courses that guided them to completion, abandoning programs not conducive to student graduation, and replacing programs with those directly affecting authentic learning including Reading, Algebra and English, with concurrent support for English Language Learner students. In contrast, Kearney, Herrington, and Aguilar (2012) conducted studies focused on high performing, high minority, high poverty schools in Texas. Their research led them to conclude that successful high needs schools exemplify strong support structures such as active stakeholder involvement, robust relationships among both internal and external school constituents, and stable leadership over time.

The work of the principal in a high-needs school is complex, in this study we focus on the areas considered by scholars around the world to be the most fundamental (International School Leadership Development Network (ISLDN—isldn. weebly.com) including: learning (as in developing a school culture that fostered learning), leadership (as adapted to the needs of teachers, students, and families), and context (situated in a high-poverty region).

METHODOLOGY

This study uses a criterion sample and a phenomenological design. Creswell (2013) clarifies that phenomenological research helps us understand "what all participants of a research have in common as they experience a phenomenon" (p. 76). Common to all schools included in this study were characteristics of high-poverty, high-minority, and high performance in at least one core discipline. Phenomenological studies often provide the opportunity to understand the essence of the phenomenon (what) by incorporating how the experiences of individuals are shared. An adapted protocol from the ISLDN was used.

With representatives from more than 20 countries involved ISLDN scholars have examined each country's unique contexts (Barnett & Stevenson, 2016), reporting back for a global research network with the goal of determining qualities of leadership critical to leading high-needs schools focusing on three areas: leadership, learning, and context. This worldwide research initiative is supported by the British Educational Leadership, Management, and Administration Society (BELMAS) and the University Council for Educational Administration (UCEA). Questions asked by these scholars relate to the vision and goals for high-need areas, including building capacity of self and others in improving the condition of students, as well as leadership that contributes to individual and organizational performance of teachers, students, and community members. In this study we focused on leadership, asking, "How do principals in high-performing high-poverty minority-serving schools in Texas enhance performance at the individual and organizational levels?"

This study considers philosophies and practices of school principals related to multiple factors influencing the leadership in high-poverty and minority-serving schools. We consider the economic, political, and social landscape of the USA as influencing the work of educators, where school principals seem to need authentic advocacy in leading schools In this study's framework we considered leader behaviors and styles. For example, the Ohio State Studies in 1945 provided a way to examine leader behaviors and styles through constructs such as "Initiating Structure" (which related to leadership performance and outcomes), and "Consideration" (strongly related to leader and job satisfaction) (Judge, Picollo, & Ilies, 2004). Principals who employ such constructs in their leadership may be involved in observable strategies for school improvement. Anderson (2009) added more complexity to these structures by articulating that especially in high-need schools, leadership is immersed in the U.S.' national context—which means that the principal must not only be focused on structures and behaviors, but also dispositions – being an advocate for the promotion and success of students in high-need schools. The author calls for advocacy among leaders—with tactics and strategies that address economic and social injustices while improving schools and students' academic experiences. In this light, "advocacy leaders are those who can hold onto the idea that social justice for low-income students is much more than a question of raising test scores or even increasing authentic academic achievement" (Anderson, 2009, p 179).

Based on Anderson's conceptual ideas, we generated an adapted advocacy leadership conceptual framework (Figure 1.1) that considers three areas of ad-

With teachers, principals:

- model authentic connections with students
- guide teachers to participate in authentic cognitive and non-cognitive pedagogies connected to real student issues
- safeguard teachers from stresses related to reform-imposed mandated policies and scripts

Advocacy in generating authentic spaces for student learning

Advocacy in generating authentic teacher investments

Advocacy in developing authentic support for students and families

Advocacy leadership is based on:

- employing ethical principles of high education quality and equitable public education
- generating a safe space for students from where they are in their academic development
- being willing to work outside of comfort zones- taking risks to seek causes not symptoms
- addressing stressors of low-income students and parents proactively

Principals advocate for community relations by:

- being skeptical of systems and policies that trap students and families in high need areas
- developing authentic connections with parents and community
- creating structures of support for students and families in high need areas

FIGURE 1.1.   Advocacy Leadership Framework in High Need Schools (adapted from Anderson (2009)

vocacy for principals in high need schools: (a) advocacy in generating authentic spaces for student learning (where students and families get a sense of safety, stability, and students are respected and recognized); (b) advocacy in generating authentic teacher investments (where teachers find support in their professional growth and are prepared to support students); and (c) advocacy in developing authentic support for students and their families (where schools consider challenges families confront in high-need areas to involve families in the students' learning).

SITE AND PARTICIPANT SELECTION

In order to examine leaders building individual and organizational capacity in high-needs schools, we used a similar selection criterion to those provided by Reeves' (2003, 2004) model, whose work sought to identify common correlates of high-performing high-poverty high- minority campuses so that such strategies can be duplicated elsewhere. Reeves himself builds off of the work of Levine and Lezotte (1990) who similarly sought to identify correlates of high-performing schools in general. We observed Geels (2002) multi-perspective approach in the analysis of these schools which argues for combining human agency, social structures, and organizations in order to observe strategies and functionalities. The author argues, "The different levels are not ontological descriptions of reality, but analytical and heuristic concepts to understand complex dynamics…" (p. 1259), which for this study, relates to school leadership.

The first step was to identify the criteria by which schools would be selected for possible inclusion within this study. The determination was made to utilize the 85/85/85 threshold in which at least 85% of students were ethnic minorities, at least 85% of students qualified for free or reduced lunch, and at least 85% of students were passing standardized achievement tests in Reading, Math, Science, or Social Studies. While it is certainly true that there are many ways to identify school success, the authors of this study were particularly interested in learning from principals of schools that had successfully closed the socioeconomic and ethnic achievement gaps on standardized tests in at least one of the academic disciplines.

To determine whether there were any schools meeting these criteria in South Central Texas, data were obtained through a criterion sample (Maxwell, 1996). Data from the state accountability reporting instrument entitled, "Accountability Ratings by Region: Region 20: San Antonio" (Texas Education Agency, 2016a) informed the preliminary screening of principals. We examined the most recent year of testing and demographic data for 709 schools in this region and identified 10 schools that met the selection criteria.

Data Collection

The data collection involved inviting principals from the high-performing campuses identified through state reports to serve on an interview panel. From the 10 principals invited, 6 agreed to participate. The panel presentation was audiotaped and transcribed. Questions for the panelists were formulated utilizing the ISLDN protocols which have been piloted in nine locations around the globe including Australia, China, Malaysia, Nepal, Sweden, and the United States. During the panel, principals reflected on the following arenas: (a) developing a culture of learning on campus; (b) strategic intentions in the first few months of appointment; (c) short and long-term goals to build capacity in the school; and (d) their most significant individual and organizational leadership contributions to this school.

We contacted the principals from the panel for possible individual interviews and possible visits to campuses. Four (N=4) agreed to do so. These four principals represented a cross section of gender and ethnicity. They similarly represented the gender/ethnic demographic characteristics of the region. Two principals were male, two were female. Two principals were Hispanic, one principal was African-American, and one principal was White. Two participants were principals of public elementary school, one was principal of a charter middle school, and one was principal of a magnet high school.

The school visits included not only interview with principals, but also classroom visits, revision of documents related to the principals' activities, and events. The interviews were recorded and subsequently transcribed. The features of the principals and schools are summarized in Table 1.1; pseudonyms are used for all principals and schools.

TABLE 1.1. Principals in High Need Schools—Campus Information*

Principal	Type of School	Gender of Principals	Ethnicity of Principals	Number of Students	Ethnicity of Students	Percent of Students Qualified for Free or Reduced Lunch	High Performance Area	Title I
Ms. Avila	Public Elementary	F	Hispanic	390	Hisp: 98.7 A.A. 0.5 White 0.5	94.4	Reading Science Math	Yes
Mr. Beal	Public Elementary	M	White	863	Hisp: 70.1 A.A. 14 White 13	90.4	Science	Yes
Mr. Cisneros	Public Elementary	M	Hispanic	379	Hisp: 92 A.A. 4 White 2	86	Reading Science Math	Yes
Ms. Dee	Charter Middle	F	African American	188	Hisp: 69 A.A. 26.6 White 3.2	93.6	Math	Yes

*Source: Texas Education Agency (2016b), results reflecting 2013–2015 patterns. Top 25% indicates that the campus is demonstrating excellence in closing performance gaps in the top quartile in comparison with 40 other schools with similar demographics in the state. Ethnicity of students' abbreviations: Hisp (Hispanic); A.A. (African American).

Data Analysis

Transcripts from group and individual interviews were coded in order to identify common themes that emerged endemically from the data. Information of schools was collected through public documents and a table was developed to treat each campus as a case. Analysis of schools, interviews, observations within campuses, and collection of documents. Data were analyzed through the conceptual framework observing principals' achievements and their advocacy in generating authentic spaces for student learning, teacher investments, and support for students and their families.

We observed the possibility of some overlap between correlates of high-performing high-poverty minority-serving schools and high-performing schools in general (Duke 2014; Herman et al., 2008). Hence, within this study, we note that the experiences of these principals were not incompatible with prior research in regard to correlates of high-performing schools. One potential limitation with both Reeves' (2004) construct and the framework forwarded by Levine and Lezotte (1990) we identified, is that the correlates in both sets of research vary markedly from one campus to another, making duplication difficult.

This is naturally a limitation of the current study as well. What is currently in place in a school, as well as transformative ideas from its principal informs each campus' uniqueness and are only replicable in similar contextual U.S. conditions. Nonetheless, we believe the data yielded from the aforementioned cases has the potential to provide lessons which may be useful to principals of similarly structured high-poverty high-minority campuses.

FINDINGS

In this study we examined principals in high-performing high-poverty minority-serving schools in Texas, observing how they enhanced performance at the individual and organizational levels. First, we report on the principals and the contextual characteristics of their campuses. We included the principals' work experience, school's mission as displayed or articulated in the school documents, as well as information on the school location in terms of high-need area characteristics and families' income and schooling. Following, we report on the identified principals' advocacy in relation to generating authentic spaces for learning, teacher investments, and the development of support needed for students and their families.

School Contexts: The Principals and their Campuses

Ms. Avila grew up in the same school district where she is a principal. She in her third year as a principal at Angelina Elementary, which is a public school. The campus is on the west side of town where she lives. She was a teacher in a middle school, and high school before leading the elementary school. The zip code in which the school resides has 58,811 inhabitants. 40% of families in this area rent their homes (City Data, 2017). 89% of the residents are Hispanic, 8% are White, and 2% are African American. The estimated median household income is $30,153. The cost of living index in the area is 13%lower than the US average. Only 12 percent of the population who are over 25 years of age hold a bachelor's degree or higher (City Data, 2017). The campus' motto is excellence, honor and pride, and the campus adopts the district's mission statement which includes the purpose of having every child graduate and is prepared to be a contributing member of the community. The average years of experience among teachers was 13 years (Texas Education Agency, 2016a).

Mr. Beal is an experienced principal and educator at Bastrop Elementary, which is a public school. He served four years as assistant principal and nine years as principal on this campus. Prior to serving this campus, he taught in rural and inner-city schools as a bilingual teacher. The zip code in which this school is situated has 21,040 inhabitants, 48% of whom rent their homes (City Data, 2017). 51% of residents are White, 30% are Hispanic, and 9% are African American. The cost of living index in the area is 12%lower than the US average. The estimated median household income is $56,628. Twenty nine percent of the adults over 25 years of age hold a bachelor's degree or higher (City Data, 2017). The school's mission expresses that all children will receive a quality education that will enable them to be successful in a global society. Their motto is to create an environment where students will work hard, but also have fun and develop as inquisitive learners. The motto is available in Spanish and English in their website. The average years of experience among teachers was also 13 years (Texas Education Agency, 2016a).

Mr. Cisneros has been a principal for 12 years with experience in Middle and High Schools and is in his first year at this Public/Magnet High School. Historically, this is one of the oldest school buildings in the heart of downtown. The zip code the school serves has 1,083 inhabitants, 89% of families rent their homes (City Data, 2017). The population is 49% Hispanic, 36% White, and 11% African American. The estimated median household income is $224,753. The cost of living index in the area is 3% lower than the US average. 25% percent of the population over 25 years of age hold a bachelor's degree or higher (City Data, 2017). The school adopts the district's mission to prepare all students to graduate and be educated so they can become contributing members of society. The school has changed focus since its inception, even changing names. Once a comprehensive high school, the decreasing student population in the area required the district to consider whether closing or changing the focus of the school to a Magnet (providing more specialized education for students with high ability in high need areas). This school is public but accepts applications from students from any area of the city. At this preparatory high school, Mr. Cisneros sees himself as a teacher of teachers, building connections fruitful for students' success. The school ranked number 13 in the city with its current focus on pre-law and pre-med career paths.

The average years of experience among teachers was 7.5 years (Texas Education Agency, 2016a).

Ms. Dee began her career as a science teacher, and was the founding principal of Cameron Middle School, which is a charter school. She had been a principal for over 15 years and sees herself as an instructional leader. The zip code in which the school is situated has 42,370 inhabitants, although students from this charter school also come from other neighborhoods. About 55 percent of families rent their homes in this neighborhood (City Data, 2017). 65% of the residents are Hispanic, 24% are White, and 3% are African American. The cost of living index in the area is 15% lower than the US average. The estimated median household income is $41,430. Twenty one percent of the population over 25 years of age hold a bachelor's degree or higher (City Data, 2017). The school purposefully targets economically disadvantaged students who are interested in learning. The school specializes in preparing these students in small classrooms using innovative strategies. The school adopts the district's mission to educate, motivate, and nurture all students with the use of evolving methods and technology, preparing them today for tomorrow's challenges. Their mission is to innovate, adapt and excel to make dreams happen. The average years of experience among teachers was 8 years (Texas Education Agency, 2016a).

Although student populations for all four campuses in this study are high minority (>85% non-White), high poverty (>85% of students qualifying for free or reduced lunch), this is not necessarily a reflection of the neighborhood's zip codes in which these schools reside. The data indicate this disparity is attributed to an aging population of wealthier white residents without school aged children residing in the same zip code with a younger, less affluent minority community with school aged children.

All principals in this study served high-need neighborhoods, with high-minority student populations. In these neighborhoods, the adult population holding bachelor's degrees is lower than the state or national average. The income level is also lower than the national average for three of the four zip codes in which these schools reside, and one of the campuses relied on its configuration to continue to serve an area with a declining population. Principals showed dedication to the high need area they served, either by creating schools, growing up as part of the community, or serving the same school district for over 10 years. Interestingly, even when prompted, none of these principals provided formulas for improving a specific discipline or grade level. Even in individual interviews, these principals were intentional about creating schoolwide support when developing a culture of learning as a way to generate high performance in different disciplines. A grounded theory approach (Corbin & Strauss, 1990) was used to develop a conceptual framework for how principals within this study provide advocacy leadership for their campuses. Following we present their insights about advocacy in high-need schools.

Advocacy as Generating Authentic Spaces for Learning: Setting High Expectations

In generating authentic spaces for learning, we focused on high quality education and equitable opportunities for students by asking principals about the development of a culture of learning. Advocacy in this case may include principals "willing to take risks to make it happen," argued Anderson (2009). These principals would be willing to work outside of their (or their teachers') comfort zone to set high expectations for all stakeholders on campus. All of these principals set high expectations. As Mr. Beal put it, "Set the expectation high and do not look back."

All four principals seemed to focus on developing a culture where all students were exposed to challenging learning opportunities regardless of the development they acquired prior to enrolling in the school. Principals emphasized they would not allow students to be railroaded by restrictions set by others or programs that seemed to be created for others. According to Ms. Dee, "On our campus everybody takes the Advanced Placement (AP) class. It's not something for a select group of students. Everybody will not make an A but everybody takes the AP class (because) that is the best curriculum." The high school principal added, "Will everybody go to college? That's not a guarantee, but everybody has to complete the Apply Texas application on my campus. That's mandatory or I won't sign their diploma."

Principals were alert and proactive about stressors in high-poverty realities for students and parents. Ms. Avila, who grew up in the same neighborhood as her students reflected:

> I tell students that things are going to get hard and things are going to get screwed up. But you know what? You have to decide whether or not you want this or not—and bottom line—that decision is yours. I try to lead by example and when people ask me where I am from, I get excited because I came from poverty and I came from probably a chance of nothing—and was able to kind of stay in my district and show my kids I can be an example…not only to the students at school and teachers, but to my own children.

In addition, these principals were found teaching alongside their faculty. Chenoweth and Theokas (2013) highlight how principals in high-poverty schools define themselves by focusing on instruction first. The principals in this study showed an authentic purpose and intent in creating a culture of learning and spaces for high expectations. Visits to campuses showed that, particularly in elementary schools, a close connection with teachers was necessary to set the tone for high expectations, as well as a continuous reminder of a safe and stable space for learning.

Advocacy as Generating Authentic Teacher Investments: Knowing and Letting Your Students Get to Know You

Content knowledge and mastery of pedagogies is a significant part of teachers' experience in order to achieve levels of success with their students demonstrating high performance. In the campuses included in this investigation, the faculty body averaged between 7.5 and 13 years of experience (Texas Education Agency, 2016a). In addition, principals developed mechanisms to support teachers. A large part of the principal's role related to the support for teacher investments. Mr. Cisneros reflected that he believes many of the teachers at Delta choose to stay at this school due to the authentic recognition they receive for their contributions. Interestingly, Mr. Cisneros, Mr. Beal, and Ms. Dee all highlighted relationships as the base for the high-performance of students. Ms. Dee put it this way:

If you have that one teacher that's really great and successful in the classroom, 100 percent of those kids will pass standardized tests at the end of the year. But if the rest of the teachers do not perform the same, you're still a low performing campus. So, it is not the one person who does it, it is the team. So, I focus on motivating everybody and encouraging everyone all the time—that is, the team work that is going to get us through in the end and we stay on that in everything we do.

Mr. Beal used faculty meetings to generate all-staff action research processes that included review of student work by peer teacher teams, reflection journals about each other's classroom visits, and a review of student work to provide input for enhanced pedagogies. This structure of collaboration took time to develop when the principal was new, but once all teachers became aware of the collective campus performance and learned how to support one another's needs.

Building relationships with students, parents and staff is a key part of the principal's job. Especially in smaller schools, principals often pride themselves in knowing every student by name. Anderson (2009), reminds us that schools with depersonalized hierarchies create inauthentic structures, generating inequitable status quo environments leading to unjust practices. This highlights the need to examine authentic relationships in high-need schools. Ms. Dee put it this way:

I know every student. One of the very first things I do at the beginning of the year is name associations, so I know every student by name and by face. You call a child by their name, and they say, 'You know who I am?' Yes, I know who you are. Because it is very important, and it is my job and I make it a key thing to know every student and to be able to call them by name so that they know I know them.

In schools with smaller populations, the task is not as challenging as in a campus with over 800 students. Thus, the size of school can threaten the impact of authentic connections with students, teachers, and families. In these cases, principals can adopt other strategies to create connections. For example, Mr. Cisneros said, "It's important for you to talk to your students. It's important for them to hear you on the PA. It's important for them to see your door open, to know that you're available to serve their needs as well."

Another strategy used by a principal in this study related to putting structures in place encouraging teachers to get to know their students. As Ms. Dee put it, "Each teacher has a small group. We try not to have more than 13 per teacher. That's your family. You know their birthdays, and you plan (based on their needs). Sometimes it's physical, sometimes it's academic, so they support each other." Classroom visits indeed showed more work in small groups, and the teachers dedicating time to different degrees of development across the groups.

Relationship building is a two-way street and an important component of authenticity. Anderson (2009) highlighted that authenticity is exceedingly difficult unless the values of equity and democracy are practiced through authentic connections. Ms. Dee explained her approach this way, "Allowing me to be me and celebrate the diversity I have in my culture allowed me to embrace the diversity of the culture of the other kids and if I wasn't afraid to celebrate me, they weren't afraid to celebrate who they were and where they came from." In creating authentic connections with students, the principal related to her own family reality to connect with students: "We could talk about my past, my family picking cotton when my dad said, 'My kids will not pick cotton. I don't know what they're going to do but they will not pick cotton.' I pick everything else [jokingly referring to picking up after students around the school], but I did not pick cotton. And to be able to share that with kids and say, hey, this is not something that was just in a book. Now, what's your story?" Ms. Dee talked about her attempts to learn Spanish:

> I don't speak (much) Spanish, but I say, 'Hijole,' and all the kids go, 'Oh Miss, you're so cool.' Hijole, yes, c'mon. You know I am not afraid to try and I do these things and we break down barriers and then it doesn't matter what gender, what race, what economic disability or whatever you have, we are all the same. We are all trying to achieve something.

An additional strategy for improving student performance was grouping students in advisory groups where the teacher could interact with a small family structure. Ms. Dee shared:

> Advisory is a very powerful thing when it is used as a proper tool. Our advisories are called Personal Learning Communities (PLC) for the students and they are named for one of the school's core values and the year of their graduation. So, you may belong to Respect 2014 or Respect 2016, depending on when you graduate. That's a small family that is built with a teacher leader for their group and that teacher becomes a surrogate parent for those students.

Connecting to real student issues help teachers understand the scope of their advocacy. The same principal told an interesting story about students supporting one another:

One year we had students who were upset, arguing in the classroom. They were brought to the office. In their PLC group they learned about one of their team members, he had never passed the Math on his end of year assessments, but he said whenever everyone gets up and turns in their test, it makes him feel dumb if he is still working. So, people in his PLC agreed that no one would turn in their test until he's done. So, the girls got into an argument. Thank God it was on a practice test day! One said, 'You turned your test in early!' And the other one said, 'I thought he was finished!' That year the young man who had never passed the test, passed the Math assessment for the first time. It was because of the work of the team.

The family structure in high-need schools seemed to bring a sense of family that was well accepted by students as they began to support each other towards academic success.

In this era of accountability, educators and administrators in high-need schools are often held accountable for low student performance. Anderson (2009) argues that "While high-stakes accountability targets underperforming schools in an attempt to 'motivate' teachers to teach better, it does so with a punitive, zero tolerance policy that lacks understanding of what motivates professionals" (p. 12). Students are not the only ones who need to feel supported. In fact, when teachers do not feel supported by their administration, this can lead to dissatisfaction and resignations. Ms. Avila got some inside information just before she stepped into her current principal role:

Prior to me getting there, one of the teachers heard that they were getting a new principal and she saw one of my teachers (who knew me) when I was an AP, and asked, "What do you know about (this principal)? How is she with discipline? And (the teacher who knew me) was like, "Oh yeah, she'll support you." She called a bunch of teachers that night and said, 'Look, pull your transfers. Let's stay. The only thing they were lacking (under the previous administration) was support.

This same principal emphasized the leader's presence in the classroom. As she put it, "I never forget what's really important, and it's that teacher in the classroom, so I always keep that in mind and I still teach on occasion, staying close to what's going on in the field, in curriculum, in instruction." Mr. Cisneros called attention to buffering district demands for every group of students (e.g., behavioral issues, special education issues, tiered guidelines) reminding teachers that these are not the only students teachers should be focused on. Mr. Beal summed up this concept by saying, "It is by focusing on every student that we will create a culture of learning."

In creating authentic teacher investments, Hargreaves and Fullan (2013) argued that when developing teachers, it is important to perceive their commitment, such as enthusiasm, and dedication to a moral purpose. They separated commitment capital from capability which relates to managing students, knowing content, and the students' different degrees of instruction. It is equally important for principals to focus on building the capacity of adults (Chenoweth & Theokas,

2013) especially in safeguarding teachers so they can develop commitment and capabilities in order to achieve success in high-need schools.

Advocacy in Developing Authentic Support for Students and Families

In their roles, principals are expected to develop connections with families and communities in high-need areas. Principals advocating for community relations according to the conceptual framework adopted, are ethical but also skeptical of systems or policies that do not contribute to students and families' engagement. Knowing what you believe is important and being willing to act on those beliefs was the final common theme connecting these four high- performing principals. Ms. Avila spoke of advocating to parents and teaching them to enforce the importance of schoolwork. She said her teachers talk to parents and "ask them to put excuses to the side." Ms. Avila focused on structures of support that families could cultivate, and continued:

> We have to be careful with how we approach things. We have to be careful with coming on too strong but at the same time we can't nurture everything because if you do that sometimes you start playing into the excuses and you don't push any further, you stay right there with them at those excuses so you kind of have to dig a little deeper and sometimes that's uncomfortable, and sometimes that's uncomfortable for me because then those parents come to me and they're like, 'She talked to me like this…or she asked this…' which I respond, 'What are your expectations? What do you want for your child? What was uncomfortable about that?' Because sometimes it is uncomfortable to hear that your child is not where they need to be.

When developing authentic connections with students, Mr. Cisneros spoke of his belief in the importance of graduation. He said:

> My first campus was an alternative school. Students used to call themselves dropouts. (I would say) You are a drop in, not a dropout, because you are here. As long as you are here, in this building, you are going to make it. And so, we would graduate 20 year olds. It was the 'can do' attitude that you had to share with your students on a daily basis. When students would miss school, we would go find them and bring them back. Our whole mission was to graduate those students.

Ms. Avila emphasized safety on her campus. She noticed a lack of order in the way children were being picked up at the end of the day, so she moved the students into the gym and dismissed them one at a time. "The parents fought me. The district called me I do not know how many times. I had to mediate with a parent because she was upset about how I organized dismissal. (The parent said) 'That's a long line.' I said ma'am, but you know what? I would want to stay in line if I knew that my kid was in a safe spot. I think that safety comes first."

Principals were proactive in creating or adapting structures of support for students and families in high-need areas. However, in developing areas of authentic support for students and their families, we recognized that these principals were mainly focused on establishing the schools as part of the community, by informing and preparing parents of the presence of schools as spaces where their children could, in a shared space, and with dedicated and authentic purpose, become more prepared to confront academic and societal challenges.

All of the neighborhoods in which these schools are located have low levels of collegiate education, as demonstrated by the percentage of adults with bachelor's degrees or higher (City Data, 2017). This could easily contribute to a culture of low expectations. Duke (2012) emphasizes that it is crucial for low-performing schools to function like high-performing schools. He says: "Little consideration has been given to the possibility that schools serving large numbers of disadvantaged and low-achieving students might be better served by developing modes of organization and operating procedures uniquely suited to their circumstances" (p. 23). Principals in this study indicated that advocating for authentic connections was more about generating, innovating, or reaffirming the development of a schoolwide culture of high expectations with families, teachers, and students, than necessarily aspiring to be like their high- performing counterparts.

DISCUSSION

This study asked: How do principals in high- performing high-poverty minority-serving schools in Texas enhance individual and organizational performance? The results of this study correlate well with much of the extant literature in this area. Based on the feedback gleaned from the principals we spoke with, we feel Medina et al. (2014) definition fits well, in which they define high needs schools as "Institutions where students come with issues, concerns, academic, economic, social, emotional, physical deficits that have not been met and have not been addressed" (p. 93). We perceive these leaders as having the responsibility to develop authentic connections with students through pride, high expectations and positive motivation.

This study employed a grounded theory approach in which a conceptual framework was employed based on Anderson's (2009) concept of advocacy leadership. The responses from the principals within this study confirm our belief that Anderson (2009) was correct in his argument that it is important for leaders to advocate for the common good, particularly in educational systems with unequal resources. We recognized the extensive work of scholars developing research on turning around low-performing schools similar to the ones observed in this study. The principals talked about common concerns as shared in previous research which included issues of leadership, processes and procedures, parents and community involvement, as well as additional issues, such as all-school professional development, small advisory support groups for students, and personal, or authentic connections with school stakeholders. According to both Anderson (2009) and the principals interviewed for this study, advocacy leadership is essential within high-needs schools.

Additionally, the responses from principals who participated in this study aligned well with many of the ISLDN protocols. Specifically, principals in this study focused on developing a school culture that fostered learning, encouraged authentic teacher investments, and were led by principals who advocated for students, and families in schools servicing a high-poverty region. All principals were deeply rooted on their campuses, having a long history with their school districts.

Conclusion and Implications

All of the principals in this study chose to work in challenging low-income areas, seeing education as a social responsibility and feeling rewarded when enriching the students' sociocultural capital to improve students' experiences, and all were highly successful at achieving student success within these contexts. We concur with Anderson (2009) that educators are held accountable for low student performance without considering larger societal and contextual limitations. Low performance is often linked to child poverty, lack of resources, health, safety and many other factors students face in high-need areas. Reflecting on educators working in high-need schools, Anderson (2009) stated:

> …It seems that society was exclusively holding them [educators] accountable for low student performance. They expected to be held accountable and wanted all mediocre teachers and principals be held accountable as well. But this new system was not accountability in the authentic sense that any professional expects to be held accountable; rather it was a kind of accountability that was punitive and humiliating, like an angry mob searching for a scapegoat. (p. 23).

Defining what authentic advocacy looks like is crucial in this age of accountability. Implications for future study include the further observation of advocacy as a consistent characteristic of high minority communities with high performing schools. According to the principals within this study, there are three specific ways that school leaders can advocate for high-need campuses, confirming some of Anderson's findings:

1. Advocate for authentic spaces for learning, where principals set high expectations, create spaces of sustainability and establish a routine for authentic student learning;
2. Advocate for authentic teacher investments, where knowing and letting students get to know adults in schools made connections for students tangible using their own stories or language; and
3. Advocate for authentic support for students and families, where parents can trust that their students will be in a safe space and receive quality education through authentic support.

This study's findings were also in agreement with studies related to school leadership and change (Duke, 2012). The critical observation of systemic economic concerns may be important in a study of school leaders that advocate for students to be successful academically. Academics and community support was evidenced as closely tied in these schools, where teaching was not only about content knowledge and test results. These principals demonstrated the essentials of relationality and connecting in authentic ways with students. We reflected on Duke's (2012) inquiry about impacting schools where he asked: "Do the practices and processes that have come to be associated with school turnarounds constitute true reforms? Or do they represent time-tested strategies that low-performing schools simply have failed to implement successfully?" (p. 22). After the development of this study, we argue that the successful implementation of practices and processes require leadership advocacy that bring about authentic relations in schools as part of educational reform. Principals in high-need schools not only chose to work in high need schools, but were a stalwartly presence, where with teachers, they generated authentic levels of individual and organizational commitments.

Questions for the Reader's Consideration

1. How can authentic commitments be developed by principals and teachers, particularly those who are new to the campus or new to the profession?
2. How can principals assigned to a new campus demonstrate authentic commitment to this school's community from day one?
3. How long does it take for a principal to learn about the community and strategize with teachers and families about the steps needed to improve students' performance? And what initial steps can a principal take to facilitate this process based on the examples in this study?

REFERENCES

Anderson, G. (2009). *Advocacy leadership: Toward a post-reform agenda in education.* New York, NY: Routledge.

Apple, M. W. (2001). Comparing neo-liberal projects and inequality in education. *Comparative Education, 37*(4), 409–423.

Barnett, B. G., & Stevenson, H. (2016). Leading high poverty urban schools. In S. Clarke & T. O'Donogue (Eds.), *School leadership in diverse contexts* (pp. 23–42). Oxfordshire, UK: Taylor and Francis.

Brookover, W. B., & Lezotte, L. W. (1979). *Changes in school characteristics coincident with changes in student achievement.* East Lansing, MI: Institute for Research on Teaching, Michigan State University.

Brown, E. (2015). In 23 states, richer school districts get more local funding than poorer districts. *Washington Post* March 12, 2015. Accessed November 29, 2017 at https://www.washingtonpost.com/news/local/wp/2015/03/12/in-23-states-richer-school-districts-get-more-local-funding-than-poorer-districts/?tid=a_inl&utm_term=.40db4897ef1e.

Chenoweth, K., & Theokas, C. (2013), How high-poverty schools are getting it done. *Educational Leadership, 70*(7), 56–59.

City Data (2017). *Zip code detailed profile.* Retrieved June 17, 2017 from www.city-data.com/zipDir.html

Corbin, J., & Strauss, A. (1990). Grounded theory research: Procedures, canons, and evaluative criteria. *Qualitative Sociology, 13*(1), 3.

Creswell, J. W. (2013). *Qualitative inquiry and research design* (3rd ed.). Thousand Oaks, CA: SAGE.

Duke, D. L. (2006). What we know and don't know about improving low-performing schools. *Phi Delta Kappan, 87*(10), 729–734.

Duke, D. L. (2012). Tinkering and turnarounds: Understanding the contemporary campaign to improve low-performing schools. *Journal of Education for Students Placed at Risk (JESPAR), 17*(1–2), 9–24. https://10.1080/10824669.2012.636696

Duke, D. L. (2014). A bold approach to developing leaders for low-performing schools. *Management in Education, 28*(3), 80–85.

Duke D. L., & Jacobson, M. (2011). Tackling the toughest turnaround—Low-performing high schools. *Phi Delta Kappan, 92*(5), 34–38.

Duke, D. L., Tucker, P. D., Salmonowicz, M. J., & Levy, M. K. (2007). How comparable are the perceived challenges facing principals of low-performing schools? *International Studies in Educational Administration, 35*(1), 3–21.

Foskett N., & Lumby J. (2003). *Leading and managing education: International dimensions.* Thousand Oaks, CA: SAGE.

Geels, F. W. (2002). Technological transitions as evolutionary reconfiguration processes: A multilevel perspective and a case study. *Research Policy, 31*(2002), 1257–1274.

Gurr, D., Drysdale, L., Clarke, S., & Wildy, H. (2014). High need school in Australia: The leadership of two principals. *Management in Education, 28*(3), 86–90. https://10.1177/ 0892020614537666

Hargreaves, A., & Fullan, M. (2013). The power of professional capital with an investment in collaboration, teachers become nation builders. *Journal of School Development, 34*(3), 36–39.

Herman, R., Dawson, P., Dee, T., Greene, J., Maynard, R., Redding, S., & Darwin, M. (2008). *Turning around chronically low-performing schools: A practice guide.* (NCEE #2008-4020). Washington, DC: National Center for Education Evaluation and Regional Assistance, Institute of Education Sciences, U.S. Department of Education. Retrieved from http://ies.ed.gov/ncee/wwc/practiceguides.

Hursh, D. (2007). Assessing No Child Left Behind and the rise of neoliberal education policies. *American Educational Research Journal, 44*(3), 493–518. https://doi.org 10.3102/ 0002831207306764

International School Leadership Development Network (ISLDN). (n.d.). *High needs group.* Accessed July 10, 2018 at https://isldn.weebly.com.

Judge, T. A., Piccolo, R. F., & Ilies, R. (2004). The forgotten ones? The validity of consideration and initiating structure in leadership research. *Journal of Applied Psychology, 89*(1) 36–51.

Kearney, W., Herrington, D. E., & Aguilar, D.V. (2012). Beating the odds: Exploring the 90/90/90 phenomenon. *Equity and Excellence in Education, 45*(2), 239–249. doi: 10.1080/10665684.2012.661248

Klein, A. (2015). No Child Left Behind: An overview. *Education Week,* April 2015. Accessed October 13, 2016 at http://www.edweek.org/ew/section/multimedia/no-child-left-behind- overview-definition-summary.html.

Levine, D., & Lezotte, L. (1990) *Unusually effective schools: A review and analysis of research and practice.* Madison, WI: National Center for Effective Schools Research and Development.

Maxwell, J. A. (1996). *Qualitative research design: An interactive approach.* Thousand Oaks, CA: Sage.

Medina, V., Martinez, G., Murakami, E., Rodriguez, M., & Hernandez, F. (2014). Principals' perceptions from within: Leadership in high-need schools in the United States. *Management in Education, 28*(3), 91–96.

Reeves, D. B. (2003). *High performance in high poverty schools: 90/90/90 and beyond* (pp. 1–20). Denver, CO: Center for Performance Assessment, .

Reeves, D. B. (2004). *Accountability in action: A Blueprint for learning organizations.* Englewood, CA: Advanced Learning Press.

Texas Education Agency (2016a). *Accountability ratings by region: Region 20: San Antonio.* Retrieved May 3, 2014 from http://ritter.tea.state.tx.us/cgi/sas/broker

Texas Education Agency (2016b). *TTIPS Cycle 5—2016–2020.* Accessed October 17, 2016 at http://tea.texas.gov/Student_Testing_and_Accountability/Monitoring_and_Interventions/ Title_I_Part_A_-_School_Improvement/TTIPS_Cycle_5_-_2016–2020/

U.S. Department of Education (2015). *Profiles of school turnaround strategies in selected sites.* Accessed October 9, 2016 at http://education.gov/programs/sif/sigprofiles/index.html

U.S. Department of Education (2016). *School improvement grants* (SIG). Accessed October 10, 2016 at http://www2.ed.gov/programs/sif/index.html.

CHAPTER 2

SUCCESSFUL SCHOOL LEADERSHIP THAT IS CULTURALLY SENSITIVE BUT NOT CONTEXT CONSTRAINED

David Gurr, Lawrie Drysdale, Fiona Longmuir, & Kieran McCrohan

This chapter reports on multiple perspective and observational case studies of the leadership of three underperforming schools, two serving communities with relatively high educational advantage, and one with low educational advantage, yet all facing challenges related to school closure and pressure to succeed. Utilizing Hallinger's (2018) context and culture framework for school improvement to analyze the cases, it is shown that whilst these schools had very challenging contexts, they have been able to meet the needs of their local community cultures through leadership from the principal, and others, that has not been constrained by context. There was a consistency of behavior that underlined the increasing evidence that there are common leadership practices that are useful in most contexts. All three principals had clear direction, two were focused on developing staff, they were all able to re-design their schools, and there were clear foci on improving teaching and learning. So, contexts do matter but not so much in terms of the core leadership practices that lead to success, but rather in the way these practices are employed.

Educational Leadership, Culture, and Success in High-Need Schools, pages 25–43.

Keywords: school leadership, principal, school improvement, context and culture.

INTRODUCTION

It is well established that context matters in terms of educational success (Teese & Polesel, 2003), and there is a rich literature on culturally responsive leadership, and from its first research findings, the International Successful School Principalship Project (ISSPP) has suggested that successful principals are able to adapt, use and influence context to foster success, whilst still being culturally responsive. For example, in considering the initial cases of the ISSPP, Day (2005. p. 68) noted that successful principals had the ability to

> ...not be confined by the contexts in which they work. They do not comply, subvert, or overtly oppose. Rather they actively mediate and moderate within a set of core values and practices which transcend narrowly conceived improvement agendas.

Similarly, when exploring a more recent collection of cases from the ISSPP, Drysdale (2011) found that across different country contexts and cultures, successful principals were adaptive and reflective, and able to learn from their practice and experience to ensure school success, whilst Gurr (2014, pp. 86–87), in a review of ISSPP research, claimed that

> Context and culture can influence leadership practice, but not as much as some might think...Successful school leaders not only develop a range of core practices we know are associated with school success, but they fine-tune their responses to the context and culture in which they lead.

In a summary book of illustrative cases from the first 14 years of the ISSPP (Day & Gurr, 2014), whilst core features of successful school leadership that work across varied cultures and contexts were articulated (Gurr & Day, 2014), the variety of cases provided evidence of the nuanced responses of successful leaders to culture and context.

This chapter builds on this evidence base by considering three new multiple perspective cases that are part of the ISSPP and International School Leadership Development Network (ISLDN). The chapter reports on case studies of the leadership of three underperforming schools, two serving communities with relatively high educational advantage, and one with low educational advantage, yet all facing challenges related to school closure and pressure to succeed.

Before we consider the conceptual framework used to guide this paper some history of the ISSPP and ISLDN is needed to locate the importance of these projects within the broader educational leadership research landscape. The ISSPP began in 2001 (http://www.uv.uio.no/ils/english/research/projects/isspp). With more than 20 countries now involved, it has been a productive research project accumulating more than 100 cases studies exploring the leadership of successful schools, and producing many publications including four project books, seven special journal issues, and more than 100 chapters, journal articles or country specific books. It is most likely the largest international educational leadership project ever undertaken. The ISLDN is a more recent construction and is a joint endeavor between UCEA and BELMAS, led initially by Bruce Barnett and Howard Stephenson, and begun in 2012. There are currently two strands of research focused on leadership for social justice, and leadership in challenging contexts and this has so far produced a special journal issue and a book, with further publications to follow.

HALLINGER'S CONTEXT AND CULTURE FRAMEWORK FOR SCHOOL IMPROVEMENT

Context can be considered to encompass many layers, from the local/school level through system and national contexts. In the ISSPP research, school leaders described how context was often more a melting pot of these many layers rather, than having a focus on one level (Gurr, 2014). Culture can refer to both the broader societal culture (at national and more local levels), and school culture. According to Peterson and Deal (2009) core elements of school culture include: a shared sense of purpose and vision; norms, values, beliefs, and assumptions; rituals, traditions, and ceremonies; history and stories; people and relationships; and, architecture, artefacts, and symbols. Culture defined in this way overlaps considerably with context and the leadership characteristics and practices of school leaders. For this paper, Hallinger's (2018) recently articulated view of context and culture will be used to frame analysis of the case studies.

Whilst Hallinger has been an influential figure in the development of instructional leadership he has recognized that instructional leadership is necessary but not sufficient for school improvement (Hallinger, 2018). As a consequence, he has constructed a new model of leadership that utilizes instructional leadership ideas, but which accounts for the influence of multiple contexts (Hallinger, 2018). The model conceptualizes school leadership that is focused on improving student learning through influencing school climate and the teaching and learning program. It is shown diagrammatically in Figure 2.1.

This model builds on Bossert, Dwyer, Rowan and Lee's (1982) earlier work that incorporated contextual factors into an instructional leadership model. How school leadership is enacted within the triumvirate of instructional organization, school climate and student learning is not the primary focus of this paper as we have discussed elsewhere the related findings from the ISSPP (Drysdale & Gurr, 2011; Gurr, 2015). Rather, we consider Hallinger's contextual elements. A brief description of the model and each context follows.

The model shows that principal leadership is derived from the personal characteristics of principal interacting with the institutional and community context to influence both the school climate and instructional organization. Both the school

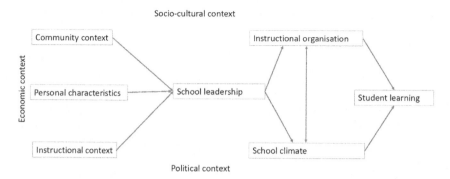

FIGURE 2.1.   Hallinger's context and culture framework for school improvement (Hallinger, 2018, p. 18).

climate and instructional organization impact on student learning. The model also shows that beyond these factors are other relevant contextual forces that influence how principals lead. The model shows that leadership is influenced by multi-level contextual factors.

Institutional Context. This encompasses the location of a school within a system or systems of education (local area network, regions, districts, state, national, religious and so forth) and how these systems influence practice through aspects such as decentralization, school autonomy, policy mandates, and work/ role expectations. The size of systems, the support systems available, and types of schools provided, all fall within the consideration of this contextual element.

Community Context. This considers the school within the community it serves, and so aspects such as challenge (resource deprivation, safety, security, success), community educational advantage, socio-economic status, location (e.g. city, urban, suburban, rural, remote), and degree of conflict in the community become important influences on leadership enactment.

Socio-Cultural Context. In this view, leadership is considered to be value-driven and leaders adapt their leadership styles to the prevailing societal values and norms. It is focused on the macro-level contextual influences on schools. For example, Raihani (2007, 2008) found that principals in secular schools in Indonesia nevertheless exhibited core Islamic values.

Economic Context. This is concerned with the economic development of the broader society. Like the socio-cultural context it is a macro-level feature to consider. The economic context has been shown to impact on features such as time at work, with principals in higher GDP countries tending to work in longer hours than lower GDP countries (Lee & Hallinger, 2012).

Political Context. This view does not subscribe to the notion that education is an apolitical public service, but rather considers the extent to which the prevailing political context shapes the beliefs, attitudes and practices of school leaders. For example, national goals of schooling are a political statement of what is valued and privileged, as is the allocation of financial support from government for the various types of schools.

School Improvement Context. Hallinger (2018) also introduces a new contextual factor that is not demonstrated in the model but is noteworthy. This is related to the historical context of a school and the school's improvement trajectory. It is a contingency-oriented approach to school improvement leadership. Utilizing a four-frame notion to describe a school's improvement state (effective, improving, coasting and ineffective) it suggests that leadership style and impact is contingent upon the school's improvement needs.

This chapter is a companion piece to a journal article (Gurr, Drysdale, Longmuir & McCrohan, 2018). The journal article has a less extensive literature section, but more engagement with the case study findings through extensive use of quotations to give participant voice to the findings.

THE RESEARCH

There is considerable overlap between the ISSPP and ISLDN especially with the more recent focus on underperforming schools in the ISSPP, and the development of the high needs strand of the ISLDN. For this paper we are drawing on recent research that fits within this overlap, and we consider three cases of underperforming schools. Two of the schools are in educationally advantaged contexts and one is in an educationally disadvantaged context. All three schools have been created from the remnants of other schools. One school resulted from the amalgamation of three failing schools, another from the resurrection of a closed school in an inner-city community, and the final from the re-birth of a school that was heading for closure as the community had lost trust with the school. All schools have been underperforming, but all were on an improvement journey when the research was conducted.

The research involved multiple perspective observational case studies. In each school, the principal, senior and middle level leaders, teachers, parents, students and school council members were interviewed individually or in groups. As well, relevant documents were collected and key events in the life of the school were observed. The focus of the research was on:

1.   What are the characteristics and practices of principals leading underperforming schools and what influences these?
2.   Who else contributes to the leadership of these schools and what are their contributions?
3.   How does the context influence the performance of these schools?

Further details of the methodology can be found at: https://www.uv.uio.no/ils/english/research/projects/isspp/

The Cases

We now consider the three cases in terms of the contextual influences on the leadership of the schools. Within the space allocated for this chapter the findings are presented as summaries with no interview quotations to support the findings. Further details can be found in doctoral theses associated with this research. The first two schools come from the doctoral research of Fiona Longmuir (Longmuir, 2017) and the third school from the yet to be published doctoral research of Kieran McCrohan.

Two Schools with High Educational Advantage: Tiverton College and Fairview High School

Tilverton College and Fairview High School are secondary schools in suburbs of Melbourne, Victoria. These two schools were characterized by cultures, reputations and educational approaches that were highly innovative and alternative. They were recognized as unusual in comparison to similar local schools that tended to be more traditional and conservative. These two schools were considered to have high educational advantage based on their parent occupation indices and the socio-economic advantage levels of the communities in which they are located. The Index of Community Socio-Educational Advantage (ICSEA) is a measure of the educational advantage of a school community based on students' family background (parents; occupation, school education and non-school education) and school-level factors (geographical location of a school, proportion of indigenous students). It is used to compare National Assessment Program—Literacy and Numeracy (NAPLAN) data which is supplied on the My School website (www.myschool.edu.au). ICSEA has a mean of 1000 and a standard deviation of 100. In 2016, both Tilverton College and Fairview High School had an ICSEA of about 1090 which places them in the highest 20 per cent of all schools in Australia for educational advantage.

In recent years, these schools had undergone significant re-establishment following a crisis. At Tilverton, this was a recommendation for closure following several years of declining enrolments, depleted reputation in the community and staff dissatisfaction. Fairview is one of the oldest secondary schools in Melbourne but was closed for a decade in the 1990s and re-opened in 2004. The principal leadership that was investigated at these two schools oversaw different phases of the improvement journeys. Michael was an external principal appointment at Tilverton around the time that recommendations for closure were being responded to. He oversaw rapid, innovative and disruptive change to the culture, structure and purpose of the school. Robyn at Fairview had been involved in the leadership of the school from the stage of planning for the school's re-opening. She had moved through leadership roles within the school until her appointment as principal in the school's fifth year of operation.

Institutional Context

These two schools are part of the Victorian Government Department of Education and Training (DET). The DET was an early adopter of autonomy and self-management practices with schools having high levels of control over aspects such as staffing and resourcing since the late 1980s (Caldwell & Spinks, 2013). This context assisted both these school to pursue their alternative and ultimately successful agendas. The flexibility and autonomy available enabled decisions such as staff appointments that were reported to be vital to gathering together aligned and motivated staff who were committed to the vision and goals of the schools.

Community Context

The communities of these two schools consisted of families from the local suburb as well as a proportion of families who by-passed other schools for their children to attend Tilverton or Fairview. Some of these families selected these schools after withdrawing their children from other secondary schools, and some students commuted for up to an hour each way to attend. Both school leaders developed strong pre-enrolment processes that ensured all those that chose their schools were well informed about the philosophies and structures they should expect. The social capital of the community along with the benefits of informed school choice had resulted in high levels of support for the school leadership and for the innovative approaches to improvement. In these schools, the community context and leadership developed reciprocal influence. The early vision and direction of the principals and other school leaders attracted community members who supported the development of further innovative and alternative approaches. These practices in turn enhanced the reputation of, and trust placed in, the school leaders which further supported them to continue with transformative improvement trajectories.

Socio-Cultural Context

The socio-cultural contextual influences in these two cases provided strong influence on the instigation of the innovative responses to the re-establishment of these two schools. The leaders demonstrated strong commitment to core values of equity, diversity and citizenship. They were both highly aware of broader social challenges including increasing prevalence of disengagement, youth mental health challenges and the need for schools to educate young people for uncertain futures. These values underpinned the provision of broad opportunities for students to engage in learning and prepare for future pathways. Although these core values are common at a macro socio-cultural level to schools in Australia, the prioritization of them was exceptional and evident broadly in structures and curriculum. Central to the principals' value-led leadership work was a strong student focus. Examination of the practice of these two principals demonstrated that they developed strong personal connections to students. They ensured that the cultures of their schools focused on enhancing connections, individualized approaches to learning and strong wellbeing structures. Further, they instigated structures and processes that were unusual in empowering students to be involved in school management and decision making. The levels of student agency and involvement demonstrated that the principals leveraged the capacity of students to contribute to innovative school improvement that is not common in most schools. This consideration of students not only as an outcome of the triumvirate of instructional organization, school climate and student learning (to return to Hallinger's model above) but as a resource for contributing to structural and educational capacity of the schools may be examples of novel ways to address modern social and educational challenges prevalent in the socio-cultural contexts that influence these schools.

Economic Context

Both schools receive most of their monetary and building resources from the state government. With relatively high educational advantage, the resources the schools are given are adequate but lower than government schools that are serving more disadvantaged communities (see the next case study), or those with similar advantage that are free to charge tuition fees as in the case of Catholic and independent schools. Tilverton College had in 2016 a per student allocation of $12,512, and capital expenditure over 2009–15 of $1,667,852. Fairview High School had a per student allocation of $12,640, and capital expenditure over 2009–15 of $5,432,498. For comparison here are two non-government schools with similar levels of educational advantage: Catholic College, had a per student allocation of $14,607, and capital expenditure over 2009–15 of $7,944,347; Independent College had a per student allocation of $14,152, and capital expenditure over 2009–15 of $13,014,300. So, as government schools they have lower per student allocations and, at least in these cases, lower capital expenditure than comparable non-government schools.

Tilverton made further use of the economic context by a focus on entrepreneurial activities. Entrepreneurship was an important part of the culture at the school and it fit well with the student-centered philosophies and values. As well as being a vehicle for encouraging student empowerment and agency, entrepreneurial activities contributed to the financial circumstances of the school. Students worked in the school in a variety of roles from gardening to reception to media liaison. Student run businesses such as animal breeding and catering contributed funds to the school. Michael was a role model in entrepreneurship by seeking every opportunity to connect with external service provides and businesses to hire out or co-locate in school facilities. These practices reflected the economic context of the school that benefited from extra revenue. They also reflected the economic context of the broader Australian community where entrepreneurial enterprise is becoming more common and highly valued.

Political Context

The response to the political context of education in Australia is of interest in the leadership and improvement of these two schools. The national goals of schooling are presented in the Melbourne Declaration on Educational Goals for Young Australians (Ministerial Council on Education, Employment, Training & Youth Affairs, 2008) and promote equity and excellence in education for all young Australians to become 'successful learners, confident and creative individuals and active and informed citizens.' These goals closely aligned with the visions and values of the two schools and the leadership developed school cultures that reflected them. Other political influences are less explicit but still prevalent in Australian schools. The most note-worthy of these is public reporting of student achievement results. Tilverton and Fairview are subject to these processes through publication of final year results (Victorian Certificate of Education) and the National Assessment Program—Literacy and Numeracy (NAPLAN) for Year Seven and Nine students. Although these two schools had seen mixed performance on these measures there was overall improvement trajectory in recent years. Both schools also utilized internal achievement accountability processes such as the development of on-line continuous assessment and reporting processes at Fairview. At Tilverton, students were significantly involved in accountability for achievement with every student developing their own individual learning plan that was monitored by a mentor teacher in combination with their families.

At both schools the tension of these accountability mechanisms was noted. As has been evidenced, philosophically, perceptions of student achievement and school success were considerably broader. The schools' internal accountability processed were a priority and other celebrated achievements included increased enrolments, high student satisfaction and provision of curriculum options for students to achieve well in areas of their specific learning interest. However, results from NAPLAN and the Victorian Certificate of Education were described as an influence on leadership and were used as tools to inform improvement whilst balancing the broader values and priorities. The leaders demonstrated strong capacity to navigate and balance the political contextual factors by selecting and focusing on achievement results in ways that strengthened the schools' re-establishment as viable, innovative and student-centered.

School Improvement Context

Hallinger's (2018, p. 16) statement of the importance of the school's improvement context as 'defining the nature of the principal's leadership challenge' is particularly relevant in these two cases. The nature of the challenge for the principals of Tilverton and Fairview was significantly influenced by firstly the 'crisis' that had occurred at each school and secondly, the maturity of the improvement trajectory to re-establish the schools. The contention from this research is that the decline of these two schools that resulted in the crisis of closure at Fairview and near closure at Tilverton provided the opportunity for a significant break with the past culture and structure of the schools. Combined with the socio-cultural and political influences described above, these 'crisis' circumstances enabled opportunity to re-engage with core values and beliefs and go beyond incremental improvement to riskier, disruptive and holistic changes. Research at these two schools provided opportunity to compare re-establishment at two different stages of maturity, with Fairview approximately five years further along a journey improvement than Tilverton. It was evident that the leadership of the principal at Tilverton was significantly more directive, explicit and visionary resulting in disruptive innovation across all elements of the school. At Fairview, while the principal was still focused on innovative improvement, it was more considered and incremental, building on the past successes and an established vision.

The improvement context, in combination with the high advantaged community and the personal and professional philosophies, histories and values of the principals, enabled the pursuit of innovative and transformative improvement that differentiated these schools and successfully re-established them.

ONE SCHOOL WITH LOW EDUCATIONAL ADVANTAGE: NORTHERN COLLEGE

Northern College is a multi-campus coeducational government school born from the amalgamation of three former failing schools in a northern suburb of Melbourne, Victoria. It consists of two Year 7–9 campuses and a Year 10–12 campus. Both Year 7–9 campuses share their sites with a local primary school, and one of these campuses also has an English language center. This language center supported the 74 per cent of students with a non-English speaking background at the school. The amalgamation of the three schools was to turnaround the suburb's entrenched educational reputation of having schools with low expectations and achievement, and to attract local students back to their local secondary school.

Northern College is considered to have low educational advantage based on their parent occupation indices and the socio-economic advantage levels of the communities in which they are located. In 2016 Northern College had an ICSEA of less than 890 placing it in the lower 16 per cent of all schools in Australia for educational advantage.

The appointment of an executive principal, the first of its kind in Victoria, to Northern College from outside of the three amalgamated schools was symbolic of the need for change. Peter, the executive principal, grew up in the local area and was intimately aware of the social disadvantage. He had experienced great success during his educational career, including evidence of turning around schools. Peter enjoyed the personal challenge that school improvement brought with it.

Peter's focus to bring about whole school change was directed towards building the leadership capacity of his staff to enact what was required to form a new college made up of three failing schools with disenchanted staff and students who, on the whole, were averse to learning.

Institutional Context

As a government school, the institutional context of Northern College is similar to that of, Tilverton College and Fairview High School. The high level of autonomy and flexibility allowed Peter to undertake significant change at the college throughout his principalship. Having said that, there was guidance sought from the DET and his regional director to support decisions that were integral to the successful foundation of the school. These included decisions, such as extending the contract of key staff that were on loan from other schools, and to introduce a minimum attendance expectation on students to make them more accountable. Peter had great experience working within the DET, and this familiarity with the system was essential in understanding when he required the regional director's support and when he could utilize the autonomy available within a Victorian government school.

Community Context

The community of Northern College was made up of students mainly from the suburb in which the school was located. The initial observations of Northern College made by Peter following his appointment was that there were many students walking past this underperforming school. The school enrolment numbers were low, and the student population experienced great disruption due to misbehavior and absence.

Except for those parents who sat on the school council, there had been a history of little, or no, parental involvement in the three schools prior to amalgamation. Parents, seemingly, placed a low value on their child's education. This feeble parental engagement did little in supporting the vision of the college. As a result, Peter identified the need for greater connection between the school and home to support the attendance of students; for some students, attendance was as low as 60 per cent, and one of the amalgamated schools had an average absence of 35 days. Greater accountability for students to attend was implemented, along with clear structures for teachers to follow in the event of low attendance. One of the significant changes was that promotion to the next year level was linked to satisfactory attendance, and so suddenly attendance became a necessity. A system of 'Time Counts' was also introduced. 'Time Counts' required students to be seated in class by 8:45am. If a student was marked as late three or more times in a week, they were required to work for 30 minutes of their lunchtime on missed learning.

Collectively, the staff worked towards a target of 90 per cent attendance for all students which it had achieved for the years 2014 to 2016. Peter realized to support the community in understanding the commitment required by students to achieve their best, he needed to implement clear accountability measures that would be noticed.

As Hallinger (2018) identified, to 'break the cycle' of failure, strong leadership was paramount. Peter recognized this and prioritized the need to build the leadership capacity of his principal leadership team in the first instance through a rigorous, *Coaching for Success program*, as well as targeted professional learning opportunities, using research literature to support the school's context and improvement trajectory. The coaching professional development built the capacity of the staff to enact change, which included pivotal parts of the teaching and learning program such as, developing a guaranteed and viable curriculum through Curriculum Design Teams and implementing a common teaching methodology across the college. Such a focus was the foundation on which a positive school improvement trajectory could be experienced.

Socio-Cultural Context

The core values of the principal of Northern College centered on his relentless pursuit of quality education, and strong moral purpose to do the best for the students. Peter's belief, that every child deserves a rewarding education that delivers a long-term benefit was evident in his catch cry of, "low socioeconomic does not mean low achievement." This phrase echoed through his leadership team, as he went about building their leadership capacity to lead school improvement. Throughout his tenure, Peter's integrity was unquestionable, yet as a result of his high expectations, there was a large turnover of staff and a high number of student expulsions from the school. Each decision required a difficult conversation but highlighted the culture Peter wanted to create to transform Northern College into an attractive school and one that the community could be proud of. Peter's trust in his leaders echoed the confidence he had in successfully leading a team. This confidence was drawn from previous experiences at leading a high performing school, and the emphasis he placed on embedding all of his decisions on sound research. Peter was comfortable to declare that he had, "never had an original idea in his life." This humble declaration reflected his commitment to evidence-based decision making. This was particularly evident through his decision to focus on areas that research identified as key to support school improvement such as strong leadership that is shared, high expectations, teacher efficacy, ensuring an orderly environment, and a focus on key priorities. To support the shared leadership, a visual representation of the key priorities of the school was developed. This clearly articulated the vision and direction of the school and it was a key communication tool with staff. For example, identified on the diagram was the key priority of a common teaching approach to address the low literacy and numeracy skills of the students, along with actions staff were required to take to fulfil this priority. This explicit approach to change was necessary to ensure the school's vision was attainable through its delivery of the identified evidence based 'best practices.'

Economic Context

The school receives most of their monetary and building resources from the state government, with a lesser contribution from the federal government and small contributions from families. With relatively low educational advantage, the resources it received were higher than government and non-government schools that serve more advantaged communities; (refer to the previous examples). The College had in 2016 a per student allocation of $17,320, and capital expenditure over 2009–15 of $5,592,319.

As well as state and federal government support, Peter recognized the opportunities that existed through seeking funding from external agencies. Any additional funding was directed towards the school's priorities. The school sought funding from agencies, such as Social Ventures Australia (www.socialventures.com.au), which offers funding, investment and advice to support schools in disadvantaged areas to help their students overcome their social barriers to success. The approach taken by the school to seek funding included being involved in ongoing projects, such as the 'Growing Great Teachers' project (www.socialventures.com.au/work/ growing-great-teachers) and the school developing their social and emotional curriculum to address the needs of students from a socially disadvantaged area. The money from such alliances was used to employ more literacy and numeracy coaches and provide professional development opportunities for staff that would otherwise be unaffordable. It was these innovative ideas that ensured Peter could build the capacity of his staff and provide every student a better chance of success.

Political Context

As outlined earlier, the Melbourne Declaration on Educational Goals for Young Australians (Ministerial Council on Education, Employment, Training & Youth Affairs, 2008), provided an over-arching vision for all Australian students. Northern College's vision for their students was prefaced by the statement, *two years of learning in one for all students.* This statement was born out of the dire situation many of its students faced when they entered Northern College in Year 7. There were a large number of students beginning high school at least two years behind their expected literacy and numeracy levels. To 'catch them up' the school embarked on an ambitious goal of delivering two years of learning growth in one year. Although the school was mandated to participate in NAPLAN testing in literacy and numeracy for all Year 7 and Year 9 students, and used this data to track performance and growth, it also used the system provided by the Department of Education and Training, *On Demand Testing* (www.vcaa.vic.edu.au/ Pages/prep10/ondemand/index.aspx) to closely monitor performance in English and Mathematics across all years 7 to 10. This data was used to track more closely how well the College met its own goal of two years of learning growth in one, and to help teachers plan their teaching goals. Each teacher was supported to achieve these goals by a coach, who helped improve their practice and supported their professional development.

Although much of the focus on schools in Australia is on achievement on standardized test such as NAPLAN, Northern College's vision embraced a long-term goal of developing a love of lifelong learning and equipping students with the opportunity to lead a purposeful and fulfilling life beyond school. This reflected the deep moral purpose that was evident in not only the Principal but in many of the staff. This belief was supported by the school's guiding principles of diversity, achievement and success, which are visible in the College's documentation and its learning environment, as well as the vernacular of its students.

The leadership team recognized that the engagement of students attending Northern College needed to be harnessed beyond the promise of academic success. This included offering courses focused on industry experience and hands on learning, as alternatives to the academic focused Victorian Certificate of Education (VCE). Such broad learning opportunities for students highlighted how Northern College lived by its vision, addressed the school's guiding principles and promoted the strong moral purpose held by its leaders and staff.

School Improvement Context

When Peter was appointed to the school he understood that it was important to establish a clear school improvement direction. Peter demonstrated directive leadership to establish a high expectation culture and a physically and emotionally safe environment for all. He also focused on developing a strong leadership team and distributing leadership ever more widely as the capacity of staff grew. Coaching, and targeted learning opportunities facilitated by internal and external personnel provided the necessary capacity building. The improvement agenda was supported through several critical friends to the school (Huerta Villalobos, 2013) who, whilst external consultants, acted on a regular basis to provide advice and professional support. One critical friend provided professional learning for middle-level leaders twice per term for more than three years.

The focus on building leadership capacity was to ultimately improve the conditions for teaching and learning. The development of Curriculum Design Teams (CDT) supported the need for a whole-school focus on teaching, learning and assessment approaches. These teams, each with their own leading teacher, created a guaranteed and viable curriculum that could then support the teaching practices of staff and promote appropriate assessment practices, such as moderation between teachers. Through the CDT, peer coaching and observations were an expectation, leading to stronger collaborative practices and a culture of relentless improvement. Developing such a culture came about from the principal's identification of the school improvement direction and the commitment Peter made to what was required to create a quality school.

DISCUSSION

As outlined in this chapter, numerous writers have attempted to unravel the mystery of how leadership interacts with context. There are three challenges in seeking to achieve this—what do we mean by leadership, what do we mean by context, and how do they interact in determining an outcome. The chapter uses Hallinger's model to identify a number of levels of context and explore how these influence leadership. Hallinger's model shows that context is multifaceted. There is the internal context (institutional context), immediate local context (community context) and the broad macro context (economic, social and political context). In this chapter we have used Hallinger's model of context to explore how three principals navigate these multiple contexts to improve schools that have troubled histories.

The most obvious aspect to note is that the contextual framework can be applied to the cases. Whether the principals or schools were fully aware of operating in these contexts is not known from this analysis, but it is clear that behaviors and intentions on the part of principals and other school leaders could be linked to each of the six contexts.

What is also evident from the findings is how the principals were able to engage with and utilized the multiple contexts to improve their schools. This was a feature of the successful school principals in the ISSPP, and it seems that the principals in these underperforming schools were operating in similar ways. Now, of course, these schools were on an improvement pathway, and one of the principals had been a successful principal previously, and so perhaps this finding is not surprising. But it does reinforce that idea that whilst context matters, perhaps it matters less than is commonly claimed. Indeed, successful principals, and the three principals described here, seem to not be constrained by context. The ISSPP has generated several models of successful school leadership, and Gurr (2015) has captured these into a single model with the suggestion that this model can describe the work of school leaders in many contexts around the world. Leithwood and colleagues (Day et al., 2010; Leithwood, Day, Sammons, Harris & Hopkins, 2006; Leithwood, Harris & Strauss, 2010; Louis, Leithwood, Walhstrom & Anderson, 2010) have for more than a decade described a four element leadership framework that includes practices associated with building vision and setting direction, understanding and developing people, redesigning the organization, and managing the teaching and learning program. These four practices are viewed as being core to principals and other school leaders around the world. Indeed Leithwood et al. (2006) claimed that it was not the practices that change across contexts but how leaders apply them. This was supported by Day et al. (2010) who also described these practices and claimed that whilst successful leadership utilized these basic leadership practices, that there was no single model for achieving success. They went further to describe how differences in context affect the nature, direction and pace of leadership actions. We see these elements in the cases described in this chapter. How the principals exercised leadership was somewhat different across their different contexts. For example, Peter and Michael could introduce more rapid and directive change as their contexts were dire, and as shown by Day et al. (2010), in challenging contexts leadership actions were often more directive and focused on core issues such as safety and setting behavior expectations. Robyn was building upon an established school direction and so was slower and perhaps more considered in what changes were introduced. However, it wasn't only that they responded to their contexts, all three principals purposefully leveraged certain contextual elements. Michael used the closure crisis, and perceptions about the system not catering for individual student need, to support his approach. Robyn also used the focus on individual student need to continue her school's trajectory. Peter used poor academic history as the stimulus for major change. These choices both played to and aligned with the needs and culture of the three communities. The high-advantage communities wanted alternative approaches that recognized and supported the individual needs of students. The low advantage community wanted their students to have a chance to achieve more, and they wanted a local school that they could trust to deliver this. All three principals had clear direction, two were focused on developing staff (Robyn and Peter), they were all able to redesign their schools, and there was a clear focus on improving teaching and learning. So, contexts do matter but not so much in terms of the core leadership practices that lead to success, but rather in the way these practices are employed.

Longmuir (2017) utilized the ideas of best practice and next practice to consider the leadership of Fairview High School and Tilverton Secondary College. Here we draw on this analysis and extend it to include Northern College. Best practice is an approach to addressing improvement needs by identifying, codifying, familiarizing and adopting strategies that have had proven successful in other settings while next practice are 'emergent innovations that open up new ways of working' (Hannon, 2008, p. 79). Tilverton demonstrated an almost consuming passion for seeking out next practice ideas. Nothing was sacred, and since Michael's arrival as principal, new ideas were introduced continuously, driven by the overarching desire to meet individual student needs. Interestingly, Tilverton has now become a best practice school, with Michael having started working with other schools to replicate some of Tilverton's key approaches. Fairview had been established as a next practice school focused on the latest ideas about middle-schooling. By the time Robyn became principal, these ideas had become best practice and were increasingly being adopted by mainstream schools. Robyn, however, was interested in next practice and so introduced new ideas, but in a careful and considered manner so that they had a good fit with the school's established direction. For Peter at Northern College, his approach was to draw on best practice to construct a school that would meet the needs of the local community. There were some next practice elements, such as the 'two for one' improvement philosophy, but most of what Peter implemented were drawn from well-known and proven ideas. To paraphrase Longmuir's (2017, p. 201) summation, the responsiveness of the leadership and community at the three schools to the broad contextual influences led to the instigation of the disruptive, innovative and transformative improvement trajectories. Leadership, appropriately balanced between 'next' and 'best' practice at these schools, worked toward a desire to 'recast today's schools in a form more suitable to the needs of tomorrow's students' (Leithwood, 2008, p. 75).

We already know that context matters for school success but how much it matters appears to be situational and dependent on the characteristics of the principal.

Papers such as Hallinger's (2018) seek to understand the relationship between leadership and context. This chapter shows that whilst context matters it is not necessarily insurmountable and can be used to influence school outcomes positively. Like a river that forges and carves through the complex terrain, successful leaders can find a pathway through the various layers and levels of context. Each river is unique but follows common processes. Rivers can meander, rush, find their way around obstacles, and cut through barriers. In some instances, the terrain can facilitate the flow of the river and help it on its journey. Like strong rivers, successful leaders are able to navigate through contextual levels to get to their destination. They are not muted or overwhelmed by context. Our research suggests that we can view the work of principals operating within distinctive context levels, and that successful principals will use a range of inventions, behave in ways that reflect their personal characteristics and values, and navigate a pathway to positive outcomes for students and the school. Our research shows that various levels of context impact and shape the task, mission and leadership challenge. The characteristics of the principal were important in how each principal perceived and dealt with the context, with their leadership approach, style and strategies being contingent on the circumstances and the stage of their school's improvement journey. The relationship is complex, but our cases give valuable insight into the dynamic processes between context and leadership. With principals that are less successful, it may be that context plays a larger part in how their leadership impacts on their school, and one that makes successful outcomes more difficult to achieve. There is certainly more research to be done into the relationship between context, leadership and school success.

Questions to Consider:

1. Where do you stand on the degree to which context matters for school success? Can school leadership exert influence that is sufficient to mitigate adverse contextual elements?
2. How does a complex consideration of context such as Hallinger's, help your understanding of the leadership of schools? What is missing from this view and what could be deleted or combined?
3. The evidence base for these cases is complex and difficult to capture in a small chapter. To what extent can you trust the findings presented here? What promotes or hinders your level of trust? Do you need to research this further and seek the full doctoral descriptions of the research to be fully convinced?

REFERENCES

Bossert, S. T., Dwyer, D. C., Rowan, B. & Lee, G. V. (1982) The instructional management role of the principal. *Educational Administration Quarterly, 18*(3), 34–64

Caldwell, B. J. & Spinks, J. (2013) *The self-transforming school.* London, UK: Routledge.

Day, C. (2005). Sustaining success in challenging contexts: Leadership in English Schools. In C. Day & K. Leithwood (Eds.), *Successful principal leadership in times of change* (pp. 59–70). Dordrecht, The Netherlands: Springer-Kluwer.

Day, C., & Gurr, D. (Eds). (2014). *Leading Schools Successfully: Stories from the field.* London: Routledge.

Day, C., Sammons, P., Hopkins, D., Harris, A., Leithwood, K., Gu, Q., & Brown, E. (2010). *10 strong claims about successful school leadership.* Nottingham, UK: National College for Leadership of Schools and Children's Services.

Drysdale, L. (2011). Evidence from the new cases in the International Successful School Principalship Project (ISSPP). *Leadership and Policy in Schools, 10*(4), 444–455.

Drysdale, L., & Gurr, D. (2011) The theory and practice of successful school leadership in Australia. *School Leadership and Management, 31*(4), 355–368.

Gurr, D. (2014) Successful school leadership across contexts and cultures. *Leading and Managing, 20*(2), 75–88.

Gurr, D. (2015) A model of successful school leadership from the international successful school principalship project. *Societies, 5*(1), 136–150.

Gurr, D., & Day, C. (2014) Thinking about leading schools. In C. Day & D. Gurr (Eds.), *Leading Schools Successfully: Stories from the field* (pp. 194–208). London: Routledge.

Gurr, D., Drysdale, L., Longmuir, F., & McCrohan, K. (2018). Leading the improvement of schools in challenging circumstances. *International Studies in Educational Administration, 46*(1), 22–44.

Hallinger, P. (2018). Bringing context out of the shadow. *Educational Management Administration & Leadership, 46*(1), 5–24.

Hannon, V. (2008). Should educational leadership focus on 'best practice' or 'next practice'? *Journal of Educational Change, 9*(1), 77–81.

Huerta Villalobos, M. (2013). *The role of the critical friend in leadership and school improvement* (M.Ed. thesis). Melbourne: The University of Melbourne.

Lee, M., & Hallinger, P. (2012). Exploring the impact of national context on principals' time use: Economic development, societal culture, and educational system. *School Effectiveness and School Improvement, 23(*4), 461–482.

Leithwood, K. (2008). Should educational leadership focus on best practices or next practices? *Journal of Educational Change, 9*(1), 71–75.

Leithwood, K., Day, C., Sammons, P., Harris A., & Hopkins, D. (2006). *Seven strong claims about successful school leadership.* Nottingham, UK: National College of School Leadership.

Leithwood, K., Harris, A., & Strauss, T. (2010). *Leading school turnaround: How successful leaders transform low performing schools.* San Francisco, CA: Jossey-Bass.

Longmuir. F. (2017). *Principal leadership in high-advantage, improving Victorian secondary schools* (PhD dissertation). Melbourne: The University of Melbourne.

Louis, K. S., Leithwood, K., Wahlstrom, K. L., & Anderson, S. E. (2010). *Learning from leadership: Investigating the links to improved student learning.* Minnesota, MN: University of Minnesota.

Ministerial Council on Education, Employment, Training & Youth Affairs. (2008). *Melbourne declaration on educational goals for young Australians.* Canberra ACT: Ministerial Council on Education, Employment, Training & Youth Affairs.

Peterson, K. D., & Deal, T. E. (2009). *Shaping School Culture: Pitfall, paradoxes, and promises* (2nd ed.). San Francisco, CA: Jossey-Bass.

Raihani. (2007). Successful school leadership in Indonesia: A study of the principals' leadership in three successful senior secondary schools in Yogyakarta (PhD dissertation). Melbourne: The University of Melbourne.

Raihani. (2008). An Indonesian model of successful school leadership. *Journal of Educational Administration, 46*(4), 481–496.

Teese, R., & Polesel, J. (2003). *Undemocratic Schooling: Equity and quality in mass secondary education in Australia.* Carlton: Melbourne University Press.

CHAPTER 3

PRINCIPALS' WORK IN HIGH-NEED SCHOOLS

Findings from Rio de Janeiro

Ana Cristina Prado de Oliveira and Cynthia Paes de Carvalho

Brazil has one of the most unequal educational systems in the world, despite having an emerging economy, our educational results in international evaluations are dismal (60th in the PISA 2015 ranking, http://www.compareyourcountry.org/pisa/country/bra?lg=en). As extensive sociological research has shown, social background is the most important impact factor on students' results. Nevertheless, educational research has repeatedly highlighted some school factors that can minimize the impact of students' social characteristics and favor satisfactory academic results despite low socioeconomic status (SES) indices. One of these key school factors is the role of the school principal. In this chapter, we choose to enlighten and discuss how the principal's leadership can make a difference in challenging circumstances. Specifically, we identified two schools in Rio de Janeiro's urban area with similar SES indices and similar contextual issues but very discrepant students' results. These two schools highlight a successful experience in a high-need situation in contrast with another school experience, where similar social challenges were faced. Interviewing teachers and principals (using the ISLDN Protocol) and observing the schools' routine enabled us to better understand how the principals manage their jobs considering their high-needs situation, focusing on student learning (or not). The qualitative

Educational Leadership, Culture, and Success in High-Need Schools, pages 45–61.
Copyright © 2019 by Information Age Publishing
All rights of reproduction in any form reserved.

research developed helped to expand our perception of the importance of building an atmosphere suitable for learning, which includes the relationships between principals and teachers, and certainly the skills to *welcome* and *discipline*, without losing focus on the main goal of the school: to prepare everyone.

Keywords: Principals, High-need schools, School climate

INTRODUCTION

In this chapter, we discuss how the principal's leadership can make the difference in challenging circumstances. Specifically, we studied two schools in Rio de Janeiro's urban area with similar Socioeconomic indices—SES and similar contextual issues but with very discrepant students' results in Brazilian national evaluations. The study highlighted a successful experience in a high-need school in contrast with another experience, where similar social challenges were faced. The immersion in these two schools, similar in terms of their population but with different academic outcomes, intended to highlight principals' different ways to deal with their challenges. Interviewing teachers and principals (using the International School Leadership Development Network—ISLDN Protocol) and observing the schools' routine enabled us to understand how the principals manage their work considering their school's high-needs situation, focusing on student learning (or not).

This chapter has 6 sections, after this introduction. The first one presents our theoretical framework on the central role of school leadership in improving students' results. The following section brings an exploratory literature review in this field, focusing on how principals build school climate. The third section presents our methodological procedures to select the two schools studied. The fourth section describes the two schools and their social contexts. The findings are discussed in the fifth section, where we present some of the rich data collected. Finally, the last section summarizes our conclusions and presents some questions for future research.

Theoretical Framework

The research on school effectiveness indicates that, if the family background has significant weight in determining the student's performance, some intra-school factors could minimize its effect, stimulating efficiency and equity in the educational opportunity (Brooke & Soares, 2008; Franco, et al., 2007; Medeiros, 2007; Sammons, 2008). Sammons (2008), as well as Alves and Franco (2008) lay out some of these intra-school factors (pedagogical actions focused on learning, teacher training and remuneration, school infrastructure, school management, monitoring the academic progress of students, among others).

This study highlights *school management*—often coupled with the principals' leadership skills—and seen as possible factor of school effectiveness, regarding what Sammons (2008) makes in the following consideration:

> Almost every school effectiveness study shows leadership as a key factor both in junior schools and high schools. Gray (1990) says that "the importance of the leadership of the Principal is one of the clearest messages from research into school effectiveness .' [...] the study of the literature shows that three characteristics were found to be frequently associated with successful leadership: strong purpose, involvement of other employees in the decision-making process, and professional authority in the processes of teaching and learning (p. 351).

Thus, school management has created increasing interest in educational research and gained prominence in the current educational policies arena. Using the concept of school leadership associated with school management, Leithwood (2009) also underscores the attention given to the topic and states that leadership is "an important goal for reform and, at the same time, a vehicle for other things to happen" (ob. cit., p. 17). Given the recent studies in the area, Leithwood stresses that school leadership accounts for a quarter of total variance when variables such as students' social origins are controlled, and only intra-school factors are analyzed (2009, p. 23).

Soares (2007) also underlines the importance of management among intra-school factors related to school effectiveness. The author points out that the positive differences found in student results that might be related to the principal's work are usually linked between the maintenance of a learning environment and a collective perception of the work with goals shared among the school team members.

Considering these characteristics, the present study seeks to deepen the knowledge about the principals' tasks related to the school climate (as maintaining a learning environment and promoting collaborative work) inside high-needs schools. This research considers also that the principal's decisions and actions are affected by the determinations of the educational system to which the school belongs and by its local social context. Given the literature on the subject and the studies about the different types of leadership in American schools, Urick and Bowers (2014, p. 27) argue that principals mediate district policies information and adapt their leaders' behavior in school according to its contextual characteristics.

The authors' argument agrees with Leithwood (2009): "successful leadership depends on considerable sensitivity to the context in which it is exercised" (p. 256). Thus, understanding the principal's role in school involves knowing the context that helps to define the profile of his or her work. This theme appears in recent international and national publications as will be presented in the next section.

LITERATURE REVIEW

As an exploratory study, we conducted a bibliographic review of publications from 2010 to 2015 in Brazilian and American journals on school management and leadership. The recognition that school leadership has a fundamental role in the organization and functioning of schools, affecting the results of the students, is reported in all the studies selected. How leading the school influences students' success, especially in high-needs contexts though, remains worthy of deeper studies.

Considering educational policies that promote large-scale assessment of student learning, the studies selected tend to focus the analyses of school leadership on its strategies to obtain academic success. Some authors highlighted the principal's interactions and mediations with teachers as conducive to a better work environment, with repercussions on student learning, as we synthesize it in the following diagram:

The studies analyzed tend to indicate the relationship between the principal and other members of the school organization (especially teachers) as a determining factor for the quality of school's work. The influence is especially important when developed in the classrooms (Harris, Ingle, & Rutledge, 2014; Higgins & Bonne, 2011; Jackson & Marriot, 2012; Leithwood & Sun, 2012; May & Supovitz, 2011; Shapira-Lishchinski & Tsemach, 2014). A more participatory/distributed/collaborative leadership, involving professionals in decisions concerning the school routine—especially pedagogical aspects—appears to be the main factor in the level of satisfaction and commitment of teachers with his or her work (Boyd, et al., 2011; Shen, Leslie, Spybrook, & Ma, 2012; Thoonen, Sleegers, Oort, Peetsma, & Geijsel, 2011) in addition to increasing the degree of team cohesion in the school (Price, 2012), since all are called on to participate and decide (Hulpia, Devos, & Keer, 2011; Mayer, Donaldson, Lechasseur, Welton, & Cobb, 2013; Supovitz, Sirinides, & May, 2010).

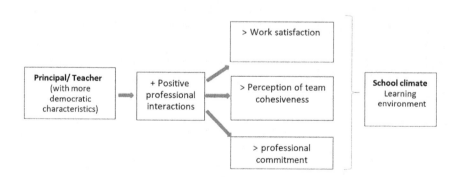

FIGURE 3.1. Findings from international studies—synthesis. (Prepared by the authors).

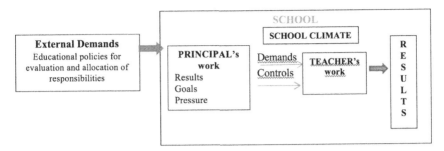

FIGURE 3.2. Findings from national studies synthesis

As shown in the diagram above, most studies have shown the relationship between leadership strategies geared to ensure the quality of the teaching work with an improved school climate, thus enabling greater academic gains by the students. Some of the studies pointed out the importance of principals' and teachers' expectations about the students' academic future, highlighting the importance of knowing the students' social context. (Bruggencate, Luyten, Scheerens, & Sleegers, 2012; Elfers & Stritikus, 2014; Nelson & Guerra, 2014; Scanlan, 2013; Urick & Bowers, 2014).

Among Brazilian publications, studies emphasized the interference of external demands on the work of the school principal, focusing on educational evaluation policies and dissemination of their results by school (Correia, 2010; Machado & Alavarse, 2014; Russo, 2011). The analyses on the school principal's work are drawn towards the discussion about external policies (formulated in the municipal system level) that directly affect the management of a school, bringing new administrative and teaching demands.

The main emphasis is on the effects of this interference on the principal's priorities and strategies, who is responsible for the school's results and the support over teachers' work based on external demands (Ramos, 2013; Silva & Alves, 2012). Some of the studies emphasized the different roles of principals leading Brazilian public schools (Conceição & Parente, 2012; Ferreira & Torres 2012). The following diagram summarizes the considerations presented:

The selected studies point out that the principal's work impact the school routine and relationships in different ways: methodologically (through organizational interventions and teaching guidelines, monitoring student learning and teacher training) and emotionally (strengthening institutional links to maintain a school environment that influences both teacher's decision to continue working at that school as well as the quality of their work).

METHODS

The municipal educational system of the city of Rio de Janeiro is the largest one in Latin America. Currently, there are 641,655 students enrolled in 1,537 school

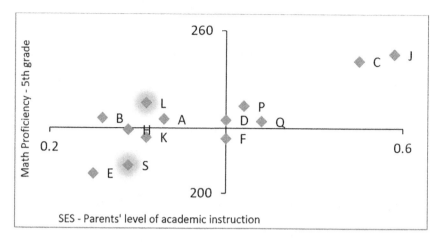

FIGURE 3.3.   Math Proficiency (5th grade) X SES. (Oliveira, 2015).

units. The school units have different arrangements and, in 2015, 163 schools served students from first to 9th grade (defined as Elementary Schools) and were chosen to be the universe of our research.

This choice had two reasons: the interest in examining leadership strategies adopted by principals who deal with a potentially larger public school, with students of different ages and needs and a wider and diverse faculty (with generalists and specialist teachers for different subjects). In addition, this option allowed a much wider view of the characteristics of principal management with information provided by teachers. We selected a representative sample of 42 schools where we applied a survey, directed to principals and teachers—Survey GESQ 2014. With the data collected, we developed a statistical study, building indices for school leadership and measuring their relationship with both students' results and teachers' work satisfaction (Oliveira, 2015). From the initial sample, we managed to gather data from 27 schools.

Then we selected two schools considering these specific characteristics: (a) low socioeconomic level—SES, (b) different academic results[1], (c) different levels of School Leadership Recognition, (d) School Climate Perception, and (e) Teachers' job satisfaction (all these indices were built in the statistic phase of the study). The graph in Figure 3.3 illustrates this choice:

Among the 27 schools of the final sample, we chose two schools in the left side of the graph (low SES) but in different vertical quadrants (with high and low academic math results), picking schools L and S.

---

[1] Here, we are considering as a proxy of academic results the 5th grade students' proficiency in Mathematics (in average per school) measured by the Prova Brasil test. Prova Brasil is an assessment applied every two years to the final grades of each stage of elementary school, in all public schools with more than 20 students in the grades assessed. The assessment includes Portuguese language and Math tests and contextual questionnaires.

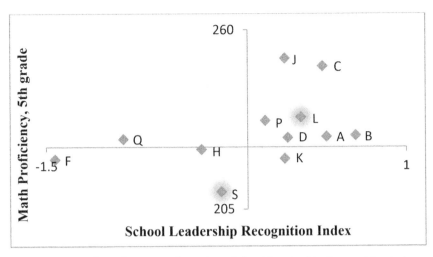

FIGURE 3.4. Math Proficiency (5th grade) X School Leadership Recognition Index. (Oliveira, 2015).

Using the information collected through the survey, we identified the level of teachers' recognition of principal's leadership in each school. Figure 3.4 shows that schools L and S had different results in this matter.

We also analyzed the teachers' level of satisfaction in working in their schools, and how they perceived its climate. The graph presented in Figure 3.5 below shows that while the School L teachers have a high level of satisfaction and a positive perception about the school climate, in school S teachers have very low level of satisfaction and a negative perception about their school climate.

For the qualitative study, we used three procedures: semi-structured interviews with 5 to 6 teachers per school, principals and management team; the *shadowing* technique (Spillane, Parise, & Sherer, 2011; Teroski, 2014) following the principal's work to identify possible trends, predominance, behaviors[2]; the observation of at least one meeting between the school management team and the teachers[3]. In all the interviews, we used the ISLDN Protocol[4]. The results are presented in the following sections.

Context: School L and School S

Both schools are in the northern part of the city but are far apart from each other. School L is located in a middle-class neighborhood, crowded and busy, which

---

[2] Follow up of the principal's work (3 shadowing days in each school).

[3] One collective meeting (Center of Studies) observed in each unit.

[4] We conducted 13 semi-structured interviews, totaling more than 9 hours of recording and 171 pages of transcription. The interview scripts followed the International School Leadership Development Network—ISLDN Protocol (Baran & Berry, 2015).

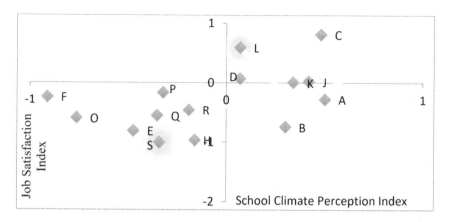

FIGURE 3.5. Teachers' Job Satisfaction Index X School Climate Perception Index. (Oliveira, 2015).

is placed between major slum complexes (some of them were still in the process of implementing a Pacifying Police Unit—UPP[5], which house the vast majority of its students. As one of the School L teachers reflected, "the surroundings, these three communities, are difficult to work with. So, you have all the odds against you, but we do everything for our work to be successful" (excerpts from the interview with Teacher 3, School L)). School S is located in a traditional neighborhood, with higher socioeconomic inequality than School L neighborhood, where there are middle-class and upper middle-class houses, surrounded by huge pacified slums, from where the School S' students come from.

Principal's years in office (at this school) 28 years 3 yearsBoth schools enroll children with similar and low SES (estimated through parents' instruction level), below the average of all other municipal schools. Even considering the socioeconomic differences between the communities of School S and School L (and within these communities), incidents involving violence, conflicts, and crime were reported in both units. The learning results, however, were very discrepant between the two schools. We present in Figures 3.6 and 3.7, the results for School S and School L, since 2007 (Math Proficiency[6] in 5th and 9th grades):

Observing the math proficiency trajectory for both schools, we note that the results of School L students were above the national and local (municipal system) average in all years in the two grades evaluated. On the other hand, the average

---

[5] Of the 6.3 million Rio de Janeiro's inhabitants, 1.4 million live in slums. According to the 2010 Demographic Census, the city has 763 slums. Since 2008, 38 of Pacifying Police Units (UPPs) were installed to improve local safety against.

[6] Considering the students' average result in Prova Brasil, a national biannual assessment applied in all Brazilian public schools since 2005.

TABLE 3.1.   School S and School L.

	School L	School S
Students enrolled (2015)	1,215	710
Students whose families are beneficiaries of Bolsa Família Program1.	50%	39%
Teachers	47	40

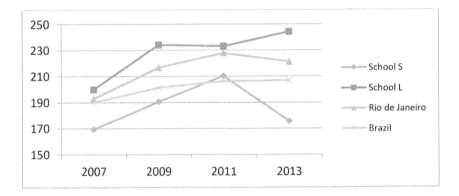

FIGURE 3.6.   Math Proficiency in 5th grade: Brazil, Rio de Janeiro, School L and School S. (Oliveira, 2015).

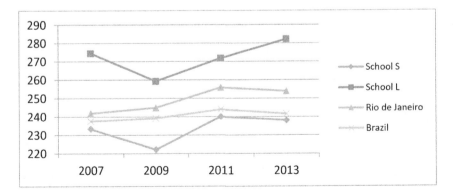

FIGURE 3.7.   Math Proficiency in 9th grade: Brazil, Rio de Janeiro, School L and School S. (Oliveira, 2015).

academic result of the School S students was lower than the national and local average in virtually all years, both for the 5th and the 9th grades.

What could explain this difference in performance between these two schools, considering that the sociodemographic characteristics were so similar? The interviews in both schools and the observation of principals' daily activities brought new elements to discussion.

FINDINGS AND DISCUSSION: WHAT FOSTERS STUDENT LEARNING IN HIGH-NEED SCHOOLS?

The Principal's Role in the Organizational Climate

It is noteworthy that the data seemed to indicate that a proactive principal, specially creating a positive environment to academic practices, is an important element for both teaching quality and student learning (Oliveira, 2015). The qualitative approach in two high-need schools pointed out two different ways in which principal's actions build "school climate," involving their leadership characteristics developed in each context.

School L: Focusing on Discipline. In interviews with teachers from School L, they were unanimous in recognizing the importance of maintaining student discipline and abiding to the school's rules as the main characteristic of the school principal's leadership style:

> Her defining trait, for me, is being a *disciplinarian*. I cannot think of another. [The Principal is] present. She is always present, something you do not see in other schools. Active, yes? She is firm when she needs be, both with students and teachers, and especially with parents. (Teachers 2 and 3, School L).

Teachers emphasized the firm and disciplinary action of School L principal, in different moments of the school routine, who exemplified it through her support for teachers' decisions. Working in an environment where students comply with rules (punctuality, use of uniform and general behavior were the most cited in the interviews) favors learning, said the teachers when asked about the school climate:

> And the greater the disciplined and calm environment, more they will understand that this is an environment ... It's not that chaotic environment, of violence and aggression. Here we come to learn. We play, we have fun, but we mostly come to learn. (Teacher 2, school L).

The information collected in the qualitative research conducted at School L revealed the profile of a principal who values school discipline and establishes dialogue with staff regarding organizational issues. These aspects appear in the teachers' testimonies regarding their satisfaction in working at the school and, especially, recognizing their principal's leadership.

School S: The Inclusive School. In School S, innumerous incidents and reports (from teachers and the principal) highlighted its' inclusive characteristic, often in order to emphasize that this school caters all students who arrive there, regardless of their difficulties or lack of adaptation at other schools. According to a teacher, listening and providing chances to the student is a school prerogative:

> We have a lot of this thing of talking to students, you know? We talk, we reveal a lot. We have this thing, we really pick up the student and: "We will try, we will improve, we will change ..." And we give every chance. We will give chance even when we should not ... until we exhaust all possibilities. So therefore, we have this policy here. (Teacher 2, School S).

The warm welcoming attitude of the principal appeared as a hallmark of his leadership at School S, recognized in his relationship with students and teachers. His accessibility and openness towards the teachers was visible, although this relationship has not appeared as an influential factor of the satisfaction level of the faculty with their work at the school. In some of teacher interviews, we saw a mix of recognition and disapproval of the flexibility of limits in the relationship between the principal and students:

> So, their [referring to principal and assistant-principal] main characteristic is: Embracing the school, always being present. [...] So, I think that, in what concerns management, I think we have to have ... because things get confused in the minds of students ... I think it is very confusing in their minds... (Teacher 1, School S).

According to the perception of teachers, the predominance of a more welcoming profile at work of the principal in School S did not completely overshadow the other characteristics of his work in school management, although they were perceived as less relevant.

To discipline X to include: Does it Need to be a Choice in High-Need Schools? It's important to consider that having a predominantly "disciplinary" profile or a predominantly "welcoming" profile as a school principal is not a simple choice... In fact, it seems to be related to the context in which these principals operate. Studying the different typologies of school leadership in US schools, Urick and Bowers (2014) remark that few studies have paid attention to the school's contextual variables to understand principals' leadership profiles. According to them, "the inclusion of variables on the school context is important as the principal adjusts his or her leadership to meet the needs of teachers and students in school" (p. 105).

Therefore, it is relevant to analyze the context in which the representations (disciplinary and welcoming) on the performance of the two principals studied were built.

Before assuming her current position, School L Principal was the Coordinator of the same unit and began to "organize the school," as she told herself. It was the late 1980s, the context was complex, and she brought from her previous experience (a rather complex school), the characteristic of "disciplinarian":

> I came to a school that was crazy, it was an open gate, here was a pingpong table, a football table, and it was ... the student from morning[7] turn could stay here in the afternoon if he wanted to stay and the students of the afternoon turn, they could come in the morning to play ping-pong and the [...] geek. And that was crazy. And I started to bring discipline in the school. (Principal, School L)

Bringing order and discipline to the school in a turbulent moment, the principal of School L met the expectations of the faculty and community of that school (at least for the most part). Since then, with successive reelections, her disciplinary characteristic has been legitimized vis-à-vis the school's leadership.

In School S, as previously mentioned, there is a negative collective representation about the students' profile attended (sent by other schools to the Special Classes[8] or for disciplinary reasons). This perception is explicit in the statements of teachers who assumed, as a school responsibility, to welcome these students and to foster their link with school life: "The main characteristic of this school is inclusion. This is a school of inclusion" (Teacher 4, School S)

The context of the school, be it real or built through collective common sense, seems to have built the need to prioritize the reception of students among educators, building what could be called the "social climate of the school," where the *emotional state* of the institution is highlighted (Mafra, 2003, p. 116). Upon taking office recently, the principal of School S belonged already to this context and, as explained by some teachers, was probably chosen for having a profile identified with this characteristic of the school.

Having a more disciplinary or a more welcoming profile does not exclude, as discussed previously, the other characteristics of school management in the units studied. We witnessed a number of situations in which the School L principal demonstrated a close relationship with her teachers and a welcoming approach to the students: preparing a snack table for teachers in the meetings, receiving the students at the door and greeting them by name, talking spontaneously with the students during recess. In School S, besides the good relationship with the students, there were numerous situations in which the principal intervened in conflicts or situations of indiscipline. In some of them, he needed to change his voice and threaten students to be suspended or even transferred to another school.

In both schools, welcoming and disciplining are not exclusive objectives in leading the schools. Added to these tasks are administrative, pedagogical and external issues. Balancing the different demands to face the challenge of running a school is not an easy task. The demands and the context of each school, along

---

[7] The most part of Brazilian schools attend in two different periods: one group in the morning and another one in the afternoon (each school period lasts four hours).

[8] The municipal system of education in Rio, offer (in some schools) different special classes to attend students with special necessities or students with academic delay above two years.

with the principals' personal characteristics, have shaped their leadership profiles, either disciplining or welcoming.

Students' Adequate Learning: What do Principals Think?

Reinforcing the importance of building an adequate climate for student learning, we observed different ways in which principals deal with the school context. As mentioned, the two units predominantly receive low-income students with quite complex social and security contexts. The School L principal has a view of the students' reality that reflects her belief in the power of social change through education. Using her own story as example, she clarifies that she has high expectations of students, and that "no one should call them 'poor things'! I hate that expression!" (Principal, School L). She proudly points out that some School L students were selected for prestigious High Schools, as an example of overcoming social origin.

School S enrolls a clientele with very similar socioeconomic profile of School L, which also experiences the intricate territorial reality of the slums in Rio de Janeiro. Educators from School S, however, seem to have a less hopeful outlook on the academic prospects of their students. Their narrative was bounded by the limitations and gaps of their students, a possible victimization by their socioeconomic condition: "The school [environment] is harsh, the reality we deal with here ... is 'punk' (Principal, School S) The problem is the raw material with which we deal..." (Teacher 8, School S).

In the interview with School S principal and his assistant, the issues related to student learning and the pedagogical work developed at the school were only briefly addressed. The answers to the questions ended up diverting focus, recovering the theme of inclusion or welcoming undisciplined students. They seemed to consider that curricular learning was a secondary issue. Teachers seem to have the same perception: "I sometimes completely forget the academic topic... to talk, to show them things they need, to show that they do not have to go that way, to do those things ..." (Teacher 2, School S).

Although we recognize that the socioeconomic origin of the students is the main factor determining the difference of academic results between the schools, several studies have already shown that the intra-school factors can minimize this social effect (Brooke & Soares, 2008; Cremers & Reezgit, 1996). Considering that the socioeconomic variable was isolated in the choice of the two schools, we tried to understand how school factors—particularly principal' leadership—could influence the variance of the students' results.

CONCLUSIONS

In a previous study (Oliveira, 2015) we had found the importance of principals' leadership recognized by faculty and an adequate school climate for students' results, as highlighted by many other studies. To deepen our understanding of how these factors operate in high-need schools, we developed the qualitative study presented here.

In his studies of *school leadership*, Leithwood (2009) defines it as: "the work of mobilizing and influencing others to articulate and achieve the shared intentions and goals of the school" (p. 20). The author asserts that effective leadership covers functions and characteristics such as: (a) a non-conformist orientation; (b) rigorous selection and replacement of teachers; (c) ensuring that the focus of school work is students' learning; (d) frequent monitoring of school activities; (e) giving importance and investing time and energy in school improvement; (f) supporting teachers; developing educational leadership; (g) ensuring the participation of the students' parents; (h) monitoring the progress of students; (i) developing successful processes for grouping of students; (j) coordinating the curricular and evaluation issues of the school; among others.

Teachers in Schools L and S recognized their principals' leadership by their main characteristics, developed through their experience and under influence of each school context. Since these features are not chosen, we must consider their importance to determine the principals' actions and strategies during school routine. Those actions are determinant to the quality of school climate. During the research, we observed that in School L all students had behavioral practices (lines to go to their classes, low conversation inside the school, respect regarding the class initial time, etc.) and we did not find groups without teacher supervision in the playground during school time. On the other hand, in School S, students did not have a regular procedure to go to their classes at the beginning of the day or after the break. We observed them listening to the bell but only going to class when they wanted to... The principal used a microphone to call each group to go to their class, but the students ignored him and went to sing in the microphone with the principal. Normally, the students lost 10 to 15 minutes of their classes after the break and even the teachers procrastinated in their coffee breaks. We witnessed many times one or more student groups not attending lessons, but in the patio, thus collaborating to a constant high-noise level inside the school. Therefore, we registered that different characteristics in leading the two schools built different organizational climates.

The principal's work characteristics relating to the maintenance of a good school environment, with appropriate conditions for teaching and, consequently, for student's learning, can be developed in different ways, with different consequences. With the data collected in this study we cannot (and do not want to) directly relate the principals' characteristics to their schools' academic results. As we know, there are many intra-school factors influencing students' learning. Considering that the school leadership and the school climate are important factors in this path, we tried to understand how they act in two different high-need schools. Some questions remain for future research: Does the socioeconomic background of the students affect the teachers' and the principal's perception of the school's main goal? And does it affect the principal's commitment to establishing disciplinary practices to ensure student learning? How does the principal's educational and professional background affect his/her ability to promote a school climate that favors high-need students' learning?

The qualitative research developed and summarized here helped to expand the perception of the importance of building an atmosphere suitable for learning in high-needs schools, which includes some tasks of principals' action, involving certainly the skills to welcome and discipline, without losing focus on the main goal of the school: to teach everyone.

Questions to Consider:

1. Does the socioeconomic background of students affect the teachers' and the principal's perception of the school's main goal?
2. Does socioeconomic background affect the principal's commitment to establishing disciplinary practices to ensure student learning?
3. How does the principal's educational and professional background affect his/her ability to promote a school climate that favors high-need students' learning?

REFERENCES

Alves, M. T. G., & Franco, C. (2008). A pesquisa em eficácia escolar no Brasil: Evidências sobre o efeito das escolas e fatores associados à eficácia escolar. In N. Brooke & J. F. Soares (Eds.), *Pesquisa em eficácia escolar: origem e trajetórias*. Belo Horizonte: Editora UFMG.

Baran, M. L., & Berry, J. R. (2015). *The international school leadership development network (ISLDN) High needs schools group research protocol and members' guide*. Washington, DC: ISLDN and UCEA/BELMAS.

Boyd, D., Grossman, P., Ing, M., Lankford, H., Loeb, S., & Wyckoff, J. (2011). The influence of school administrators on teacher retention decisions. *American Educational Research Journal, 48*(2), 303–333.

Brooke, N., & Soares, J. F. (Eds.). (2008). *Pesquisa em eficácia escolar: Origem e trajetórias*. Belo Horizonte: Editora UFMG.

Bruggencate, G., Luyten, H., Scheerens, J., & Sleegers, P. (2012). Modeling the influence of school leaders on student achievement: How can school leaders make a difference? *Educational Administration Quarterly, 48*(4), 699–732.

Conceição, S., & Parente, J. (2012). Um estudo multivariado do perfil do diretor das escolas públicas de Itabaiana—SE. *RBPAE—Revista Brasileira de Política e Administração Escolar, 28*(2), 479–494.

Correia, J. A. (2010). Paradigmas e cognições no campo da administração educacional: Das políticas de avaliação a avaliação como política. *Revista Brasileira de Educação, 15*(45), 456- 497.

Creemers, B., & Reezigt, G. (1996). School level conditions affecting the effectiveness of instruction. *School Effectiveness and School Improvement, 7*(3), 197–228.

Elfers, A., & Stritikus, T. (2014). How school and district leaders support classroom teachers' work with English language learners. *Educational Administration Quarterly, 50*(2), 305–344.

Ferreira, N., & Torres, L. (2012). Perfil de liderança do diretor de escola em Portugal: Modos de atuação e estratégias de regulação da cultura organizacional. *RBPAE—Revista Brasileira de Política e Administração Escolar, 28*(1), 86–111.

Franco, C., Ortigão, I., Albernaz, A., Bonamino, A., Aguiar, G., Alves, F., & Sátyro, N. (2007). Qualidade e equidade em educação: reconsiderando o significado de "fatores intraescolares." *Ensaio: Avaliação e Políticas Públicas em Educação, 15*(55), 277–98.

Harris, D., Ingle, W., & Rutledge, S. (2014). How teacher evaluation methods matter for accountability: A comparative analysis of teacher effectiveness ratings by principals and teacher value-added measures. *American Educational Research Journal, 51*(1), 73–112.

Higgins, J., & Bonne, L. (2011). Configurations of instructional leadership enactments that promote the teaching and learning of mathematics in a New Zealand elementary school. *Educational Administration Quarterly, 47*(5), 794–825.

Hulpia, H., Devos, G., & Keer, H. (2011). The relation between school leadership from a distributed perspective and teachers' organizational commitment: Examining the source of the leadership function. *Educational Administration Quarterly, 47*(5), 728–771.

Jackson, K., & Marriott, C. (2012). The interaction of principal and teacher instructional influence as a measure of leadership as an organizational quality. *Educational Administration Quarterly, 48*(2), 230–268.

Leithwood, K. (2009). *¿Cómo liderar nuestras escuelas? Aportes desde la investigación.* Santiago: Salesianos Impresores.

Leithwood, K., & Sun, J. (2012). The nature and effects of transformational school leadership: A meta-analytic review of unpublished research. *Educational Administration Quarterly, 48*(3), 387–423.

Machado, C., & Alavarse, O. (2014). Avaliação interna no contexto das avaliações externas: Desafios para a gestão escolar. *RBPAE—Revista Brasileira de Política e Administração da Educação, 30*(1), 63–78.

Mafra, L. (2003). A sociologia dos estabelecimentos escolares: passado e presente de um campo de pesquisa em reconstrução. In N. Zago, M. Carvalho, & R. Vilela (Eds.), *Itinerários de pesquisa: Perspectivas em Sociologia da Educação.* Rio de Janeiro: DP&A.

May, H., & Supovitz, J. (2011). The scope of principal efforts to improve instruction. *Educational Administration Quarterly, 47*(2), 332–352.

Mayer, A., Donaldson, M., Lechasseur, K., Welton, A., & Cobb, C. (2013). Negotiating site-based management and expanded teacher decision making: A case study of six urban schools. *Educational Administration Quarterly, 49*(5), 695–731.

Medeiros, V. G. (2007). *Clima escolar: um estudo sociológico de uma instituição pública de excelência.* 2007. 151 f. Dissertação (Mestrado em Educação Brasileira)—Departamento de Educação, Pontifícia Universidade Católica do Rio de Janeiro, Rio de Janeiro.

Nelson, S., & Guerra, P. (2014). Educator beliefs and cultural knowledge: Implications for school improvement efforts. *Educational Administration Quarterly, 50*(1), 67–95.

Oliveira, A. C. P. (2015). *As relações entre Direção, Liderança e Clima Escolar em escolas municipais do Rio de Janeiro.* 2015. 283 f. Tese (Doutorado em Educação) -Programa de Pós-Graduação em Educação, Pontifícia Universidade Católica do Rio de Janeiro.

Price, H. (2012). Principal-Teacher interactions: How affective relationships shape principal and teacher attitudes. *Educational Administration Quarterly,* 48(1), 39–85.

Ramos, G. P. (2013). A política educacional Paulista (1995–2010) e seus impactos na identidade da escola e do professor. *RBPAE—Revista Brasileira de Política e Administração da Educação, 29*(3), 537–556.

Russo, M. (2011). Trabalho e administração da escola: desenvolvimento e apropriação do sentido que assumem no processo de produção pedagógica. *RBPAE—Revista Brasileira de Política e Administração Escolar, 27*(3), 361–588.

Sammons, P. (2008). As características-chave das escolas eficazes. In N. Brooke, & J. F. Soares (Eds.), *Pesquisa em eficácia escolar: origem e trajetórias.* Belo Horizonte: Editora UFMG.

Scanlan, M. (2013). A learning architecture: How school leaders can design for learning social justice. *Educational Administration Quarterly, 49*(2), 348–391.

Shapira-Lishchinski, O., & Tsemach, S. (2014). Psychological empowerment as a mediator between teachers' perceptions of authentic leadership and their withdrawal and citizenship behaviors. *Educational Administration Quarterly, 50*(4), 675–712.

Shen, J., Leslie, J., Spybrook, J., & Ma, X. (2012). Are principal background and school processes related to teacher job satisfaction? A multilevel study using Schools and Staffing survey 2003-04. *American Educational Research Journal, 49*(2), 200–230.

Silva, L., & Alves, M. (2012). Gerencialismo da escola pública: Contradições e desafios concernentes à gestão, à autonomia e à organização do trabalho escolar. *RBPAE— Revista Brasileira de Política e Administração Escolar, 28*(3), 665–681.

Spillane, J., Parise, L., & Sherer, J. (2011). Organizational routines as coupling mechanisms: Policy, school administration, and the technical core. *American Educational Research Journal, 48*(3), 586–619.

Soares, J. F. (2007). Melhora do desempenho cognitivo dos alunos do ensino fundamental. *Cadernos de Pesquisa, 37*(130), 135–160.

Supovitz, J., Sirinides, P., & May, H. (2010). How principals and peers influence teaching and learning. *Educational Administration Quarterly, 46*(1), 31–56.

Terosky, A. (2014). From a managerial imperative to a learning imperative: Experiences of urban public school principals. *Educational Administration Quarterly, 50*(1), 3–33.

Thoonen, E., Sleegers, P., Oort, F., Peetsma, T., & Geijsel, F. (2011). How to improve teaching practices: The role of teacher motivation, organizational factors, and leadership practices. *Educational Administration Quarterly, 47*(3), 496–536.

Urick, A., & Bowers, A. (2014). What are the different types of principals across the united states? A Latent Class analysis of principal perception of leadership. *Educational Administration Quarterly, 50*(1), 96–134.

PART II

LEADERSHIP FOR LEARNING

CHAPTER 4

SCHOOL LEADERSHIP FOR SOCIAL JUSTICE AND STEM

Findings from a High Need Secondary School in Belize

Lorenda Chisolm, Noemi Waight and Stephen Jacobson

This chapter reports the efforts of two school leaders to establish a secondary school on a small island off the coast of Belize, a developing nation in Central America. This case study uses a theoretical framework synthesizing research on social justice school leadership and student achievement and the methodology and interview protocol developed by the International School Leadership Development Network (ISLDN). This case study tracked the social justice impetus that led to the school's establishment by two women from North America, as well as their attempts to implement a curriculum that would address the environmental and ecological future of the island. Their intent was for this Science, Technology, Engineering and Mathematics (STEM) orientation to create career opportunities for students in the island's emerging eco-tourism industry. We focused on the leaders' efforts to promote social justice by ensuring that every child on the island has access to a secondary education, regardless of prior academic performance or financial circumstances, in a country where secondary education is not compulsory and less than half of the nation's youth are enrolled. From our findings, we draw tentative conclusions for

Educational Leadership, Culture, and Success in High-Need Schools, pages 65–83.
Copyright © 2019 by Information Age Publishing

policy, practice and future research that can inform similar efforts in other developing nations attempting to broaden access to secondary education and implement STEM curricula that can support both the academic needs of students and the future needs of the local economy.

Keywords: School Leadership, Social Justice, Social Justice School Leadership, STEM Curriculum, and Developing Nations

INTRODUCTION

School leaders across the world struggle with the challenge of providing a quality education that can improve both the life chances of their nation's youngsters and the future economic wellbeing of the country. Nowhere is this challenge more arduous than in developing countries, such as Belize, where universal access to secondary education is limited based on a lack of both human and fiscal resources. Examining the practices of leaders for social justice cannot be fully understood without first considered the educational context and governance of the nation in which their efforts occur. Therefore, the chapter begins with a snapshot of the context of education in Belize, where education beyond primary school is not compulsory and has come only recently to some parts of the country, such as Blue Cove Caye[1] in 2008. This overview is followed by a brief literature review of existing research on school leadership, social justice, and STEM. Next, we present a conceptual framework for successful leadership practices based on the work of Leithwood and other scholars, particularly a Wallace Foundation (2013) study that found important linkages between leadership and improved student learning. These researchers affirmed that while classroom instruction is the most significant in-school practice related to learning, leadership follows as the next most important variable. With that as our grounding, we report the methods used and the demographics, development and evolution of Social Justice Academy (SJA), a school committed to providing equitable access to secondary education for the children on this island.

Next, the paper reports on the findings from a case study of one school, and how they related to the work of the school's co-founders who also serve as co-principals, Ilene and Heather, including their efforts to develop a STEM curriculum supportive of local needs. We consider courses that offer site-based learning opportunities that align with an emerging eco-tourism economy (e.g., fly-fishing and scuba diving) intended to provide a more prosperous future both for the students and the island's community. We conclude with implications for policy, practice and future research that can inform similar efforts in other high need schools

---

[1] Blue Cove Caye and Social Justice Academy are pseudonyms. It remains the only secondary school on the island at the time of this writing.

and developing nations and pose two questions to prompt further thinking about these issues.

LITERATURE REVIEW: EDUCATIONAL LEADERSHIP AND THE CASE OF BELIZE

Although Belize's Ministry of Education has placed a stronger emphasis on the importance of secondary schooling in recent years, education beyond primary school is still not compulsory. Secondary education in Belize consists of four years of high school that requires passage of a comprehensive exam for entry. A student's ranking on the test determines, in large part, which secondary school s/he can attend. Still yet, access to secondary school may be limited or inaccessible due to charges for tuition, books and other fees which are often beyond the means of many families. In addition, the lack of schools within a village community or within reasonable distance, may also prevent access to secondary schooling. Consequently, secondary schools currently serve only half the children who complete primary school in Belize. In practice, it is available primarily to those students who have excelled academically, who do not have a history of significant behavior problems and whose families can afford the costs associated with tuition, fees and uniforms.

Based on the British educational system, Belizean schools are divided into three levels: *primary, secondary and tertiary.* Within these levels, students transition through a series of 'Standards' and 'Forms' (See Table 4.1). Standards are equivalent to the elementary grade levels in the USA, while forms are equivalent to junior and senior high school. Students must take and pass the Belize National Selection Examinations for promotion. All students take the Belize Junior Achievement Test (BJAT) in the sixth grade, the Primary School Examination (PSE) in eighth grade, and then grade twelve students wishing to pursue tertiary (post-secondary) education take the Association of Tertiary Level Institutions of Belize (ATLIB). In other words, while promotion at each level is predicated on

TABLE 4.1.   Education Levels in Belize

Education Level	US Grade Equivalent	Age	Years	Assessment for Promotion	Additional
Primary (Infant I and II, Standards I through V, and 1st Form)	K–8	5–13	8	Belize Junior Achievement Test (BJAT)	Compulsory
Secondary (2nd Form—4th Form)	8–11	13–17	4	Primary School Examinations (PSE)	
Post-Secondary (Tertiary or Vocational)	12-University	17-	2	Association of Tertiary Level Institutions of Belize (ATLIB)	

successfully passing a standardized exam, only the first 8 years of schooling are mandatory.

School Leadership

There are numerous descriptions of leadership offered throughout the literature, typically focusing on the skills, traits and/or attributes of a leader. Chemers (1997), for example, describes leadership as a "process of social influence in which one person is able to enlist the aid and support of others in the accomplishment of a common task" (p. 1). Considering leadership from the context of an educational organization, McDougall, Saunders, and Goldenberg (2007) describe it as an artful combination of "pressure and support in a way that moves schools relentlessly toward accomplishing student achievement goals, utilizing indicators, cultivating assistance and collaboration, and building productive school settings" (p. 53). In addition, school leaders must have an understanding of who they lead and the nature of complexities in which they serve (Brown & Conrad, 2007).

Studies of school leadership have focused on principal preparation, styles of management, successful practices, and principals' impact on student achievement through instructional leadership (Blasé & Blasé, 2004; Bush, 2009; Chemers, 1997; Jacobson, 2011; Ylimaki, 2007). Findings from this research have contributed to educational reforms and policies designed to address the expanding roles of school principals, increasing accountability and other complexities of school contexts in the 21st century (Bush, 2009). However, Watson (2003) posed the question of whether such reforms hold at their core the needs of the individual, the school and/or the national system. Although the individual, the school, and the national system should presumably strive towards the same goal(s), there are often competing needs among them (Chisolm, 2017), and ultimately, it is the goals of the national system that become primary (Watson, 2003). This is especially important in the developing world.

School Leadership in Developing Nations

Research studies on school leadership and successful principal practices have been conducted primarily in developed nations such as Australia, Cyprus, Denmark, England, New Zealand, Norway, Sweden and the USA (Jacobson & Day, 2007; Leithwood & Riehl, 2005; Pashiardis, Kafa, & Marmara, 2012; Santamaria, Santamaria, Webber, & Pearson, 2014; Ylimaki & Jacobson, 2011). This is often attributed to the fact that industrialized nations have greater access to resources and financial stability (Cohn & Rossmiller, 1987), more efficient systems of accountability, and a longer history of organized education systems (Chisolm, 2017). Moreover, these industrialized nations do not still experience the long-endured, negative effects of colonialism, such as the consequences of British colonialism that has oppressed and "influenced subsequent educational systems" (Fanon, 1963, p. 21) as in Belize, and other nations such as Ghana, Jamaica, and

Trinidad and Tobago, to name a few (King 1987; Lall, 2007). Nevertheless, research from developing nations can inform important aspects of leadership practice in the developing world. For example, Johnson, Møller, Pashiardis, Vedøy, and Savvides (2011) studied the leadership of two elementary principals in rural schools with large minority (immigrant) populations in Cyprus. They found that these principals were successful because they were able to mobilize school community stakeholders (parents and teachers) through the creation of a shared vision and the communication of clear expectations for their minority students. In these cases, the principals demonstrated a willingness to employ a sense of social justice leadership by challenging the status quo to create a deep "culture of socio-political consciousness…in order to empower the diverse community of the school" (Johnson et al., 2011, p. 93).

But more often, the results of studies in developed nations can lead to reforms and policies derived from a Western perspective (Lall, 2007) that are often impossible "for any society in a globalized era to refrain from 'borrowing.'..especially from Western, more industrialized societies" (Brown & Conrad, 2007, p. 183). According to Cohn and Rossmiller (1987), there are two polarizing differences between developed and developing nations that impact academic achievement. First, schools in developing nations operate on a considerably smaller budget such that school expenditures for these nations are but a small fraction of industrialized nations. Second, there is the issue of locale that is a cultural [and geographical] factor that cannot be ignored, especially as it relates to 'access.' Many rural schools in developing nations, as is the case with Social Justice Academy, are physically located too far from the Ministry of Education to benefit from governmental resources necessary to support school leaders, teachers and students (Cohn & Rossmiller, 1987). Both issues, limited resources and an isolated location, underlie the circumstances confronting the secondary school we studied in Belize.

Social Justice

The concept of social justice is neither narrowly nor easily defined and there are several definitions offered throughout the literature. Marshall and Ward (2004) describe social justice as a means of 'fixing' inequities in access, while a broader definition is provided by Goldfarb and Grinberg (2002), who describe it as "the exercise of altering these arrangements by actively engaging in reclaiming, appropriating, sustaining, and advancing inherent human rights of equity, equality, and fairness in social, economic, educational, and personal dimensions, among other forms of relationships" (p. 162). Jost and Kay (2010) define social justice as being when, "(a) benefits and burdens in society are dispersed in accordance with some allocations principle (or set of principles); (b) procedures, norms, and rules that govern political and other forms of decision making preserve the basic rights, liberties, and entitlements of individuals and groups; and (c) human beings…are treated with dignity and respect not only by authorities but also by other relevant social actors, including fellow citizens" (p. 1122). Taken together, these perspectives suggest that 'social justice' can be seen as a broad set of social concepts that are dependent upon the settings in which they are applied. This becomes especially important in less developed nations where issues of limited access and inequitable allocations of resources have long had serious consequences for student achievement (Chisolm, 2017).

In addition, just as the roles of the school leader are extended and inter-woven into various aspects of their responsibilities, many of the roles of a successful school leader are found among those who consider themselves to be leaders for social justice. Focusing on the principal's role in professional development for social justice, Kose (2009) identified the school principal as a change agent or transformative leader, with the transformative leader being someone who enacts leadership that seeks to influence the motives of followers, particularly in under-performing schools in need of improvement (Denmark, 2012). Leithwood (1994) adapted the business model of transformational leadership to educational institutions where the focus was on the leader's ability to influence the school community towards positive school improvement. In this capacity, the school leader uses his or her agency to employ transformative leadership for social justice as a means of challenging and addressing disparities (Chisolm, 2017). Brown (2004) considers social justice and transformational school leadership from a critical theory perspective, which is grounded in evaluating how social structures devised by the dominate class effect the daily lives, structures and cultures of others. These perspectives informed the lens through which we examined the role of our two leaders in Belize.

Conceptual Framework

The role of a social justice school leader from the critical theory perspective is to alleviate inequities found within educational institutions by challenging policies that maintain the 'status quo.' Social justice leadership, particularly in a developing nation, requires a unique set of skills to efficiently and effectively shift a school's culture, which is often just a microcosm of problems that exist in the larger societal culture. The 'socially just' school leader strives to bridge the 'opportunity gap' by acknowledging inequities and advocating for all students. Drawing on the definition provided by Larson and Murtadha (2002), social justice school leadership is a set of "theories and practices of leadership that are vital to creating greater freedom, opportunity, and justice for all citizens—citizens who, through public education, are better able to participate in and sustain a free, civil, multicultural, and democratic society" (p. 136). This definition holds at its core the belief that education is the key to access and opportunities. In applying this definition to the role of educational leaders among developing nations, social justice not only stems from the desire to act but comes with special consideration for disparities in the quality of educational services. This includes, among other things, access to and equity in the allocation of resources, incorporating concerns of others in daily practice, and the need to address institutional systems and policies (decision-making bodies) that continue to marginalize segments of the population based on race, gender and/or religion (Cohn & Rossmiller, 1987; Jost & Kay, 2010; Larson & Murtadha, 2002).

The role of social justice school leaders within developing nations does not vary greatly from the roles of those in the USA and other industrialized nations, particularly when working in high-need schools confronting inequities to marginalized groups, specifically students of color, students with disabilities, and English as new language learners. In fact, the social justice framework for schools in developed nations such as England and developing nations (e.g. Venezuela, Tanzania, and Ghana) keep central to their focus, an interdisciplinary understanding of their historical, political, cultural, religious, and economic contexts as it relates to disparities between groups of people (Bosu, Dare, Dachi, & Fertig, 2011; Goldfarb & Grinberg, 2002; West & Currie, 2008). The school leader can influence building-wide practices by setting expectations and exercising behaviors that often times are not in alignment with an educational system established by those with 'power' (Chisolm, 2017). However, what varies between many developing nations and developed nations is the focus of the school leader as a social justice leader in providing not only equity, but *access* to the curriculum (formal and informal) and, in the case of Belize, education beyond primary school.

School Leadership and STEM Curriculum Development.

A critical component of social justice education involves preparing students with knowledge and skills for career and economic opportunities in the 21st century. Research documenting the state of STEM education in developing countries like is Belize is almost non-existent. Thus, given the context of this study (primarily its proximity to the Barrier Reef and its environmental impact), it was important to understand how the school leaders were conceptualizing, designing, and implementing the STEM curriculum.

Reform efforts in STEM related domains often focus on the school, classroom, teachers, and students and associated dynamics as the unit of analysis. Naturally, outcomes are often evaluated within the bounds of these units and/or agents. However, a significant but often overlooked variable involves the role of school leadership and the nature of decision-making and school support related to STEM teaching and learning. Indeed, the Wallace Foundation (2013) reported, "Education research shows that most variables, considered separately, have at most small effects on learning. The real payoff comes when individual variables combine to reach critical mass" (p. 4). Other researchers offer support for this perspective and have also documented that while classroom instruction is the most significant in understanding outcomes of practices related to teaching and learning, understandings of school leadership follow as the next most important variable (Wahlstrom, Louis, Leithwood, & Anderson, 2010). Wahlstrom et al. (2010) highlighted that school leadership has a strong and positive effect on teaching, learning, and associated student achievement. While the above work has examined school leadership and achievement, very few studies have examined the role of school leadership, STEM reform efforts and STEM enactment at the high school level. Indeed, Bairaktarova, Cox, and Evangelou (2011) identified this gap and in response, conducted some preliminary work in the Bulgarian context. The authors emphasized that promoting development of STEM skills and knowledge is as much the business of teachers and school leaders. Here we wanted to understand how school leaders navigated this domain of teaching and learning in the context of SJA.

Brown, Brown, Reardon, & Merrill (2011), explained that STEM education is a "standards-based meta discipline" (p. 6) that focuses on math, science technology and engineering. The emphasis on STEM also involves an integrated approach where content is viewed as dynamic. In this regard STEM teaching and learning is intended to address the dynamic nature of STEM fields through authentic practices that involve inquiry-based, problem solving, and innovative pedagogical approaches intended to solve human wants and needs. The Next Generation Science Standards (NGSS) (NGSS Lead States, 2013) also reinforces these practices. The focus on STEM in the Belizean context offers an opportunity to address interdisciplinary understandings of ecology and environmental sustainability. In this regard STEM is contextual; content knowledge is directly located to student's ecological environment and livelihood.

METHODOLOGY

For this case study, we used an adaptation of the multi-perspective interview protocol originally developed for the International Successful School Principalship Project (ISSPP) (Jacobson & Day 2007) and then adapted by the International School Leadership Development Network (ISLDN). Through interviews of school leaders, teachers, parents, students and community members, as well as field notes and official school and government documents, we sought to understand how a sense of social justice influenced and guided the work of these two leaders. Additionally, we examined how their STEM curriculum (specifically biology/life sciences and environmental education) was developed to take advantage of the environmental resources that are accessible to this island community. Classroom observations were also conducted during STEM classroom sessions

Research Participants

There were two main participant groups in this study, primary and secondary. Table 4.2 shows the demographics for each of the individual participants. The primary participant group consisted of the former school principal (retired) and two of the three school founders, both of whom currently serve as co-principals as well as teachers in the school. The third school founder is a real estate investor, whose primary role in the development of the school was the acquisition of the school property and the preliminary financing of its construction. This individual does not play a leadership role within the school, and therefore, was not included

TABLE 4.2. Participant Demographics

Participant	Role	Gender	Educational Background	Experience at Social Justice Academy (Yrs.)	Experience in K–12 (Yrs)	Interviews Conducted
Heather	Principal	F	M. S.	9	9	3
Ilene	Co-Principal	F	M. Ed.	9	9	3
Dr. Lazala	School Counselor	F	Ph. D.	4	4	2
Tricia	Teacher, Science	F	B.D.	9	9	1
Marco	Teacher, Computer	M	A.D.	3	3	1
David	Teacher, Mathematics	M	A.D.	2	2	1
Arlene	Former Principal (2010–15)	F	A.D.	5	10	1

in this study. Secondary participants included the school counselor, three classroom teachers, and a 10-member student focus group comprised of mixed genders and mixed grade levels.

Data Collection

For this study, the main data sources were 40–60 minutes semi-structured individual and group interviews and observations of the school leadership team and other school agents. Follow up interviews were conducted, as needed, to further expound on ideas or provide clarification for a deeper analysis of the data. All interviews were audio-recorded and transcribed.

Data were collected via Skype interviews, through online correspondence and while on site in Belize over a 10-day period. Semi-structured interviews were conducted with the following: 2 school leaders, 1 school principal (retired), 1 school counselor, 3 teachers, and a 10-member student focus group. Interviews were conducted in English, which is the official language of Belize.

Data Analysis

Participant interviews were audio taped and transcribed utilizing Rev.com and analyzed using Hyper RESEARCH software. Open coding, focus coding, and document analysis was conducted. Emphasis was placed on the synthesis and triangulation of information in order to make meaning of, and substantiate participants lived versus perceived experiences.

When Social Justice Academy (SJA) was founded in 2008 it was the first secondary school on the small island of Blue Cove Caye. Beginning informally with just 10 students on a front porch, the two founding school leaders opened the doors to SJA with 35 students. Since then, the school's enrollment has doubled to over 70 students with equal numbers of male and female students. SJA has three school administrators, eleven teachers (eight full-time and three part-time), and approximately 15–20 volunteer instructors. In addition to serving as the school's leadership team, the two school founders also serve as teaching principals, responsible for classroom instruction. SJA provides instruction in all four forms and an academic intervention program for students who require additional academic support for the transition from Form 1 to Form 2. There are currently 19 courses offered including site-based learning opportunities that focus on supporting the eco-tourism local economy of Blue Cove Caye.

In order to reach its current level of success, school leaders had to galvanize parent and community support, while negotiating with the Ministry of Education for a level of funding that would provide basic services for a functioning school, such as funding for teacher salaries, instructional materials and even the physical infrastructure (e.g., classrooms, clean water and toilets) that is still a work in progress as a third story is being added to accommodate the growth in enrollment.

FINDINGS

Leadership for Social Justice and STEM at SJA

Social justice influenced the work of the school's leaders daily as they strived to provide *all* students the opportunity for equitable access to a secondary education. In SJA, unlike most secondary schools in Belize, access is not just for those students who have passed the PSE and can afford tuition, but rather, access is available to any student on the island wishing to get a secondary education. "In the context of Belize, Blue Cove Caye and Social Justice Academy, social justice right now is tied into resources" (Ilene, School Leader).

The school's leaders are 'risk-takers' who enact social justice by creating a culture of care and providing students with 'windows of opportunities.' SJA's leaders identify themselves as leaders for social justice and members of the school community (students and teachers) view them the same way. The first act of risk-taking was not only in identifying a local need to address the number of 'at-risk' school-aged children who were on the streets during the day instead of enrolled in school.

> I started talking about wanting to open a school, just as an idea. I was in a coffee shop and there was cook behind the counter. She ran around and said, 'I heard you talking about wanting to open a school.' And she came at me with such desperation...I called the Ministry of Education and was thinking of about five students on my porch. How could I be allowed to share the education I had because it seemed so sad to me that they didn't have the opportunity (Heather, School Leader).

Risk-taking was not only in the school leaders' ability to identify this need, but more so in their ability to navigate educational and cultural systems and structures as 'outsiders' or non-natives.

Additionally, school leaders have made personal investments, both emotionally and financially, to ensure the school succeeds. Oftentimes their personal investment is at the expense of de-prioritizing their own families to ensure the school is operational and able to serve its students. Heather, the current school principal reflects,

> I sometimes wonder, like on a spiritual level, where this comes from…I sacrifice so much about myself or my life or my finances…I siphon money from my family to pay teachers when it's needed or to carry out some initiative I want to do, and sometimes I do that maybe at a level that makes me wonder why (Heather, School Leader).

In this case, the founding school leader sometimes uses her personal money to help to cover teacher payroll.

Outside of school, the school leaders have consistently gone above and beyond, often times serving as social workers, making home visits to check on students with high–absence and/or families who are struggling themselves, due to other mitigating factors such as alcoholism, drug abuse, or family illnesses, as well as using home visits as a means to recruit non-enrolled school-aged students. It is in these efforts that the school leaders are considered 'risk-takers' by staff and students alike.

> Heather does quite a bit of home visits. I tend to sometimes hesitate because I'm often not sure how comfortable they [the families] are. I sometimes question the extent to which we should go into homes (Dr. Lazala, School Counselor).

Heather shared, "we knock on doors and we sit, sometimes for two hours with the child and their parents and just talk with them about why they shouldn't leave education, why they need to be in school."

In addition to providing the island's youngsters access to a secondary education, these leaders have developed an informal science and environmental curricula that provide 'windows of opportunities,' i.e., 'pathways' and 'connectors' between students and resources that may create future career opportunities for their graduates both on and off the island, "On an island where resources are scarce, education is the key to everything. The school leaders are "excited by the 'opportunities' for students [that are] so limited on Blue Cove Caye…" (Ilene, School Leader).

Locally, the school leaders enact leadership for social justice through the planning and implementation of the school's instructional program design. The focus on STEM was an important component of the curriculum for SJA because of the location of Blue Cove Caye and the relevance of ecology and environmental education. Blue Cove Caye is within close proximity to the largest barrier reef in the western hemisphere and because of high volumes of tourist traffic on the Caye, the school leaders were cognizant that students needed to understand the ecology of the marine and coastal environment. School leader Ilene (Interview 1) emphasized:

> I would say our science program is one of our most popular and successful programs. I forgot to say early on environmental education is another one of our core values as a school. Our school motto is preserving our heritage, creating our future."

Likewise, School leader Heather also reinforced ecology and technology: "Some of the areas of focus include tourism, marine biology, and protection of our reef and our ecosystem." In this respect, the goal was to ensure that students understood the ecological value of their community and in turn this would inform a sustainable approach to tourism. This approach involved both formal science content and informal learning through the applied learning program. Students engaged in several 'site-based learning' opportunities through physical education (PE) classes and internships. Students participate in physical education courses, also known as 'site-based learning' opportunities, such as kayaking, fly-fishing, scuba diving, tour-guides, and biking. As part of the school's entrepreneurial programs, the PE program offered at SJA is connected to sports and activities on the island that are pathways to some of the highest paid jobs and the most growth in industry.

> It [SJA] has opportunities that other schools in the city don't have. For example, they have the Fish with Purpose, which is a PE and it teaches the students to interact with tourists and fishing and so much more. When I first started here, I had a PE, which was Scuba Diving, and I got certified for Advanced Scuba Diving. In the future, if I want to work as a tour guide, I already can dive. I just need to get certified as a tour guide (Robert, Student).

The goal is to teach students entrepreneurship, where students are able to create small businesses, and volunteer groups and tourists can have students accompany them and interpret the local marine ecosystems and the cultural history of the island. Compensation for these services go back to the student to offset the costs associated with schooling; thus minimizing one of the many barriers to accessing education.

Supplemental to the prescribed Belizean curriculum, there is also an Applied Learning course which is co-taught by the school's leaders. This course is designed to have students start to think about what they are passionate about pursuing as a career and how to be successful in both the world of work and academics. Ilene said, "If you don't have a high school education your opportunities are very limited, so that applies to the Applied Learning class that Heather and I teach… identifying what students career goals are and exposing them."

Career and Technical Education (CTE) refers to a specially designed instructional program that provides students with the academic and technical skills and certification required to prepare students to succeed in a skills-based economy

(US Department of Education, 2012). Comparable to Career and Technical Education (CTE) programs in the USA, these courses are designed with the purpose of equipping students with the knowledge, job skills, and attributes necessary for viable employment in the most prominent careers on island and full participation in the nation's eco-tourism. In addition to working in the community, students are required to give back to the community by completing 40 service hours towards graduation. For example, students volunteer at a local animal shelter and tutor at the primary school. In addition, students participate in environmental education and advocacy in such programs as the Marine Biology Apprenticeship with Belize Fisheries and the Ocean Conservancy International Beach Clean Up. These activities are important because a key component to social justice and social justice teaching is participation in service-oriented work (Kose, 2009). What differentiates this service-oriented work from the school's entrepreneurial program is the incorporation of a sense of advocacy.

The work of these two social justice leaders extends beyond the school and the local island community in their ongoing effort to connect to an even wider global community. Students participate in many national and international competitions focused on recycling, conservation of the land and ocean, as well as mathematics and technology. The students of SJA have won several awards garnishing local recognition and funding for the school and individual students, e.g., the United Nation's International Children's Emergency Fund (UNICEF) Sports in Education Award (International), National Sagicor Visionaries STEM Competitions Most Creative and Innovative Project (National), and Belize Department of Youth Service's National Youth Award for Environmentalism (Local).

> Even with the tourism, I think the students who do the kayaking and the bike tours and all, they are getting recognition and a name for how pleasant they can be, how articulate. The school's performance in these national events, there are lots of little innovations that we do here that not just the people on the island hear about... (Dr. Lazala, School Counselor).

Participation in these competitions helps to close the 'opportunity gap' for students by allowing them to engage in advocacy, innovative problem solving, and develop a collective responsibility for their local community and beyond.

STEM Curriculum and Enactment

For school leaders, expectations for STEM curriculum reflected the urgency of preparing youth for global STEM careers within their own communities. As was explained above, understandings of ecology and marine biology were essential in empowering students to protect their environment and address the growing tourism industry in a more sustainable manner. School leader Heather explained that in addition to the national curriculum, they understood that students' education should also include their experiences at home and in the community. She explained it this way: "... what do you think that child really needs to know and understand to be successful in the world and field of math? I don't always think that the curriculum, as it comes to us, is like that… would we include it in that answer. So, we start to look at [Blue Cove Caye] students, what is it that they need in each of those subject areas?" While resources were limited and infrastructure such as a science lab were lacking, students still had opportunities to develops habits of mind with scientific investigation.

Classroom observations revealed that science inquiry experiences were provided through field-based investigations and applied learning experiences. For example, students engaged in a field-based ecology activity where they explored field sampling techniques used by biologists to estimate population. This involved identifying and tagging soldier crabs, which was repeated several times to estimate the population of soldier crabs in a protected area near to the school. In addition, to formal classroom experiences, students also conducted ecology labs during evening and weekend internships with the fisheries department. In this respect, students learned about ecological interdependence of various species of aquatic organisms. In a third example, science content learning was also linked to school-based extracurricular experiences that fostered entrepreneurship and community productivity. As Robert explained above, the opportunities offered by scuba diving extended beyond schooling. The emphasis on entrepreneurship and P.E. activities such as scuba diving also involved understanding of scientific phenomena. This included understanding of the ecology of the environment, fisheries, and important physics concepts associated with scuba diving such as understanding gases and pressure.

In the case of technology, school leaders did not have access to programming experts, so they provided access to students via online programs such as Hour of Code, a curriculum available in California schools (see https://hourofcode.com/ for more information about this program). Principal Ilene stated that "all of our students this year are doing what's called Hour of Code. It's an online free curriculum, and the reason we started doing that is we were introduced to the woman who coordinates it." In addition, the school leader Ilene also confirmed that the decision to implement this program was based on students' previous exposure and enthusiasm about the potential of programming in their school: "After that summer experience the students were so excited that we actually implemented this Hour of Code across all computer classes." She continued to explain that this programming exposure helped students to develop technology skills that they could then use beyond the context of Belize: "…with those kinds of technology skills students can stay in their own country and yet have a living, sort of like an international scale of business." It is notable that these experiences essentially highlighted how STEM knowledge and skills was very contextual. In other words, students had relevant experiences that made scientific and technological knowledge tangible and meaningful.

DISCUSSION AND CONCLUSIONS

Globally, a school and its leader's success are most often measured by standardized student achievement tests, often in the areas of English language arts and mathematics (Blasé & Blasé, 2004; Cayetano, 2011; Leithwood & Louis, 2012; Levy, 2010; Pashiardis, et al., 2012; Santamaria et al., 2014). Even in Belize, school success and the success of the school leader is attributed to student achievement on the Caribbean Examination Council (CXC) Examination (Cayetano, 2011; Levy, 2010). However, in the context of Social Justice Academy, successful leadership is not necessarily synonymous with academic achievement, as it is with providing a marginalized group of students' access to the curriculum and opportunities to increase their social capital as social entrepreneurs.

The school leaders of SJA provided students with 'windows of opportunities' by providing access to secondary education and by placing a greater emphasis on exposure to an informal curriculum intended to equip students with the skills necessary to participate and contribute to the growing eco-tourism economy of the island. The school leaders of SJA have redefined the "metrics" of success for the students of SJA and the children of Blue Cove Caye.

Some students interviewed, like Lara- an immigrant from neighboring Guatemala who "applied straight to the university," spoke of aspirations for higher education beyond secondary school. In the case of SJA, the school leaders must also recognize the importance of these aspirations and prepare students for life beyond the island by placing a greater emphasis on developing a more rigorous formal curriculum. This will enable students to not only gain access, but persist in tertiary school programs, thus providing them the opportunity to return to the island and serve in much needed careers that currently do not exist on Blue Cove Caye such as doctors and lawyers. Unfortunately, many of the students who transition to tertiary education do not persist due to the "costs associated with schooling and cost of living on the mainland" (Heather, School Leader).

Benefit to Students

The school leaders established SJA with a clear vision and mission of providing 'equitable access to universal education' for all children on the island, regardless of academic level or financial need. This is of particular importance in the context of education in Belize because for many students, they are often the first in their families to receive a secondary education because never before was there a high school on the island, and so unless their parents actually left the island, they did not have this opportunity. Particularly for those 'at-risk' school-aged children who had been on the streets before SJA, the efforts of these leaders provide several obvious benefits. First, the establishment of SJA has made secondary schooling accessible to all students on Blue Cove Caye due to its proximity and affordability. Students now have access to a curriculum and experiences that they were not previously afforded. In addition, SJA provides a viable option for students from neighboring islands, and even the mainland, who wish to explore careers in the field of eco-tourism. Students at SJA not only gain access to a secondary education, but also access to learning opportunities outside of the classroom through service learning and site-based learning.

Over the long term, these students who receive career and technical education have greater earning potential than their counterparts who have simply completed high school. "...the high payoffs associated with vocational education (relative to secondary) is consistent with findings that the labor market in Belize need skilled labor in the areas in which the country is doing well such as tourism" (Näslund-Hadley, Alonzo, & Martin, 2013, p. 17). It is through such concerted efforts that the school's leaders play a pivotal social justice role in challenging an educational system, societal norms and social politics that have led to a systemic cycle of poverty through education and work readiness skills. Besides the benefits to human capital, this evidence further supports the importance and benefits of education in Belize beyond primary school.

Benefits to Island Community

In addition to the many benefits to students, the social justice work of these two SJA leaders also benefits the local community. The site-based learning opportunities and entrepreneurship programs not only enhance community relations, but also serve to supply valuable human resources necessary to achieve and advance local economic goals. Through national and international competitions, students at SJA have worked to solve real-world problems related to the environmental and economic sustainability of Blue Cove Caye, both in the short- and long-term.

Why STEM?

Given the global urgency for equitable STEM access and the adoption of the NGSS (NGS Lead States, 2013), the outcomes of the school leaders' efforts at SJA have implications for the roles of school leaders in designing and enacting STEM curriculum, providing support and access and understanding the contextual value of STEM knowledge and skills. In other words, the quality and sustainability of STEM efforts reflect a reciprocal relationship with school leaders, the STEM curriculum and the role of teachers and students. Indeed, this study reinforced that the role of school leaders was critical in ensuring that students received meaningful experiences for both in and out of school STEM teaching and learning (Wahlstrom, et al., 2010; Waight, Jacobson, & Chisolm, 2016). Please note that we engage in extensive discussion of the role of STEM and school leadership in Waight, Chisolm & Jacobson (2018)

While this study was conducted in the context of Belize, it has global implications for understanding the roles of school leaders, the decision-making process and support for STEM implementation and enactment. Specifically, it offers insight to understand the contextual and cultural nuances of STEM implementation and enactment in high needs schools.

Questions to Consider:

1. What lessons can be learned from SJA about using social justice leadership to develop an informal curriculum designed to improve both the life chances of students and the long-term economic sustainability of the school community, particularly in developing nations?

2. What knowledge and skills do school leaders (who do not hold STEM expertise) require in order to make informed decisions about STEM curriculum and enactment that meaningfully impacts its students?

REFERENCES

Bairaktarova, D., Cox, M. F., & Evangelou, D. (2011). Leadership training in science technology, engineering and mathematics education in Bulgaria. *European Journal of Engineering Education, 36*, 585–594.

Blasé, J., & Blasé, J. (2004). *Handbook of instructional leadership: How successful principals promote teaching and learning* (2nd ed.). Thousand Oaks, CA: Corwin Press.

Bosu, R., Dare, A., Dachi, H., & Fertig, M. (2011). School leadership and social justice: Evidence from Ghana and Tanzania. *International Journal of International Development, 31*, 67–77.

Brown, K. M. (2004). Leadership for social justice and equity: Weaving a transformative framework and pedagogy. *Educational Administration Quarterly, 40*(1), 77–108.

Brown, L., & Conrad, D. A. (2007). School leadership in Trinidad and Tobago: The challenge of context. *Comparative Education Review, 51*(2), 181–201.

Brown, R., Brown, J., Reardon, K, & Merrill, C. (2011). Understanding STEM: Current Perceptions. *Technology and Engineering Teacher, 70*(6), 5–9.

Bush, T. (2009). Leadership development and school improvements: Contemporary issues in leadership development. *Education Review, 61*(4), 375–389.

Cayetano, J. (2011). *Instructional leadership and student achievement in Belizean secondary schools.* (Published doctoral dissertation). Oklahoma State University.

Chemers, M. (1997). *An integrative theory of leadership.* Mahwah, NJ: Erlbaum.

Chisolm, L. D. (2017). *Social justice leadership that matters: An evaluation of school leadership practices in a high-need secondary school in Central America-Belize.* (Unpublished doctoral dissertation). State University of New York at Buffalo.

Cohn, E. & Rossmiller, R. (1987). Research on effective schools: Implications for less developed countries. *Comparative Education Review, 31*(3), 377–399.

Denmark, Vicki. (2012). *Transformational leadership—A matter of perspective.* Retrieved from http://www.advanc-ed.org/source/transformational-leadership-matter-perspective

Fanon, F. (1963). *The wretched of the Earth.* New York, NY: Grove Press.

Goldfarb, K. P., & Grinberg, J. (2002). Leadership for social justice: Authentic participation in the case of a community center in Caracas, Venezuela. *Journal of School Leadership, 12*, 157–173.

Jacobson, S. (2011) Leadership effect on student achievement and sustained school success. *International Journal of Educational Management, 25*(1), 33–44.

Jacobson, S., & Day, C. (2007). The international successful school principal project (IS-SPP): An overview of the project, the case studies and their contexts. *International Studies in Educational Administration, 35 (3)*, 3–10.

Johnson, L., Møller, J., Pashiardis, P., Vedøy, G., & Savvides, V. (2011). Culturally responsive practices. In R. Ylimaki & S. Jacobson (Eds.), *US and cross-national policies, practices, and preparation* (pp. 75–101). New York: Springer.

Jost, J. T. & Kay, A. C. (2010). Social justice: History, theory, and research. In S. Fiske, D. Gilbert, & G. Lindzey (Eds.), *Handbook of social psychology*. Hoboken, NJ: John Wiley & Sons, Inc.

King, R. (1987). *Education in the Caribbean: Historical perspectives* (online). Mona: U of West Indies.

Kose, B. W. (2009). The principal's role in professional development for social justice: An empirically-based transformative framework. *Urban Education, 44*(6), 628–663.

Lall, Marie. (2007). *A review of concepts from policy studies relevant for the analysis of EFA in developing countries.* Consortium for Research on Educational Access, Transitions and Equity (CREATE). London, UK: University of London.

Larson, C., & Murtadha, K. (2002). Leadership for Social Justice. *Yearbook of the National Society for the Study of Education, 101*(1), 134–161.

Leithwood (1994). Leadership for school restructuring. *Educational Administration Quarterly, 30*(4), 498.

Leithwood, K., & Louis, K. S. (2012). *Linking leadership to student learning.* San Francisco, CA: Jossey-Bass.

Leithwood, K., & Riehl, C. (2005). What we know about successful school leadership. In Firestone, W. & Riehl, C. (Eds.), *A new agenda: Directions for research on educational leadership* (pp. 27–47). New York, NY: Teachers College.

Levy, L. (2010). *Exemplary leadership: A study of leadership practices that enable sustained academic achievement in high-need schools.* (Published doctoral paper). Arizona State University, Arizona.

Marshall, C., & Ward, M. (2004). "Yes, but ...": Education leaders discuss social justice. *Journal of School Leadership, 14*, 530–563.

McDougall, D., Saunders, W., & Goldenberg, C. (2007). Inside the black box of school reform: Explaining the how and why of change at *Getting Results* school. *Journal of Disability, Development, and Education, 54*, 54–89.

Näslund-Hadley, E., Alonzo, H., & Martin, D. (2013). *Challenges and opportunities in the Belize education sector.* Inter-American Development Bank.

NGSS Lead States. (2013). *Next generation science standards: For states, by states.* Washington, DC: The National Academies Press.

Pashiardis, P., Kafa, A., & Marmara, C. (2012). Successful secondary principalship in Cyprus: What have "Thucydides" and "Plato" revealed to us? *International Journal of Educational Management, 26*(5), 480–493.

Santamaria, L., Santamaria, A., Webber, M., & Pearson, H. (2014). Indigenous urban school leadership (IUSL): A critical cross-cultural comparative analysis of educational leaders in New Zealand and the United States. *Canadian and International education, 43*(1), 1.

Wahlstrom, K. L., Louis, K. S., Leithwood, K., & Anderson, S. E. (2010). *Investigating the links to improved student learning: Executive summary of research findings.* New York, NY: The Wallace Foundation.

U.S. Department of Education. (2012). *U.S. Department of Education Releases blueprint to transform career and technical education.* Retrieved from https://www.ed.gov/news/press-releases/us-department-education-releases-blueprint-transform-career-and-technical-education

Waight, N., Jacobson, S., & Chisolm, L. (2016, April). *School leadership and STEM enactment in a high needs secondary school in Belize.* Paper presented at the Annual Meeting of the National Association for Research in Science Teaching, Baltimore, MD.

Waight, N., Chisolm, L., & Jacobson, S. (2018). School leadership and STEM enactment in a high needs secondary school in Belize, *International Studies in Educational Administration, 46*(1), 102–122.

The Wallace Foundation. (2013). *The school principal as leader: Guiding schools to better teaching and learning.* New York, NY: The Wallace Foundation.

Watson, L. (2003). Issues in the headship of schools. In L. Watson (Ed.), *Selecting and developing heads of schools: 23 European perspectives* (pp. 5–16). Sheffield, UK: European Forum on Educational Administration.

West, A., & Currie, P. (2008). School diversity and social justice: Policy and politics. *Educational Studies, 34*(3), 241–250.

Ylimaki, R. (2007). Instructional leadership in challenging US schools. *International Studies in Educational Administration, 35*(3), 11–19.

Ylimaki, R., & Jacobson, S. (2011). Comparative perspectives: An overview of seven educational contexts. In R. Ylimaki & S. Jacobson (Eds.), *US and cross-national policies, practices, and preparation.* New York, NY: Springer.

CHAPTER 5

LEADERSHIP PRACTICES FOR EQUITY AND EXCELLENCE

An Exploratory Narrative of Two Principals of High-Need Elementary Schools in California

Betty Alford

The purpose of this exploratory narrative study was to identify the leadership practices that fostered student learning in two successful high-need elementary schools in Southern California in one of the 20 highest poverty districts in California. Through the leadership of the two principals, these two elementary schools received awards for consistently improving academic achievement and reducing the achievement gap for high poverty students. In each of the two urban schools, over 88% of the students were Latina(o), over 85% were from low-income families, and over 36% were English learners. This study identified the practices that these two principals demonstrated in implementing new, more rigorous content standards. Data were collected from two in-depth interviews with each principal followed by a member check with each principal after the data were transcribed. Field notes of on-site observations and document review were additional data sources. The protocol developed by members of the high-need strand of the International School Leadership Development Network (ISLDN) (Baran & Berry, 2015) served as a guide for the study. After transcription of the interviews, the researcher coded the interview and field notes to discern themes using an iterative, recursive process of data analysis. The nar-

Educational Leadership, Culture, and Success in High-Need Schools, pages 85–101.
Copyright © 2019 by Information Age Publishing
85

ratives of these two principals and observations clearly demonstrated their strong moral commitment to ensure quality learning and hold high expectations for all. The principals demonstrated consistent integrity in modeling their values through leadership of quality, culturally responsive school-wide instructional practices, professional development, and parent engagement opportunities. These leaders' ethical, socially just behavior shaped school cultures of respect and high expectations while establishing and maintaining consistent structures for collaboration, ongoing learning, and parent engagement. The study illuminated specific practices influencing students' academic success through the voices of participants.

Keywords: Elementary School Principal Leadership, Equity and Excellence, Moral, Ethical Leadership, High-need School Contexts

INTRODUCTION

Blankstein and Noguera (2015) argued that courageous leaders are needed whose actions and words stem from a strong moral purpose grounded in an inherent belief in the importance of equity and excellence for all students through shared leadership for student success: "Pushing for excellence through equity requires great courage and conviction. . ... The members of a society share a moral imperative to assure that every child gets what he or she needs to succeed" (Blankstein & Noguera, 2015, p. 9). Nationwide within the US, achievement gaps continue in graduation rates, college enrollment, and college attainment between ethnic groups of White, Asian, Latino, and Black, with White and Asian populations attaining a higher percentage of success (National Center for Education Statistics, 2014). Gaps in educational attainment between students of low-income families and middle and high-income families continue to persist across the US in high-need school contexts where low expectations for students of low-income backgrounds and low student academic achievement have often prevailed (Blankstein & Noguera, 2015; Chenoweth, 2009). In these contexts, "Advancing equity is both morally and practically the right thing to do" (Blankstein & Noguera, 2015, p. 9).

Although high-need schools often share characteristics of low academic achievement, high populations of students from low-income families, limited resources, and a high percentage of students of minority ethnic groups (Duke, 2012), some high-need schools are succeeding in achieving strong academic student performance (Chenoweth, 2009; Murakami, Garza, & Merchant, 2010). This exploratory study of two principals of successful high-need elementary schools in Southern California identifies practices that contributed to the academic success of students as the schools implemented new, rigorous content standards. Specifically, the researcher explores what principal practices fostered student learning in two successful high- need schools that have achieved recognition for students' academic success. Each of the schools has at least 85% Latino(a) students and at least 85% of students qualifying for free and reduced lunch, an indicator of poverty in the US.

Rationale

School leaders can make a significant difference in high-need settings in promoting student achievement and eliminating achievement gaps between students from low-income families and students from middle or high-income families (Blankstein & Noguera, 2015; Chenoweth, 2009). Leaders' communication of the importance of high expectations and their advocacy for the success of all students while building support systems for success and demonstrating a commitment to ongoing learning and continuous improvement are pivotal in promoting increased learning in high-need schools (Bromberg & Theokas, 2013; Dantley, 2005; Papa & English, 2011; Stanford-Blair & Dickman, 2005). Across multiple contexts, successful principals in high-need contexts have demonstrated that a moral commitment to helping all students to achieve to high levels matters (Gillett, Clarke, & O'Donoghue, 2016). Through their actions and words, successful principals exemplify their commitment to making a positive difference beyond the boundaries of a set role description (Drysdale, Gurr, & Goode, 2016), to establishing strong connections with the community (Barnett & Stevenson, 2016; Khalifa, Witherspoon, & Neucomb, 2015), and to building strong relationships characterized by trust (Gillett, et al., 2016). The voices of successful school principals in describing practices that foster student learning in high-need contexts contributes to our understanding of leadership for enhanced learning.

REVIEW OF THE LITERATURE

Both district and school leadership are important in achieving goals of equity and excellence in schools (DuFour & Fullan, 2013). Although in the US, gaps in performance exist relative to ethnicity and the number of students who are from low-income schools, the gaps do not exist in all schools (Bromberg & Theokas, 2013). School leaders can enact practices, processes, and policies that support both equity and excellence for all students (Griffin & Dixon, 2017), and principals play a key role in school improvement through caring leadership (Beck, 1994; Noddings, 2013), purposeful leadership (Dantley, 2005), and ethical leadership (Bredeson, 2005; Sergiovanni, 1992; Starratt, 1994, 2004, 2017).

Caring is a primary attribute that is demonstrated by successful school principals (Beck, 1994; Pellicer, 2003). In school leadership, caring is a reciprocal process wherein leaders engage in sustained relationships characterized by actions to meet needs (Noddings, 2013; Pellicer, 2003). As leaders of high-need schools in urban, diverse contexts recognize achievement gaps and work to eliminate these gaps to increase the educational success of all students, caring is consistently displayed through focused actions. In these contexts, principals eliminate barriers that limit students' learning as well as consistently foster a shared vision of equity and excellence for all (Donaldson, 2006).

Dantley (2005) stressed the need for purposeful leadership in which school principals' actions are guided by a central purpose of helping each child to grow to his or maximum potential. As leaders of social justice, school principals ask the hard questions pertinent to existing challenges and engage in proactive ways of meeting these challenges through a shared vision and a sustained focus on equity and excellence (Dantley, 2005). As social justice leaders, they serve as advocates for students and parents who have been marginalized and promote culturally proficient leadership (Papa & English, 2011). Murphy and Torre (2014) points out that instructional leadership is not at the peripheral of their work. Instead, it is central to each day's work. However, instructional leadership is not narrowly defined as supervision of work. Instructional leadership that matters in achieving positive results in learning is an ongoing process enacted as a co-learner and an advocate for continuous improvement (Murphy, 2014).

Applying concepts of ethical leadership to the broader context of schooling, Dewey (1916) wrote about schooling as essentially a moral practice. Within the field of educational administration, from the 1980s to the present, the focus of school administration preparation programs moved from an emphasis on managerial concepts alone to concepts of management and leadership, particularly as these concepts apply to school improvement, social justice, and caring (Murphy & Torre, 2014). In the 1990s, ethics became widely accepted as part of the knowledge base for the field (Beck, 1994; Sergiovanni, 1992; Starratt, 1994). In the 90s, Sergiovanni (1992) stressed, "Schools are moral communities requiring a distinct leadership based on moral actions" (p. 11). Starratt (1994) added, "Learning itself is intrinsically a moral act, and leadership within this environment requires leaders to attend to ethics" (p. 2).

Starratt (1994) provided an ethical framework for school leadership stating, "Ethical leadership requires a deep commitment and moral purpose guided by the leadership virtues of vision, authenticity, and presence" (p. 10). The principal's words and actions communicate a vision of high expectations for all students. The consistency of stated beliefs and actions demonstrate the authenticity of the principal in modeling a commitment to learning for all. This commitment is demonstrated as the principal is fully engaged in the school improvement process and fully present in the work of the school and analysis of the needs. In demonstrating these virtues, ethics of critique, justice, and care are important (Starratt, 1994, 2004, 2017). The principal raises questions regarding issues of social justice and demonstrates caring to design systems and interventions to meet student needs. Caring is demonstrated through words and actions.

METHODOLOGY

This exploratory narrative study was conducted by a member of the International School Leadership Development Network (ISLDN) established in 2010 and sponsored by the British Educational Leadership, Management and Administration Society and the University Council of Educational Administration. The IS-LDN has two strands of research with one strand focusing on social justice school leadership practice and development and the other strand focusing on leadership and development in high-need schools (Barnett & Stevenson, 2016). The present exploratory study was conducted as part of the high-need schools research strand to identify what principal practices fostered student learning in two high-need elementary schools in order to give voice to the two successful school principals in these high-needs settings.

The district where the two principals served as leaders of elementary schools was nationally recognized three years in a row by The Education Trust, a national educational advocacy organization, for the district's unwavering commitment to and success in serving students from low-income families. Students in this district were attaining goals of high academic achievement *despite the demographic odds* of a high-need, urban setting wherein the majority of students qualified for free and reduced lunches, a poverty indicator in US schools. In 2012, the Education Trust rated this school district as third in achieving high academic performance from the 20 highest poverty districts in California and as third among all 142 large, unified districts in California for eliminating the achievement gap between Latino(a) and White students in academic performance. For improvement among low-income students from 2008 to 2012, The Education Trust recognized the district's accomplishments in improving student performance by awarding an A rating. This success in promoting student learning in a high-need context continues to the present. With 94% of students classified as low-income through qualification for the Free and Reduced Lunch Program and 91% of the student population Latino(a), this district of 11,439 clearly represents a high-need district.

This study was designed to illuminate principal practices that contributed to the academic success of students in two of this district's high-need elementary schools. The criteria for selection of the schools included:

- Elementary schools recognized for academic performance,
- Sustained academic ratings that exceeded the state's percentage of students demonstrating mastery of learning outcomes as measured by the state's standardized, criterion referenced test,
- A student population of over 85% Latino(a) students and 85% students whose families are low income, and
- Principal leadership at the school for at least seven years.

In the two schools selected for this study, one principal had served as principal for the campus for seven years and one for eleven years, providing stable leadership for the schools.

Setting and Data Sources

Based on the criteria, the principals who were selected for this study served in elementary schools with over 88% Latino(a) students, over 85% children of poverty, and over 36% designated as English learners. For five years prior to the state's changes in accountability measures in 2015, both schools' ratings exceeded the Adequate Performance Indicator (API) of 800, the target for the state, on a statewide mandated standardized examination. California and 47 other states in the US transitioned in 2016 to new academic standards that promote college and career readiness with a new computer-based accountability test titled *Smarter Balanced Assessment*. In the transition to this new accountability state test, the principals focused on increasing student learning through an emphasis on critical thinking skills and student engagement. These two elementary schools have sustained stable teacher and principal leadership. This study identified the practices that these two principals demonstrated as they implemented new content standards while sustaining a strong commitment to equity and excellence for all students. In this exploratory, qualitative study, two individual interviews of 60–90 minutes per interview with each of the principals, on-site campus observations, and document review were the data sources.

Data Analysis

The interviews were audio-taped and transcribed before being analyzed to discern themes through open and axial coding (Lichtman, 2014; Merriam, 2009). Field notes from on-site campus observations were analyzed as part of the triangulation process as well as archival data of student academic performance results as measured on state tests. Trustworthiness of the data was maintained through member-checks and an audit trail. Pseudonyms were provided for the participants and the schools to guard confidentiality.

FINDINGS

This exploratory study identified leadership practices that two elementary principals perceived as influential in their sustained success in fostering student learning in high-need schools serving a primarily Latino student body with over 85% of the students from low-income families. The schools were located within a school district in Southern California.

Principals and School Contexts

Bello Elementary School offers a dual language program of Spanish and English that is available to students from transitional kindergarten through 5th grade, a program that has been offered for 19 years despite legislation in California that emphasizes sheltered English programs instead of bilingual programs. A high percentage of students qualify for free and reduced lunch of 85%. Ninety-three % of the students are Hispanic with 5% Asian and White and 0% African American. Forty-three % of the students are dual language students. The school enrollment is 600 for grades transitional kindergarten through 5th grade. In 2016, the school was one of three schools in California to receive the Seal of Excellence award for outstanding achievement from the California Association of Bilingual education. Charlotte has been the principal at Bello Elementary School for 7 years with 12 years of experience as a principal and 22 years of experience in the district.

The school has a strong sense of community. On how to encourage parent engagement, she said:

> First, you have to listen to the parents. They need to know you, and they need to be able to trust you and to see you are working for their child. . .. . I let the parents know that we're a partnership, and I'm working with you.

From weekly parent meetings of 35–45 parents every week to 100% parent partic-ipation at events, such as, Back to School night, the principal engaged the parents as full partners in the school. Initiatives were provided, such as "Random Acts of Kindness Week" to emphasize, "It isn't just about test scores, but it's having good character as well, understanding that they are connected to everyone in the community and that they must give back." Several of the parents in the commu-nity went to school at this elementary, and some staff members and faculty live in the neighborhood of the school. The school is in an urban setting, and there is some gang activity around the neighborhood as identified by the police. Many single-family homes characterize the attendance zone for the school with limited apartment buildings.

Although the campus accountability results had just reached 800 in the year before Charlotte became principal, she explained that the students' aggregate per-formance score on the state's standardized test "grew another 35 points, which is difficult to accomplish when the scores are already at a high range." As the state shifted to a new accountability test for students, a focus on enhancing critical thinking and writing has prevailed. The school culture when Charlotte arrived as principal was strained from the previous principal's autocratic style of leadership. However, Charlotte described her focus on strengthening a positive school culture reflecting a team approach by adding a "beneficial structure, support, funding for needed materials, and the time for faculty to get to know, trust, and respect her as their principal." She views the school's goal as preparing the students for high school and college even at 1st grade.

Elway Elementary School, a school of 718, serves predominately a Latino(a) student population of 88% and an Asian population of 7%. Ninety-one % of the students are from low-income families and qualify for the free and reduced lunch program. In 2011–2012, the school was identified by California Business for Edu-cational Excellence as a high-performing public school that is consistently im-proving academic achievement and reducing the achievement gap for high pov-erty students. Celia became the principal of the school in 2005 as interim principal and has served as principal for 11 years at this school site and 20 years in the district. Before assuming the role of principal, Celia had served as an instructional leader as a resource and reading recovery teacher. When she assumed the role of principal at the school, she described the school culture as "a dark cloud around the school." She remembered that as the assistant superintendent introduced her to the faculty and staff as the new principal, the assistant superintendent said, "You guys need to get along." The previous principal had been principal for the school for 17 years, and at the time of her leaving, the faculty members were divided in their allegiance to the former principal. As Celia arrived, she shared that she was quickly accepted as they recognized that she had participated in the same professional development sessions that they had experienced and that she was very knowledgeable about good instructional practices. She described the faculty as "feeling validated" because she had experienced the same training as many of them in her work as a reading recovery teacher. She encountered, however, negative comments from faculty indicative of low expectations for students, such as, "These students, they will never get to college." When the faculty realized that Celia had been a product of this district, she said, "It changed mindsets." She says that she realized that she needed to not become defensive, but she had to educate them to hold high expectations for all.

The school was high performing on the API rating which was already above 700 when Celia became principal. She recounted that, "Our school was the first school in the district to attain 800 on the API." In four years, the school experienced 70 points growth." By the fifth year of Celia's leadership, the financial crises occurred in California, and nine teachers were *laid off* due to the need to cut expenses within the district. The students' scores lowered that year as support services were curtailed; however, the principal was able to rehire all the nine teachers except one when funding in the district increased, and these teachers returned to the campus. She described the faculty as very hard working. She also described herself as a constant learner. She expressed a very strong working relationship with faculty who she quoted as saying, "We can tell that you love what you do." Celia added, "Sometimes they look at me, and say, 'Oh no, she's getting another idea. Oh, she's snapping that gum.'" Celia's enthusiasm for learning is contagious. As she says, "It's not easy, but I love seeing the sparks when students are learning. I have a passion for this community and for teaching literacy. My mother was a teacher in all that she did although she only completed 9th grade." As a second-generation Mexican-American college graduate of immigrant parents, Celia easily understands many of the challenges that her students and parents face as Latinos(as).

PRINCIPAL LEADERSHIP PRACTICES THAT FOSTERED INCREASED STUDENT LEARNING

Principal leadership practices in these two schools that fostered increased student learning included focusing clearly on critical thinking, engagement, and high expectations; engaging parents as partners; shared leadership with structures for collaboration; and strengthening professional learning.

Focusing on Critical Thinking, Engagement, and High Expectations.

At the time of this study, each elementary school was situated within the context of change in the state's required student examination to the *Smarter Balanced Assessment* in 2016, a computer-based examination that emphasizes increased critical thinking and writing skills. Analyzing test scores and planning instructional strategies to help all students to reach instructional goals was an ongoing collaborative process in the schools. In this academic context, the messages of the principal with all stakeholders were consistent in delving deeper than merely a concern for raising test scores. The messages continually voiced by these principals were messages of social justice and a commitment to high expectations. The emphasis of the importance of raising test scores, prompted nationwide by the *No Child Left Behind* legislation in 2001 (NCLB, 2001) and statewide through state accountability examinations, was not expressed by the principals. Instead, they spoke of the importance of high expectations.

Charlotte described ways the dual language program assisted in promoting 21ˢᵗ century skills:

> We provide a dual language program in grades K–5, but the English language is very important to us as is respecting and valuing each student's culture and home language. We try to respect and support each student's culture, and we want to give the students exposure to different cultures. We have students from Columbia and San Salvador, for example. Dual language is part of our goal. We have high expectations. We want high levels of literacy. It is our responsibility to make sure that all are on a college path. What we are doing is preparing them for high school and college, even at 1ˢᵗ grade.

Celia emphasized that the shift from an emphasis on basic skills to the knowledge and skills needed to develop students as global citizens as California implements the Common Core presented new goals. Celia stressed, "We are here for a common purpose. We want to provide opportunities for our students to go above and beyond."

Celia shared her personal experiences as a member of the community and a product of the district with the faculty in order to heighten expectations. As Celia related that she was a product of the district, comments regarding the future of these students changed: "When teachers began to share lower expectations for students of our district, I said, 'I am a product of this school district.'" When individual comments were heard that reflected low expectations for students, both principals were united in addressing the statements forthrightly. Willingness *to take a stand* in support of high expectations was illuminated by each principal's words and actions.

While the two principals consistently provided communication reinforcing their beliefs in the importance of high expectations for all students, the need to remove barriers that might be prohibiting any students' success led to a focus on establishing a positive school culture where teachers expected students to graduate and go on to postsecondary education. The principals and their faculty members had participated in sustained professional development emphasizing the importance of believing that students would graduate and continue their education. The principals began reinforcing this vision of a pathway to college through aesthetics. Charlotte described this process stating,

> First, we started with aesthetics, adopting a university and posting where each teacher graduated. We named our accelerated reader levels as bachelor's degree, master's degree, and doctoral degree for them to get acquainted with these terms.

However, the impact on the culture in these two schools was stronger than aesthetics alone and was founded in a shared belief that was fostered and supported in parent outreach meetings and faculty development opportunities. Charlotte shared, "We held parent workshops to explain what it means to go to college and how to save for this." Celia added,

> My dad had a third-grade education, fourth grade at the most, and my mom went a little beyond junior high, but their philosophy was that schooling is the answer to getting out of poverty, and I've shared that with my staff. One of my sisters is an architect, and one brother is an engineer. One of my other sisters is a supervisor in a corporate office, and another brother is a manager.

Celia explained that she recognizes that not all will go to college, but she said:

> I'm not going to make that decision for them. I'll do all I can to get them ready. . ..
> We need to prepare them to the highest of their ability. Our process is about removing any barrier and giving them that choice.

Engaging Parents as Partners

Each of the principals discussed the importance of engaging the community as partners and shared ways that parental support had been attained. Charlotte shared her experiences as a White woman principal, who was also fluent in Spanish,

> The parents were curious about me at first. I did a lot of listening and responding to their needs. Trust was established. We shared what we wanted to accomplish. We have a workshop for parents every Tuesday morning. We post announcements and information about our school on the website. I have become stronger with working with parents partly from our learning of professional learning communities and the importance of being intentional about putting structures in place for conversation and collaboration.

Part of the success of these principals in making the vital connections to the community was influenced by their abilities to identify with the community and communicate in Spanish to Latino(a) non-English speakers. As the Asian population is now increasing in Celia's school, she expressed a desire to learn Mandarin, the dialect of Chinese spoken in Beijing and adopted as the official language of China. Celia explained the response when she asked Asian parents the language she should learn to communicate with them in their first language: "They told me, 'You should learn Mandarin.' My goal is to learn Mandarin next."

Both principals were working to further strengthen their partnerships with parents. They expressed a goal to help students to understand that even if parents can't speak English, their support in reading to the child in their native language at home is very important. The principals wanted the community to view the school as a place where they are welcome. Charlotte described the culture she promotes:

> I want to provide teachers and students an environment where they can be their best and do their best. I tell parents, "I have two jobs, to keep everybody safe and everybody learning." We put in a million structures to support this.

Celia also emphasized the importance of communicating in Spanish to many Latino(a) parents and her desire to be able to do this for all English learners:

> I translate for the Latino parents who speak Spanish only, but I want to be able to translate for all parents. I think being from the community and having the passion to change the cycle helps in my leadership. It's about caring about children and the future. I've broadened my horizons to think about the larger community. If we encourage other schools to get better, we all improve. It's about all of us.

Celia shared a positive orientation to student success that was contagious. She further explained that she liked the philosophy described at the Seattle Pike's Place Fish Market of choosing one's attitude. She related that this philosophy related to her own viewpoint that we should, "Never let anyone decide your mood or color your world."

Shared Leadership with Structures for Collaboration

Each of the two principals voiced the importance of shared leadership, and structures were designed to foster collaborative planning. For example, dialogue was fostered through providing a structured time that teachers could meet for collaborative planning. Structures were established to facilitate planning. As Charlotte explained,

> Shared leadership is very important so that all the school improvement will be sustainable without you as the principal. Our culture of the school is very professional and standard based. We work as a team where people may have differences, but we are working toward common goals. Lesson study assisted us in opening doors. We focused on the lessons, and the students and teachers learned to trust each other.

In our first year of implementation, I hired two substitute teachers, so the teachers could participate in lesson study twice. They planned the same lesson, taught it, and talked about it. The teachers then engaged in dialogue over lunch off campus. Then, when they return for the afternoon, they did the cycle again. In watching each other, they were able to consider what will work with their students.

We also have leadership teams of one per grade level who meet once a month, and we set SMART goals and analyze our data considering where we want to be and how to get there. We do benchmark tests and consider what are our strengths? We try not to operate from a deficit viewpoint primarily, but from a strength perspective. We do realize that if there is an area of difficulty, we need to acknowledge this and address this.

Celia also found the structure of vertical team meeting and common meeting times as essential to school improvement:

We have a common meeting time every Wednesday for 45 minutes. The students engage in learning through enrichment activities such as a Powerpoint lesson about the galaxy from a community liaison who grew up in the community. During this time, we have professional development and once a month collaborative planning as a group. The teachers are strategically placed in vertical teams. Twice a year, the students are not at school, and we engage in planning on those days.

She also described ways that she sought to promote team accountability as part of the professional learning community with asking, "How do you know they understand?" She described the team approach and stated, "My teachers are here because they want to make a difference. . .. Although in urban high-need schools, there is often high teacher turnover, over 80% are still here over eleven years. Our success is a team effort."

Professional Learning

Providing appropriate support included determining what was interfering with learning and implementing strategies to address the need. Providing monitoring and follow-up were vital parts of ensuring that learning was occurring. Observing students' and teachers' work was an integral part of each principal's day. A goal of each was "getting into the classroom to see the instruction." Each principal clearly maintained a focus on instructional improvement. Charlotte described her daily walk-throughs in classrooms and the notes she left for students as well as for teachers. She said, "Students often show me with pride the notes I have written." Celia emphasized the constant focus on formative assessments. If teachers needed resources, the principals saw this role as one of "securing whatever was needed."

In campus professional development opportunities, instructional aides, teachers, and the principal engaged in learning together to strengthen the support systems for student success. Teams of teachers and the principal engaged in off-campus professional development activities for strengthening implementation of the professional learning communities. Celia emphasized, "It all comes down to data. When we see concerns, we plan strategies to meet the need."

The two principals described district supports that contributed to their professional growth as a risk-free environment as established by district leaders, collaborative sharing and data analysis that was fostered, and meaningful professional development that was focused on ways to achieve equity and excellence. Three initiatives with a clear district and campus focus were provided with provision of resources for implementation and professional development.

The principals also shared that the district established structures for collaborative engagement among principals. A primary district support according to the principals was that each principal's growth was encouraged and fostered through ongoing professional development meetings, through structured opportunities to network with fellow principals and to collaboratively plan; through resources for sustained, ongoing professional development; and through the opportunity to serve as active members of professional networks.

An ongoing practice of the principals was modeling a growth mindset. An asset approach to problem solving was also shared. Principals sought to build on students' strengths and adopt an asset rather than a deficit approach to problem solving. For example, instead of saying that students do not have access to technology at home, the principal explained that most have cell phones although many were unfamiliar with the school's technology of a keyboard and a mouse for computers. Celia and Charlotte both shared, "School monitors were smudged by the children trying to turn the page by touch." Teachers were encouraged to connect to the students' current understanding as they taught the keyboarding skills that were required for students to take the state test. Student learning was enhanced by an ongoing focus on learning with principals, teachers, and aides as co-learners with a focused commitment to sustained professional development on targeted initiatives. All of the actions to foster learning led to increased individual and organizational performance.

REFLECTIONS

The primary theme emergent from the data sources was the importance of the development of a positive school culture in enhancing individual and organizational performance. Both principals consistently emphasized the importance of trust—trust by the parents that the principals were listening and responding to needs as well as trust by the teachers that the principals were always seeking to do what's best for students. The principals maintained an "unrelenting focus" on school improvement. As Charlotte stressed, "We're going to give students every possible access to learn. We are going to do everything we can. . .. We are getting students ready as citizens of the 21st century."

Promoting a growth mindset was an integral part of each principal's work through a "strength-based viewpoint instead of a gap-filled viewpoint . . . in preparing students for a future that hasn't been invented yet." Charlotte stressed, "In setting a very positive and energized school culture, the work is about the students and removing barriers from the staff members' way so that they can do their best." As she further shared, "If you don't have that positive mindset, or that positive culture, then the engagement [in learning] isn't there." Charlotte emphasized, "Servant leadership is a big part of a principal's role in a high-need context in doing whatever is needed and whatever is necessary to move the school forward and being sincere."

Celia also reinforced, "It's a team effort. I've also believed that it's not about me. It's about what we can accomplish together." She also added, "I think my success comes from being able to be positive. I can't think of everything, and the great thing about the success achieved comes in encouraging all people to be leaders." She added:

> I think it all comes down to the respect that we hold for everybody. . ... I try to model that. It's all about respect. If we have that professional respect or just the professional relationships, positive results occur. . ... There should be echoes of commonality in our educational system.

The internal school contexts reflected highly positive school cultures. In these high-need schools, there was very small turnover of faculty. A culture of caring, respect, and high expectations was established by principals, and that culture influenced student success.

The principals were able to engage fully with their communities and faculties to earn and sustain respect and trust and to strengthen strong school cultures where beliefs in the importance of high expectations as well as of equity and excellence were shared collaboratively by faculty members, parents, and the community. In short, these schools were good places to work and good places to learn. Never satisfied with the status quo, the principals shared a moral commitment to assisting all students to reach their maximum potential. As Charlotte shared, "My goal is to change the world." Her context for doing so was the school. As Celia added, "I feel I am here for a reason."

These leaders serve as an example of the importance of a moral commitment in making a positive difference in school leadership. From showing initiative in implementing a dual language program to interventions as support for student needs, these campus leaders improved educational opportunities to learn for all students. Increased student learning was fostered for these campuses through the leadership of principals who clearly demonstrated a strong moral commitment to ensure quality learning and hold high expectations for all. These individuals demonstrated consistent integrity in modeling their values through ethical leadership.

Starratt (1994, 2004, 2017), refers to the importance of ethical school leaders demonstrating vision, authenticity, and presence while modeling the virtues of critique, care, and collaboration. These two principals reflected all three virtues through their words and deeds. They maintained a clear vision of helping each child to reach his or her potential and be prepared for the 21st century through character development and increased learning. Initiatives in the schools included students providing service to the community as well as promoting a vision of college attainment as a next step following high school graduation. From observations and interviews, each principal's authenticity was clearly evident through actions and words. They both approached their roles as servant leaders who are intentional in modeling respect, care, and culturally responsive leadership with a willingness to do "whatever it takes" to assist in promoting learning for all. They each were fully present in conversations with parents, students, and teachers and modeled that presence through listening, responding to concerns, implementing collaborative ideas that were shared, participating in joint professional development, and engaging with teachers and students through frequent visits to the classroom with follow-up comments on work that was observed.

Although extremely positive in their viewpoint and approaching all issues through an asset rather than a deficit orientation, the principals also modeled critique of barriers to student learning and parent engagement that might exist and collaboratively planned strategies to overcome the barriers. Data were consistently attained through surveys of parents and students and through formative and summative assessments to determine needed next steps and to lead implementation efforts when gaps between student groups were evident. The principals also "took a strong stand" in terms of justice to teach responsible behavior to students and to ensure the safety of students. The examples of ways they demonstrated their care and concern were tangible and could be replicated by other educators. Respect and integrity prevailed in all they did, in all they said, and in all they communicated; however, recognition of the power of their perspectives did not lead to views of superiority. They were not benevolent dictators. Instead, they were humble, facilitative leaders who were aware of the importance of their position power as principals, but cautious to always work with others in the collaborative learning process. They each demonstrated a strong sense of mission to make a positive difference in students' lives, but they also communicated a deep understanding of important elements in school improvement. In short, these principals' words and actions can serve as continued inspiration to achieve the shared goals of enhanced learning. Their work contributes to our understanding of ways that principals in varied contexts strive to meet the needs of diverse students, while recognizing that school leadership is "complex and contextual" (Stanford-Blair & Dickman, 2005, p. xii). The principals' modeling of ethical, socially just behavior served as a shaper of school culture for the schools and exemplars of successful leadership in high-need contexts.

Questions to Consider:

1. In what ways, if any, did the practices and processes that were implemented by these principals in high-need contexts resonate with your experiences in observing or leading school improvement in high-need contexts?

2. What are specific ways that educators can engage parents as partners in strengthening student success in high-need contexts to achieve both equity and excellence?

REFERENCES

Baran, M. L., & Berry, J. R. (2015). *The international school leadership development network (ISLDN) High needs schools group research protocol and members' guide*. Washington, DC: ISLDN and UCEA/BELMAS.

Barnett, B. G., & Stevenson, H. (2016). Leading high poverty urban schools. In S. Clarke & T. D. Donoghue (Eds.), *School leadership in diverse contexts* (pp. 23–42). Abingdon, Oxon: Routledge.

Beck, L. G. (1994). *Reclaiming educational administration as a caring profession*. New York, NY: Teachers College Press.

Blankstein, A. M., & Noguera, P. (2015). *Excellence through equity: Five principles of courageous leadership to guide achievement for every student*. Thousand Oaks, CA: Corwin Press.

Bredeson, P. V. (2005*).* Building capacity in schools: Some ethical considerations for authentic leadership and learning. *Values and Ethics in Educational Administration, 4*(1), 1–8.

Bromberg, M., & Theokas, C. (2013). *Breaking the glass ceiling of achievement for low-income students and students of color*. Washington, DC: The Education Trust. Retrieved from edtrust.org/resource/breaking-the-glass-ceiling-of-achievement-for-low-income-students-and-students-of-color

Chenoweth, K. (2009). *How it's being done: Urgent lessons from unexpected schools*. Cambridge, MA: Harvard Education Press.

Dantley, M. E. (2005). Moral leadership: Shifting the management paradigm. In F. W. English (Ed.), *The Sage handbook of educational leadership: Advances in the research and practice* (pp. 34–46). Thousand Oaks, CA: SAGE Publications.

Dewey, J. (1916). *Democracy and education*. New York, NY; Simon & Schuster, Inc.

Donaldson, G. (2006). *Cultivating leadership in schools: Connecting people, purpose, and practice* (2nd ed.). New York, NY: Teachers College Press.

Drysdale, L., Gurr, D., & Goode, H. (2016). Dare to make a difference: Successful principals who explore the potential of their role. *International Studies in Educational Administration, 44*(3), 37–51.

DuFour, R., & Fullan, M. (2013). *Cultures built to last: System PLCs at work*. Bloomington, IN: Solution Tree Press.

Duke, D. L. (2012). Tinkering and turnarounds: Understanding the contemporary campaign to improve low-performing schools. *Journal of Education for Students Placed at Risk (JESPAR) 17*(1–2), 9–24. https://doi.org/10.1080/10824669.2012.636696.

Gillette, J., Clarke, S., & O'Donoghue, I. (2016). Leading schools facing challenging circumstances: Some insights from Western Australia. *Issues in Educational Research, 26(*4), 592–603.

Griffin, A., & Dixon, D. (2017). *Systems for success: Thinking beyond access to AP*. Washington, DC: The Education Trust. Retrieved from edtrust.org/resource/systems-success-thinking-beyond-access-ap/

Khalifa, M., Witherspoon, A. N., & Newcomb, W. (2015). Understand and advocate for communities first. *Phi Delta Kappan, 96*(7), 20–25.

Lichtman, M. (2014). *Qualitative research for the social sciences.* Thousand Oakes, CA: SAGE.

Merriam, S. (2009). *Qualitative research: A guide to design and implementation.* San Francisco, CA: Jossey-Bass.

Murakami, E., Garza, E., & Merchant, B. (2010). Successful school leadership in socio-economically challenging contexts: School principal creating and sustaining successful school improvement. *International Studies in Educational Administration 38*(3), 35–56.

Murphy, J., & Torre, D. (2014). *Creating productive cultures in schools: For students, teachers, and parents.* Thousand Oaks, CA: Corwin Press.

National Center for Education Statistics. (2014). *The condition of education 2014.* Retrieved from https://nces.ed.gov/pubsearch/pubsinfo.asp?pubid=2014083

NCLB. (2001). *No Child Left Behind Act of 2001,* Public Law 107–110.115STAT.1425.

Noddings, N. (2013). *Caring: A relational approach to ethics and moral education* (2nd ed.). Los Angeles, CA: University of California Press.

Papa, R., & English, F. W. (2011). *Turnaround principals for underperforming schools.* Lanham, MD: Rowman & Littlefield Publishers, Inc.

Pellicer, L. O. (2003). *Caring enough to lead: How reflective thought leads to moral leadership.* Thousand Oaks, CA: Corwin Press.

Sergiovani, T. J. (1992). *Moral leadership: Getting to the heart of school improvement.* San Francisco, CA: Jossey-Bass.

Stanford-Blair, B., & Dickman, M. H. (2005*). Leading coherently: Reflections from leaders around the world.* Thousand Oaks, CA: Sage Publishing.

Starratt, R. J. (1994). *Building an ethical school: A practical response to the moral crisis in schools.* Abington, Oxon, OS: Routledge Falmer.

Starratt, R. J. (2004*). Ethical leadership.* San Francisco, CA: Jossey-Bass.

Starratt, R. J. (2017). *Ethical leadership.* Skype presentation to doctoral students at Cal Poly Pomona State University, Pomona, CA.

CHAPTER 6

CREATING A CULTURE FOR LEARNING IN A HIGH-NEED INNER-CITY USA SCHOOL:

The Unique Leadership Challenges

Mette L. Baran and Glady Van Harpen

The challenges facing leaders of high-needs schools are extremely complex. Students often come to school ill prepared due to various social, personal, and emotional issues taking place at home. Principals and other school leaders need to address these issues to create a productive learning environment. Time is of the essence when turning a school around and there is a plethora of internal and external demands. While the most challenging issue is closing the achievement gap, one needs to ensure that a culture for learning has been cultivated within the school and that all stakeholders are committed to this vision. The research site is a K–8 school located in a large Midwestern city, serving a high percentage of impoverished African American students. Due to the unique leadership structure and focus on creating a learning culture, the school has made a remarkable turnaround in a very short amount of time. The purpose of this qualitative case study was to reveal how the principal and the leadership team successfully turned the school around by promoting a culture of learning and character building.

Educational Leadership, Culture, and Success in High-Need Schools, pages 103–128.

Keywords: achievement, context, education, high-needs, leadership, poverty, principals, poverty, stakeholders

INTRODUCTION

This is the story one K–8 school located in Milwaukee, Wisconsin, a vibrant city situated on the shores of Lake Michigan. With a population of well over one half million people, it is the largest city in Wisconsin and the 31st largest city in the United States. Milwaukee is the International headquarters for six Fortune 500 companies and hundreds of thriving corporations and businesses. Like other major US cities Milwaukee has 5-star restaurants, hotels, shopping, professional sports teams, and the arts. Opportunities for higher education exist at more than a dozen universities and private colleges. But there is another side to this story, which reveals disparity and despair for some, especially the poor. "In almost no metropolitan area is there a greater difference in black and white income" (Romell, 2013, Para. 4). Additionally, 73% of the people living in poverty are concentrated within the city limits. This level and concentration of poor individuals creates high-needs for municipalities and the educational system.

Within this relatively isolated geographic area, Milwaukee Public Schools (MPS) supports an enrollment of over 76,000 students, 88% are students of color and 80% are economically disadvantaged (Milwaukee Public Schools [MPS], n.d.). Like other major metropolitan cities, these statistics influence factors like student achievement, high school completion, and other social issues related to lack of school success. The story could end here, but this is the beginning of a turnaround school. Due to one committed school leader, a leadership team, and a partnership with a private charter organization, over 490 students per year are finding academic success.

Background

This study revealed how the principal and leadership team promoted a culture of learning and character building in a high-needs urban charter school. Through careful leadership and planning the administration, teachers, and staff were able to turn the public charter school around. The authors used definition of charter schools from the National Alliance for Public Charter School (n.d.): "Charter schools are unique public schools that are allowed the freedom to be more innovative while being held accountable for advancing student achievement. Since the schools are public, open to all children, do not charge tuition, and do not have special entrance requirements" (para. 1).

The purpose of the study was to reveal how the principal and the leadership team promoted a culture of learning in a high-needs urban turnaround school. The research was guided by the overarching question: What fosters student learning in high-needs schools? The research question focused on three areas: student learning and character building, school leadership, and school context. The students were labeled as high-need based on several cultural and socio-economic factors including, but not limited to race, ethnicity, geographic boundaries, low academic performance, and family income.

Other risk indicators are apparent, such as a Wisconsin DPI Task Force, which began taking measures focusing on the unique challenges social and educational challenges facing urban areas such as Milwaukee. One such measure has been to identify strategies to close the achievement gap. The result of this endeavor has been the focus in a new document entitled, *Promoting Excellence for All* (Wisconsin Department of Public Instruction, 2014). The document also identifies four categories, which influence school improvement: effective instruction, student-teacher relationships, family and community engagement, and school and instructional leadership (p. 15). The hope is that Wisconsin school leaders, who focus on implementing these categories, will drive the turnaround efforts in the state to reduce the achievement gap.

LITERATURE REVIEW: LEADING TURNAROUND EFFORTS IN HIGH-NEEDS URBAN SCHOOLS

Lipham (1981) urged that the principal makes the difference in a successful school. He noted, "The principal as head of the school, which is a social system, has great potential to refine or renew its educational program" (p. 1). As early as 1982, Bossert, Dwyer, Rowan, and Lee noted that principals could significantly influence two school level factors—school climate and instructional organization indirectly by engaging more systematically with instructional practices. Principals can build a positive school climate and work with teachers and other staff to create a vision of high learning expectations and build supportive work relationships. Individuals working in leadership positions in urban schools have unique challenges and roles (Spillane, Hallett, & Diamond, 2003). As a public charter, the school context is distinct from others in the surrounding urban school district, in terms of governance, culture, and identity; however, the challenges leading a turnaround school are formidable no matter the context. The effectiveness of school leaders' performance needs to be viewed within the context of the environment. Leaders within this school context are derived from several formal and informal roles such as, chief executive officers (CEOs), administrators, principals, and leader teachers and they are all committed to the turnaround work. Effective school turnaround leaders place emphasis on policies, structures, resources, and personnel in order to rapidly and significantly improve struggling schools (Day, 2009) There has been a long history of research (Leithwood, Seashore Louis, Anderson, & Wahlstrom, 2004; Waters, Marzano, & McNulty, 2003; Youngs & King, 2002) around the notion of the importance of the principals' instructional leadership influence on school success. Furthermore, Leithwood, Harris, and Hopkins (2008) conducted wide-ranging review of over a decade of literature and came up with seven strong claims as evidence for successful school leadership (p. 27).

A turnaround effort is identified by the development of goals based on performance data derived from by assessments, which drives the turnaround vision (Duke, 2015). In leading turnaround one most challenging issues is probably closing the achievement gap. The state of Wisconsin has some of the worst academic results in the nation for students of color and the widest race-based gaps in the nation (Mulvany, 2013). The National Assessment of Educational Progress (NAEP, 2013), often called the Nation's Report Card, "showed no other state had wider gaps in both of the assessments aligned with Agenda 2017 (fourth-grade reading and math and eighth-grade reading and math" (Wisconsin Department of Public Instruction, 2014, p. 9). Identifying strategies to close the achievement gap has been the focus in a new document entitled, *Promoting Excellence for All*, in Wisconsin. By implementing a set of four categories: effective instruction, student-teacher relationships, family and community engagement, and school and instructional leadership, Wisconsin turnaround leaders hope to drive the turnaround efforts in the state to reduce the achievement gap.

Moreover, much research has focused on the unique aspects of leading teaching in high-needs schools. The principals and school leaders play an important role in improving school conditions and retaining teachers (Deal & Peterson, 2009). Petty, Fitchett, and O'Connor (2012) urged that effective leaders: lead aspirational vision and culture, define high expectations, reward high academics and behavior, support relationships that protect every student, and influence the aspiration for others to achieve.

Effective Teaching in High-needs Urban Schools

Creating an effective learning environment is pivotal in order to accelerate learning in high-needs schools. The focus needs to be on what constitutes the best environment for teaching and learning in order to close the achievement gap. Research connected to effective turnaround strategies in high-needs schools addresses the importance of building strong relationships between students and teachers and teachers and parents built on a foundation of caring (Baran 2008; Muller, Katz, & Dance, 1999). Baran (2008) noted that adolescent students had a higher level of academic motivation towards school and performed better both academically and socially when they felt cared for by their teachers. Teachers' high expectations of their students' performance can also be interpreted as a form of caring. Muller et al. (1999) found a correlation between teachers' high expectation and students' academic performance. According to Goldstein (1999) caring is important for successful outcomes.

Education is largely a relational process occurring in context rather than abstraction and in relation rather than isolation as noted by Noddings' (2002) care theory. Noddings affirmed that a true caring relationship depends on the teacher's ability to care about students and to identify and meet students' needs. Moreover, students need to confirm this perception. Students must recognize that they feel cared for by the teacher. Effective teachers in urban high-needs schools understand the tension their at-risk students feel in their lives and must create a "system that is adaptable to those needs (Brooks, et al., 2012, p. 94). In addition, relationships between parents and teachers are known to influence student outcomes (Epstein & Van Voorhis, 2010; Michael, Dittus, & Epstein, 2007; Sheldon, 2003; Sheldon & Epstein, 2002; Walker, Shenker, &Hoover-Dempsey, 2010).

Communities of Practice

A key construct for this research assumes that learning is a "situated activity" (Lave & Wenger, 1991, p. 29) where knowledge is constructed through relevant and engaging learning activities within a specific context. Like other social learning theories, the assumption is that people acquire knowledge and skills in a social context. The ideas, issues, and challenges shared by individuals within a system or organization make up the practice. According to Lave and Wenger (1991), individuals within the relevant system participate in exchanges of information and knowledge becoming "communities of practice" (p. 29). Wenger, McDermott and Snyder (2002) further define the elements of communities of practice to include "groups of people, who share a concern, a set of problems or a passion about a topic and who deepen their knowledge their knowledge and expertise in this area by interacting on an ongoing basis" (p. 4). These communities of practice (CoPs) can be either formal or informal and exist across many disciplines including: business, healthcare, and education. Understanding CoPs helps to answer the questions related to student learning, leadership, and the impact of school context of the high-needs schools in the study. For learners and leaders in the high-needs schools of this study, CoPs may be used to understand knowledge acquisition and learning within their unique context.

Distributed Leadership

The influence of distributed leadership in education has been widely reported in the last several decades (Harris, 2008; Heck & Hallinger, 2009; Leithwood, Mascall, & Strauss; 2009, Spillane, 2006; Spillane et al., 2003). Additionally, several researchers have shown a connection between school leadership, culture, structure, social, and academics (Hallinger & Heck, 2010; Heck & Hallinger, 2009; Leithwood & Jantzi, 1999; Leithwood et al., 2004; Leithwood et al., 2009). Spillane (2006) contextualized leadership in a "distributed perspective...as the interactions between people and their situation" (p. 144). In this context, the idea of distributed leadership is applied to the context of the high-needs charter school and their leaders.

METHODOLOGY

Research Design

The researchers utilized a qualitative case study design. A protocol developed by the International School Leadership Development Network (ISLDN) focusing on how leaders develop a culture of high-needs learning, was followed (Baran & Berry, 2015). In the study the researchers acknowledge a philosophic worldview that embraces constructivism, a belief that knowledge is a "human construction" (Gredler, 2001, p. 71). Using the lens of constructivism allows the research to be contextualized as a social process whereby people work together to create new knowledge (Ormrod, 2012, p. 155). The constructivist view allowed the researchers to analyze data, relationships, and circumstances that exist between leaders and learners affecting school culture qualitatively.

The research was conducted utilizing qualitative case study design to explore how the school leadership placed emphasis on developing a learning culture in a high-need setting. The researchers utilized the definition of at-risk students from the State of Wisconsin as their operational definition of a high-needs school: "pupils in grades 5 to 12 who are at risk of not graduating from high school because they are dropouts or have 2 or more of the following indicators:

- One or more years behind their age group in the number of high school credits attained
- Two or more years behind their age group in basic skill levels
- Habitual truants
- They are parents themselves
- Adjudicated delinquents
- Eighth grade students whose score in each subject area on the standardized test administered was below the basic level, 8th grade students who failed the standardized test, and 8th grade students who failed to be promoted to the 9th grade." (WI Stat. (2012). §118.153)

School Context

The focus of this paper is on the research site, which is Milwaukee College Prep's Lloyd Street Campus. Lloyd Street Campus is a K–8, a former Milwaukee Public School, is located in the Lindsay Heights area, one of the most impoverished neighborhoods in the city. The school serves approximately 500 students. The former school closed due to chronic underperformance. In fact, the closing school reported some of the lowest academic scores in all of Wisconsin with less than 20% of the students scoring advanced or proficient on the Wisconsin Knowledge and Concepts Examination (WKCE) test in Math and less than 30% in Reading. In addition, 97% of the students qualified for free or reduced lunch (Milwaukee College Preparatory School, n.d., p. 29), with over 85% free. In July 2009, MCP responded swiftly to open the campus, when more than "400 four to fourteen-year olds were left without a school in the fall with few high-quality options" (Milwaukee College Preparatory School, n.d., p. 27). This was a watershed moment for the families of the Lindsey Heights area.

Just eight weeks after the school closed, the school reopened as MCP, Lindsey Heights Campus, a Turnaround School. The school was renamed Lloyd Street

TABLE 6.1.   Student Demographics 2013–2014 K5–8

Enrollment	493
Attendance	96.0
Black	96.3
Hispanic	2.2
Other	1.5
Students with Disabilities	14.4
Economically Disadvantaged	85.6

Source: Wisconsin Department of Public Instruction (2018).

Campus when the school changed sites in year 2. The administrators promptly set high expectations for the students and the results were immediate: "students nearly doubled their scores on the WKCE tests in 8 short weeks of being introduced to the MCP instruction and curriculum" (p. 10). Table 6.1 lists the school demographics at the time of the study.

Milwaukee College Prep and Schools That Can

Milwaukee College Prep (MCP) is a Charter Management Organization (CMO) that currently has four K–8 schools. As of 2014, this CMO encompasses four K–8 campuses, two of which are within the Milwaukee Public School system. The students served by the CMO live in some of the most impoverished areas in the urban metropolis. This organization is the brainchild of Rob Rauch, the Chief Education Officer (CEO). Rauch is a visionary leader who did not give up on the Milwaukee schoolchildren when so many others did due to the dismal state of urban schools in Milwaukee and the rest of our nation. Since its inception in 1997 and guided by its motto—new leaders for new schools—MCP "bases its success on the belief that every child is full of possibility if given the right tools of knowledge and character" (Milwaukee College Preparatory School, n.d., p. 27). Since their inception, the CMO schools are producing some remarkable results culturally, socially, and academically.

Accomplishing this goal requires collaboration and partnerships with school and community leaders, and STCM coaches. Specifically, the STCM coaches joined forces nation-wide to create high-impact systems focusing on "Vital Behaviors" (Andrietsch, n.d.) and training. These eight behaviors include: 1) Teachers are immensely committed to student success, 2) Time on task, 3) Sweat the details, 4) Focus on student performance data, 5) Academic intensity in Math, English and Language Arts, 6) Joy, 7) Student Attendance, and 8) Alumni are Tracked. These strategies and behaviors guide national reform efforts at STCM to establish high-performing cultures in urban school districts that promote outstanding student achievement gains.

Data Collection Instruments

To reiterate, a qualitative case study design was selected to conduct research at one urban PreK–8 school, MCP Lloyd Street Campus managed by Charter Management Organization (CMO), which is also in partnership with the Schools that Can Network. The ISLDN researchers developed an interview protocol for school leaders, teachers, governance bodies, and parents to delve more deeply into what fosters learning, and how principals and school leaders, as well as internal and external contexts, impact individual and organizational performance. The ISLDN protocol was used for Phase One of the research focusing on how leaders develop a culture of learning in high-need school settings. The four participants were the Principal, the Dean of Students, the Academic Dean, and the Chief Operations Officer and Talent Recruiter, who are the day-to-day leadership team at the K5–8 school research site. During Phase One, the interviews required either one sitting of approximately 1¼ hours or two sittings about 45 minutes each. Phase Two of the research involved one 45-minute on-site interview with the Chief Executive Officer by the two researchers.

Data Analysis

Qualitative data, in the form of audio files, were transcribed into text and checked for accuracy to increase reliability. Researchers applied descriptive and pattern codes (Miles & Hueberman, 1994, p. 57) to the textual data. The constant comparative method for analysis and to identify patterns and themes in the data (Glaser & Strauss, 1967; Strauss, 1987).

PRESENTATION OF FINDINGS

The findings align with the purpose of the study, which involves how leaders develop a culture of learning in high-needs setting. The specific research question was: What fosters learning in high-needs schools? The general themes were: student learning and character building, school leadership, and school context. The findings are organized in a blended format including the perceptions of interviewees under each related emergent theme, which are under the theoretical framework offered through the concept of situated learning and communities of practice (Lave & Wenger, 1991).

The Lloyd Street Campus community belongs to Milwaukee College Prep (MCP), situated within a network of schools, which places strong emphasis on learning, character and academics. Additionally, the results and findings support the notion that the study of leadership in high-needs schools is both challenging and controversial at times, and that families play a critical role in their children's performance. The findings also reflect what has been adopted by the Wisconsin Department of Instruction defining "urban," the magnitude, urgency, and complexity that beleaguer urban schools (Hipp & Weber, 2007). This is particularly true in the school under study, which reflects a poverty level that provides a significant number of students in a "free" lunch program. Furthermore, experience plays a significant role in leadership, and particularly at Lloyd Street Campus that reflects the greatest poverty level of all MCP schools. All formal leaders revealed several varied experiences in urban settings and worked their way through many levels to achieve their current positions.

The following sections summarize the findings from the study to facilitate further discussion and conclusions. These seven themes are discussed in the following sections: Organizational Leadership, Distributed Leadership, Academic Achievement and Behavior, Character Building and Celebrating Students, Relationships and Emotional Connections, and Expectations and Relationships with External Partners. Finally, we offer a discussion of the findings related to the literature and concluding statements.

Organizational Leadership

Lloyd Street Campus reflects a strong focus on attendance, which is gradually improving year after year. The principal shared, "We've agreed to cut our suspension data by 25% every year, and we've actually done that the last two years." Additionally, the principal, asserted, "Our vision is that this becomes a world-class K–8th grade facility for others to see what's happening, where our proficiency levels are 80–90% or higher… and that our kids are fully prepared to be successful in life." This year students Lloyd Street campus surpassed 96% for attendance, but the goal is to strive higher. Students need to attend daily to accomplish this goal.

School staff begins the academic year engaging in a dual purpose—character development, academic excellence, and deepening a culture of learning that will help them be successful in life. The principal added, "Whatever students choose as their career, the emphasis is on the students' belief in self, that it's about dictating their destiny, not their zip code, not their free lunch status, and not whether or not they could pass a test." As the school year progresses, professional development is designed on a weekly basis consistent with the mission, responsive to test data that is collected daily revealing students' most challenging curricular and instructional needs, and involves a variety of programs.

Character building is an equally significant part of the mission and strengthens the academic focus and according to the principal, "Knowledge plus character pave the road to college and beyond" and the vision is: "To close the achievement gap in Milwaukee for our scholars and put all of our scholars on a path to college or to some location that will lead them to success." The principal tells students, "Our city needs you to be better than what you were or better than what you think you can be." Furthermore, the principal stated, "A school can't exist with the idea that we're going to tell kids that they're going to go to college and then treat them like they're going to go to prison." In the end, if students are not learning, the principal asserted, "Adults fail, not students."

All leaders and teachers noted that personnel are hired very selectively and undergo a careful selection process. Staff are expected to take learning seriously on all MCP campuses and follow Marva Collins' philosophy, *"Education is painful and not gained by playing games,"* as noted by the Academic Dean. Additionally, she contended when our students want to give up, "Sometimes it's teaching our scholars about the *Grit*, about how even when something is hard, and teachers who are stressed and overwhelmed too, to just dig in and show some grit; just get the job done." Furthermore, she noted that Lloyd Street Campus is a school where people are encouraged to make mistakes and learn from them. There is a sense of unity that defines the culture of Lloyd when everyone chants one of many expressions, according to the dean, "If you can't make a mistake, you can't make anything." She went on to explain that it is not only acceptable, but a significant step in learning and "getting students to places academically that we've never seen before." Coincidently, the Academic Dean explained,

> There are more challenges in a Turnaround model. What makes the work easier is hiring well . . . great people who are mission aligned. We find amazing people and find out what they do amazingly and have them do those things, not others, but those they do so well.

It is important to note that it is common to let teachers go if they were not a good fit, and during the last academic year, half of all teachers were new.

The principal discussed the importance of goals for everyone—adults and students. Short and long-term goals were not mutually exclusive. "We focus on the big three: attendance, behavior, and academics. To attain long-term goals, we work with short term components." He clarified, "Inherently short-term goals become long-term goals; they play off one another. For instance, with attendance, the school struggles with adaptive problems and engages in technical fixes like getting kids rides, bus tickets, etc." The Leadership Team has goals that include unique strengths and areas from which to grow. This is difficult, yet critical in a Turnaround School that deals with reverse trends and changing mindsets among the other day-today operations.

Accomplishing these goals also requires collaboration and partnerships with school and community leaders. One organization, which provided coaches, was Schools That Can Milwaukee (STCM). Specifically, the STCM coaches joined forces nation-wide to create high-impact systems focusing on "Vital Behaviors" (Andrietsch, n.d.) and training. These eight behaviors include: 1) Teachers are immensely committed to student success, 2) Time on task, 3) Sweat the details, 4) Focus on student performance data, 5) Academic intensity in Math, English and Language Arts, 6) Joy, 7) Student Attendance, and 8) Alumni are Tracked. These strategies and behaviors guide national reform efforts at STCM to establish high-performing cultures in urban school districts that promote outstanding student achievement gains.

The following three pathways combined reflect STCM's commitment to its vision:

1.   Supporting the currently identified high-performing schools through strategic planning and shared advocacy to overcome barriers;
2.   Moving high-potential schools to high-performing school, by identifying successful practices of high performing schools including district, charter and choice. The intent is to replicate and accelerate processes to achieve excellence and close the achievement gap; and
3.   Collaborating with other agencies and organizations to recruit high quality school operators and leaders to the city. (Schools That Can, 2012)

Once goals are set, the school leader must assure that all stakeholders are on the same page. The principal maintained, "Each person knows I have their backs and look to them for answers. The answers can come from anyone in the room." He added that this demands openness and risk, "it means letting go and living with the results, which is part of the learning" to build security, confidence and competency. He continued, "Consistency breeds a sense of security and safety for staff and students." The leader must assure that everyone speaks the same message and understands how their practices align with the mission and vision.

A significant challenge is retaining teachers for various reasons. The Dean of Academics lamented, "Building great teams is maintaining great teams." People move on, or out of state, that could move into leadership positions. She added, "I'm hoping for some consistency and a solid team." This was also apparent at another MCP school at first until teams became more established. The Academic Dean stated, "I want to be in a position where you're not starting over every year. This year half of our elementary teachers are new. But, we have our best results yet, so it's at least good to have the best people in the right spots and then try to keep them."

Distributed Leadership

The organizational make-up of the school ensures that several formal leaders are involved in the decision-making process. The principal noted that since there are two Deans of Students, they get very much involved in handling the academic and the discipline side of decision-making. Furthermore, the principal reportedly engages teachers in "big perspective ideas, incentives, educational opportunities." In addition, the Academic Dean is also highly engaged and meets weekly with her teachers to review lesson plans as well as staying engaged in observation of teachers. The principal noted, due to the strength of the people employed at the school, he can "empower those that are working with me and I don't say below I really say with, because the reality is the amazing things that are happening in this school are because of the people who are here." The CAO noted that they are

"Standing on the Shoulders of Giants," indicating that they are all learning from each other within this unique learning community.

Academic Achievement and Behavior

The Academic Dean offered that they assess using standardized test scores three times a year to measure individual growth. In the fall of each year, staff and leadership team meet to analyze data to determine areas of greatest need. They use these data to form student groups and to reassess targeted goals in order to affect student performance. According to the Academic Dean, "Significant growth has been evident in our MAP data" over the past two years. The Principal described student expectations clearly demanding, "We expect 125% growth for every classroom that takes the MAP, and that's K5–8th grade. When we don't see that kind of growth, then it becomes a source of conversation and requires support for classroom teachers. It's not enough just to have 125% growth, we actually need at least 75% of the kids in every room to meet their MAP goal or target... that's the marker for what we are going to do here." On any given day, the halls and classrooms are predictably alive and booming with students learning.

The school continues to produce notable growth in student performance since its inception only five years ago showing that the high expectations set for students are working.

Table 6.2 outlines recent achievement performance data for Eighth grade students. While 59.5 % of students still met "few academic expectations" this percentage shows a significant increase in reading and math as eighth grade students outperformed state growth last year in reading (35.4/31.6) and were close to meeting state growth in math (29.8/31.1). In 2016 a new State-wide assessment was introduced. The Forward Exam assesses third through eighth grade students in the areas of: English Language Arts (ELA), Mathematics, Social Studies, and Science. Results from this year's exam show that MCP students narrowed the proficiency gap in ELA from 11% to < 4% and in mathematics the proficiency gap went from 22% to 10%. The number of students who were advanced or proficient

TABLE 6.2. Student 8th Grade Achievement in Reading and Math 2013–2014

School Priority Areas: Lloyd Street 8th grade Proficient	State
Reading 14.4/100	29.7/100
Math 23.4	37.4
Reading Growth 35.4	31.6
Math Growth 29.8	31.1

Source: Wisconsin Department of Public Instruction (2018).

in mathematics fell state-wide, while MCP reported a 9.7% gain. Additionally, while the State ELA advanced or Proficient scores decreased 8.9%, MCP levels remained stable (Milwaukee College Prep, n.d.). These results explain what is possible when adults believe in students caught in the gap, hold high expectations, advocate on their behalf, and provide them with the necessary tools to excel.

The positive results are due in part to a focus on academic excellence as well as character building "MCP scholars are poised to be proactive and productive participants in the world" (p. 27). MCP also uses a proactive discipline system. "The discipline system is based on a Proactivity Chart, which is based on the tenets of Steven Covey's (1989) 7 Habits of Highly Effective People. The first premise of this program is teaching the students that they are always responsible for the decisions they make; they are taught to be "proactive, not reactive" (p. 4). Students are taught several skills to apply when making decisions about "their lifetime Aims, Goals and Objectives" (Milwaukee College Preparatory School, n.d., p. 4). In addition, MCP adopted the following core values: Trust, Respect, Excellence, Courage, and Knowledge (T.R.E.C.K.) to help guide students through college and beyond: Trust, Respect, Excellence, Courage and Knowledge.

The four MCP campuses are highly data-driven and teachers must adhere to a significant part of the academic focus, *standardized and consistent curricular, instructional and assessment expectations*. The Academic Dean spoke of the connection between learning and culture:

> With our culture becoming stronger, with our instruction becoming richer, even our educational assistants have goals of three pull-out groups a day and we require them to use data for small group interventions. The data shows that learning is increasing dramatically. What we are doing is working, even better than last year. I'm spazzing out! That's the proof and we just have to stay the course and transfer that to our scholars.

While there was an unrelenting focus on the academics, leaders saw the need to implement celebratory moments into the day. The power of a common Lloyd Street language was apparent and the focus on *Fun* as well as *Learning*, was witnessed by cheers and chants and several expressions that were repeatedly shouted throughout the day. These jovial rituals facilitated consistency across classrooms and grade levels, creating distinctive situational learning experiences.

Character Building and Celebrating Students

Everyone in the school attends the school's daily morning assembly. The purpose of the assembly is to shout out and be part of choral responses, to get involved, and to build community and celebrate character and commitment to the mission and goals. The principal maintained, "Each day is to advance that everyone is on the same page, recite the mission and what good behavior looks like, and know the overarching expectation." Lloyd Street Campus also has a declaration of excellence that is shouted out in the daily assembly, "*I'll never rest until my good is better and my better is best.*" The principal insisted, "You can't just say it, you've got to live it in practice."

The morning assemblies at all MCP campuses are scheduled to help students become aware of how special each person is, and to prepare them for the day. This means "in some cases helping students leave the baggage they come to school with from home." Throughout the school the researchers observed students and staff being recognized and supported. The assembly we visited burst full of energy, pounding, stomping, choral shouting, just as the principal described, "Our students and staff are incredibly exciting and awesome!"

Relationships and Emotional Connections

The principal found it key to believe and respect that people work very hard. However, when they are not successful he feels "you can't fault people for doing their best and it just isn't good enough sometimes." He shared that the administrative staff tries reinforcing effort while building relationships, which might often result in,

> Making positive phone calls and writing texts from teachers to scholars reinforcing staff. We envision uniting these beacons of people doing really amazing things, especially in this city. It's helping teachers get to the next level by learning from one another and sharing best practices.

It is the role of administrators to "bring awareness to people and then support them on their journey to get to the next level. We cover classes to give teachers a 10-minute break now and then and other things that add an element of surprise."

> When contemplating his greatest contribution, the principal revealed the help of others. This identity that we've created for ourselves. We call ourselves 'us.' When a school begins as fractured as MCP was, you need to start with the adults. At the end of the day when all the students are gone, what do we have left—us. If we don't have each other, we won't be good for anyone, especially the kids on Day 1 or Day 181.

The principal maintained this promotes trust, respect, and caring relationships. "I have no space in this building for negativity. When there are pockets of negativity, I deal with them quickly and harshly. It's fine for people to vent and feel frustrated, but there's no space for being frustrated or angry without looking to solutions." Furthermore, he asserted, "I'd rather have 1% of the efforts of 100 men than 100% of the efforts of one." Further still, "Everyone must feel supported, valued and appreciated, because it is not me, it's about them doing the work and the reality is they are doing it." This is substantial evidence that relationships and emotional connections matter at the Lloyd Street Campus.

Expectations and Relationships with External Partners

The Charter Management Organization (CMO) works with the four Milwaukee College Prep (MCP) K–8 campuses. Additionally, the schools work in close partnership with a national organization founded in 2010, Schools That Can Milwaukee, Inc. (STCM). Schools That Can Milwaukee (STCM), which is a nonprofit organization, partners with other identified high-performing and high-potential Milwaukee schools serving low income urban populations and is applying practices that are making dramatic differences in school achievement across the nation. STCM works as a catalyst for transformation. The organization expresses a clear vision and goal to place 20,000 Milwaukee children in high-performing urban schools by 2020. Currently, more than 50 high-performing schools, serving over 10, 000 students in Milwaukee, have joined this STCM reform effort seeking similar results. There is a strong sense of collective efficacy in the organization's commitment not to accept student failure. Rather, those involved with STCM hold high expectations and believe students can and will learn if placed in appropriate environments.

The principal indicated, "We reach out in many ways to support our families, whether it's through programs like wrap-around services or community clinics, where a social worker is constantly connecting with our families to support their health needs, or their mental and emotional needs." Also, the school is involved with an agency that supports them in developing a conservation area as part of a beautification project where the students create the space. In turn, the school partners with area businesses that support the students.

At the school parents also play a key partnership role in the culture of the learning community. The principal shared that is important, "Our parents can rattle off the mission of the school as well as the students and everyone at Lloyd Street Campus. And that's key. Everyone has to know what's happening and what every member intends to achieve." This expectation begins at parent orientations and is a part of everyday operations. The principal stated, "A mission is only as valuable as all those who know it and live it. We model what good character is and what good scholarly work looks like." Parental partnership success and trust is built through setting expectations and then providing support.

The Academic Dean shared that the mission at MCP is to get scholars to college and beyond, "to provide every student who walks through these walls and our doors the best education we can. We do our best to not waste a single minute; every minute is precious." The challenges that face MCP are significant and highly apparent to everyone in the school. She clarified, "the intent is not to play. It's a place to get an education, our top priority." However, the focus is equally on "being a good student, a good person," she added, and living their TRECK values—Trust, Respect, Excellence, Courage, and Knowledge. When students are ready to leave for college, "we want them to be prepared to make their own choices, rather than someone deciding for them," according to the Academic Dean.

The Academic Dean also shared another perspective "that in some cases community involvement and support from parents are external school contexts that are missing and impact individual and organizational performance at Lloyd for better or worse." Unfortunately, the successes at MCP are not well-known in the community and she confessed that the school could do a better job marketing and sharing the work that's being done. "It's a special place, but we need to get to know our community better too." She maintained that the community:

> Is a big influence and we are starting to build a reputation. Outside expectations are not greater than what we expect from ourselves. Influence can be positive or negative. Although we can't let negative influences drive us. We are fortunate in that we are shielded, which frees the principal, Deans, and teachers up to support, guide, teach, and celebrate people and their successes.

The parents started an MCP Parent Leadership Council and have put on events and fundraisers for the school to celebrate students' successes, according to the principal who shared,

> It's a good community builder and it's neat because a lot of kids have siblings here so you get to know kids from a lot of different grade levels. The parents are really connected with teachers at different levels.

The principal explained that MCP requires a lot from parents,

> Every night the kids have to bring home homework in every grade level and the parents have to sign their homework every night. And if the parents don't sign it's a deposit . . . and the parents have to come to conferences for quarter one and quarter two.

Furthermore, the principal went on to say,

> This is an expectation and if they don't come, the kids aren't allowed back in the classroom and I know, I mean at my first school... that was like a huge, huge issue. I would have one parent show up for conferences each time and I would like . . .. so, this is huge glow for our school because bringing the parents into the classroom and making personal connection with the teacher does a lot for each of the students.

Resources and Support

The Academic Dean provided a brief history of Lloyd Street Campus's progression from a failing school to a turnaround school. She learned from another MCP campus that "Teachers there engaged in numerous tools, techniques, and strategies, and through trial and error, were able to identify and share those that have caused most success. Now Lloyd School has integrated and honed those skills and is seeing results." She maintained this is due to the efforts of Ms. F, the Chief Academic Officer (CAO), who serves all MCP campuses to share practice, and ensure consistent expectation across campuses. "Change comes when we do it!" If teachers are not employing these tools, she meets with the teachers to determine "what systems need to be put in play and how I can support them." She also checks lesson plans for "the whole week for every teacher and make notes as to what's great and what seems to be vague." There is also emphasis placed on lines of questioning presented by teachers so, "tips can be provided as to how to dive a little deeper as to what they are trying to accomplish."

Support and visibility are evident as the Academic Dean works with teachers on their unit plans as well and meets with each grade level every week to keep track of teacher data and identify things that go well, the *Glows*, and the *Grows*, what needs to improve. She is also responsible for MAP testing and prepares student goal-setting worksheets. MCP sets goals for teachers to achieve. These efforts have paid off. She shared, "The Math growth for K–5 was set at 130 and they made 135%. We also have a goal set for a minimum of 70% for students to either meet or exceed their end targets. These results show that 72% of students met their targets. Reading was 135% with 74 meeting targets." Up to this point, they had never seen such results. "We've done well in terms of progression. We push individual student targets along with class targets and keep asking ourselves what we can do strategically to bring the numbers even higher." The staff works consistently, daily, to help students meet or exceed their goals. "They get so excited when they get a golden ticket. Not much, but they dive in for even the smallest rewards. When we get excited, they get excited, and then you have buy-in for learning. Just these little things are something they can take home and tell their parents."

There is a heavy emphasis on professional development (PD), which is offered weekly to teachers. The Academic Dean addressed lower than expected reading scores:

> We have a lot of PDs throughout the year and they introduce new challenges for the teachers throughout the year like in the third quarter. We take tests called AR (Accelerated Reading) and kids read books and then take independent tests and we noticed that our AR scores were kind of lower. So, they made this huge push school wide to get kids to take more AR tests.

This effort was viewed as a successful push on the part of the administrators.

The findings from question one regarding the role of *learning* reveal a strong mission-driven, collaborative culture with a strong academic focus that demands high expectations for staff, students and families; consistency and rigor regarding a highly structured standard curriculum, instructional strategies and programs, data-driven assessment and behavior; celebrations of good work; plentiful resources and support systems, yet mixed feelings voiced by teachers. On one hand, the teachers felt restricted by the hierarchical structure and administrative demands, but pleased to be a part of a united community that provides rigor and continues to show evidence of student results.

The Academic Dean expressed a passion for lifelong learning and for her work, "I learn so much here; it's such a great place to be. MCP is more than just a school or a job to me. It's a part of my life so I will give whatever it takes." She feels that if the teachers fail or do not feel supported, she fails. "Being transparent with them promotes openness and trust when teachers can share their frustrations and challenges. She described herself, "I am that ear, the person they can go to and problem-solve what's causing the issue. When they are successful, I get to be successful too."

A strong advantage at Lloyd School, unlike other schools, is that the principal is required to do limited paperwork, which is done primarily by the CEO. The Principal emoted,

> It is fantastic! I don't have to worry about a budget. I don't have to worry about charter paperwork for the district or compliance reports. My sole responsibility is to create, nurture and sustain an environment where teachers are valued, respected, supported, coached, and in some rare cases, exited out.

Teachers are aware that they will be supported and, according to the principal, "they are ours." As a result, the Principal claimed to spend as little time in his office as possible, so he could be visible in the school throughout the day. As a leader, one has "a finite amount of time in front of people. So, what we *say* and what we *do* become critically important; we need to be intentional... What a principal says is remembered."

The Academic Dean performs leadership in several ways. She visits classrooms daily to observe instruction and uses specific tools for note taking. She observes whether teachers are using the strategies, tools, and programs they have been taught, like collecting data (i.e., Accelerated Reader, Compass, Learning Odyssey), and then offers feedback following teacher lessons. A large part of the Academic Dean's role is to monitor data and work with teachers on specific areas that need to be covered and which strategies, techniques and tools might work best. Even though the curriculum is very structured, teachers write their own lesson plans and spend a long time writing them. The Academic Dean review each one and meet with all teachers every week to review. Each lesson has eight parts.

There are significant structural differences between MCP and other schools in the city of Milwaukee. One is having two adults in every classroom through 4th grade, usually a teacher and an educational assistant, and trying to limit each class to no more than 25 students. The structure has been facilitated by raising outside funds that align to the beliefs and mission of the school. However, "This small ratio comes with some consequences like not providing transportation for students and families. This becomes a sacrifice on the part of the parents, but on another level, we look at it as a huge bonus because we get to see our parents every day dropping kids off, walking them in or visiting our school. This as a win-win versus a huge loss." The principal stressed:

Teacher benefits are equal to those in the city, but salaries are slightly lower than the average, so it is critical to provide a "unique environment for our staff to live and work in, to be a part of a community. So, they pride ourselves on doing the small things for our staff that help them realize that this is an amazing space to call home for 10–12 hours a day."

Students in the third grade and above are now departmentalized. The structure led to one teacher teaching Math and another Reading. This was an attempt to address the problem that teachers agree was "our content is so much so the new structure will allow teachers to be great"—growing an expert in one area, so each can be groomed to be the expert in that subject area. Teachers also share their lesson plans within their school team and with teachers on other MCP campuses. "We find that whenever a teacher is focused on writing the specific subject area plans, the students perform better on those assessments."

Lloyd School's leadership with a principal, two school deans, one Chief Academic Officer, and educational assistants in every classroom, support teachers and problem-solve learning problems impacts learning as witnessed in the MAP results. Leaders generate and monitor several opportunities for teacher learning. They cover classes to allow teachers, who are struggling with specific problem, to observe other teachers at Lloyd or other MCP campuses, and successfully identify schools with which they also share successful interventions. "The principal is all over the building all day long." The Academic Dean specified, "Some teachers model well for new teachers; we offer many opportunities to build leadership in teachers. We say if someone is amazing at something, come teach us at staff meetings, show us your way. It raises people up." Interestingly, when teachers visit other classrooms, the culture is such that they are there to observe; there is an inviting, open door policy. Teachers do not visit to evaluate but to "steal effective strategies. If you tell them they are rocking; let me see what I can steal from you, so I can rock!" Additionally, Learning takes place in the "Z Suite," a specific conference center, located in the heart of the building, where teachers and administrators gather to discuss critical issues and learn from each other.

Summary

The findings reveal a strong mission-driven, collaborative culture with a strong academic focus that demands high expectations of staff, students, and families connected with Lloyd Street Campus community. This educational community is sustained with continued support; building relationships with parents while promoting adherence to expectations; consistency regarding instructional issues; constant recognition, reinforcement and celebration of student and staff efforts; and the need to forge more partnerships with the community. Formal leadership includes the principal, two deans, and the CAO who concentrate on two main functions: character building and academics. The Dean of Students focuses on behavior and character development. She was described as needing to be reactive at times, when dealing with discipline, but prefers to be proactive when engaging teachers to strengthen the classroom culture. She concurred with the principal's view of himself, as "captain of the ship" and supported this image. The principal described his role to "revive a sense of mission and vision and encourage, empower and support, clean up when necessary, and take the lead based on the needs of the school." Further, "I empower those who are with me, not below me. The amazing things happening are because of those doing the work; I watch it all happen."

The principal shared that intentional efforts to build teacher leaders happen through professional development. Also, teachers learn from peers in other neighboring charter schools. The principal noted that "teachers are autonomous within specific models and practices." The teachers concurred with the opportunities afforded them but did not perceive leadership beyond those in formal leadership roles. These learning and leader-building opportunities come from the community of practice that exists within the unique situational context of the CMO and the STCM.

The findings reveal that prior urban experience is critical in turnaround efforts in urban settings. Specifically, a mission-driven culture needs to exist with significant levels of consistency in academic and behavioral practices; relationships need to be developed, intentionally, across staff and students; support and adequate resources are necessary to address the gaps that are apparent to all; and leadership is perceived as supportive, but hierarchical with limited distribution. Intentional efforts are also pervasive in creating "the joy factor that is huge here," as described by the principal, adding, "Everything involves chants, cheers, smiling, happiness to really get kids invested."

The Academic Dean discussed the importance of consistency around mission and values, which begins, and can be facilitated in the hiring process, by finding people who are mission-aligned, who have the same beliefs. The teachers' jobs are the hardest by far in the building and support and celebration of efforts are key. We are like family here, but we know that there is a job that must get done. If not them, who? They need to get the job done. If teachers have a bad day they've got to get on the stage and turn it on. Buck up! Yet we find our teachers are amazing and we do *Shout Outs* to let them know.

A strategic action is that staff "sweat the small stuff" and that means that they act with consistency around several seemingly small things. Adults are proactive and try to model consistency around policies and procedures in the handbook by checking uniforms, giving violations, "minor things that build up to create something bigger or cause a backward slide." These actions of adults give credibility to the student disciplinary code and expectations that are equitable throughout the community.

The Academic Dean described, "This school has a vibrant culture… We play hard, but we work hard." That takes creating a "culture that is enjoyable for scholars but also making sure it's also a place where expectations need to be met. We are on this journey and everyone has to be a part of it." Goals developed from school-wide on down, both individual and organizational, have made a difference. She disclosed data that indicated, "Last year our K5 and 1 were at grade level; this year K5–2 are continuing the trajectory. I feel that without a doubt it will happen. Our 3rd grade scholars are on grade level now and have great 3rd grade teachers."

DISCUSSION

In summary, several themes repeatedly emerged in response to the three research questions. First, to embark on a turnaround effort hiring and retaining staff with urban experience was deemed critical at Lloyd Street Campus. This supports the findings of Day (2009) regarding the need for personnel, resources, and structures to be in place in order to be an effective turnaround school. Additionally, having people who are situated within a unique context, have an understanding of the community with whom they serve, and are passionate about building knowledge within that community, connects the findings with the theoretical framework offered by a community of practice (Lave & Wenger, 1991; Wenger, et al., 2002). Moreover, the expectation for staff is that they need to fit into a school with unalterable commitment to the mission, vision, and goals unique to the school.

There existed an unwavering focus on academics, as the staff clearly understood the tremendous challenges in turning around a failing school. The staff were also aware of the effort and time it would take to realize the vision, that is, to become a world-class school where "proficiency levels are 80–90% or higher and students are prepared "to be successful in life." Ample resources were noted, and significant academic support was provided by the CAO and the Academic Dean. The principal was viewed as a visible, dedicated culture and character builder; an overseer of instructional effectiveness and student progress, and a link to students, staff, family, and the community—in other words, the "captain of the ship." The research on the importance of the principal's instructional leadership influence on academic achievement (Leithwood, et al., 2004; Waters, et al., 2003; Youngs & King, 2002) is confirmed by the findings in this study.

Second, consistency played out in the school's balanced focus on academics and character in all endeavors across the MCP schools. Academically and behaviorally, students and staff at Lloyd School chanted daily expressions that revealed a strong sense of unity, efficacy, and beliefs that mirrored the school's mission and vision, both in and outside of the school's daily morning Assemblies and in classrooms. With each visit, the researchers witnessed a school exuding warmth, joy, and alive with a cacophony of sound maybe where students were highly engaged in learning. Academically, high expectations were demanded of everyone: teachers, students, staff, and parents. Every classroom in every MCP school at every level needed to look the same every day. Teachers can step into any MCP classroom and students would have the same expectations. All MCP schools follow a standard curriculum and are data-driven linked to daily assessments and standardized test results; results of any day's assessments must be shared on a moment's notice. The notion of academic turnaround, as a direct result of data-driven performance goals found by Duke (2015), is demonstrated through the findings in this study. Additionally, several instructional programs and strategies are expected to be applied in every classroom and every detailed lesson. If not apparent, support is promptly provided, similar to the findings of Bossert et al. (1982) which found the principals' influence on school climate and instructional organization to be key in creating a culture of high expectations and building supportive relationships.

There is evidence of continuous student growth as evidenced by standardized test scores and adequate support, the hierarchical leadership structure allows for limited freedom in instructional content or practice. Standardized test scores were reviewed and shared three times per year and there was an expectation of 125% academic growth in all classrooms. Again, in accessing and utilizing the knowledge created within the community of practice (Lave & Wenger, 1991; Wenger et al., 2002) there is a culture of understanding, which develops between all participants.

CONCLUSIONS AND RECOMMENDATIONS

The purpose of this study was to determine how leaders promote a culture of learning in high-needs schools. The findings indicate it is apparent that several variables blend together to place Lloyd School Campus and other MCP schools on a path to success, academically and behaviorally. Learning is the focus as noted by the school's mission driven belief that "zip code does not define one's destiny." A relentless focus on "academic performance, consistency, and exceptionally high standards for all" are propelled by the notion of grit and character building. This is apparent in a standardized curriculum, detailed lesson planning, and frequent testing that have shown results. Systems of support are in place to assist teachers to meet the high-performance goals provided by a community of practice consisting of the Chief Academic Officer (CAO), the Academic Dean, teacher assistants in every K5–5 classroom, and colleagues across schools. Lloyd Street Campus is highly data-driven, and results are monitored and managed by the Academic Dean.

Urban experience in formal leadership roles, and in the teaching ranks, is a catalyst for developing a successful urban learning context. Moreover, freed from having to spend time on bureaucratic paperwork and assignments, such as budgeting and scheduling, this principal was able to lead by being visible, present, and engaged with the entire school community. Drawing access to other leaders in MCS and STCM the principal is able to tap collective wisdom, of the community of practice that exists within the context of high-needs urban schools, to answer questions and share knowledge.

Humor and fun were pervasive in the Lloyd Street Campus creating a positive, joy-filled learning culture. The fun is balanced with strict expectations for behavior and students are indoctrinated with common language, strategies, and social tools to ensure success. All stakeholders, parents, and community partners are welcome to share the vision, support the mission, and assist students in becoming successful scholars and productive citizens. While the short-term goal is successful academic achievement at the elementary level, the long-term goal is matriculation to higher education.

The leaders of four high-needs urban schools, which make up MCP, have worked together over the past several years to establish a shared curricular model of success. The Milwaukee College Prep Curriculum model, when implemented with integrity, completeness, and consistency, has proven to be an effective framework for improving academic performance among urban learners. Through the framework of communities of practice (Lave & Wenger, 1991), teachers and leaders of MCP schools continue to utilize a social learning structure for knowledge building for employed by all stakeholders in this unique urban high-needs educational setting. Despite this success, there are still questions about replication of this leadership model in other similar high-need urban settings. Additionally, since we know anecdotally, that parental involvement places a key role in student academic success, further study would uncover these factors in the context of high-needs schools.

Questions to Consider:

1. How can leaders of high needs schools involve all stakeholders in increasing student achievement and success?
2. How can parents become more involved with students and school engagement in high needs communities?
3. What can institutions of higher education o to better prepare teachers and school leaders to work in communities of high need?
4. What leadership initiatives exist to foster learning in high need schools?

REFERENCES

Andrietsch. A. (n.d.). *Rocketship education is ready to launch in Milwaukee.* Schools That Can Milwaukee. Retrieved from https://app.e2ma.net/app/view:CampaignPublic/id:1409000.7472661032/rid:71865a86f40ca62519fe6e752cf402eb

Baran, M. L. (2008). Assessing the effects of a middle school looping program. *The International Journal of Learning, 15*(7), 185–192.

Baran, M. L., & Berry, J. R. (2015). *The international school leadership development network (ISLDN) high-needs schools group research protocol and members' guide.* Unpublished manuscript.

Bossert, S. T., Dwyer, D. C., Rowan, B., & Lee, G. V. (1982). The instructional management role of the principal. *Educational Administration Quarterly, 18*(3), 34–64.

Brooks, J. S., Armstrong D. E., Bogotch, I., Harris, S., Sherman, W., & Theoharis, G. (2012). *Social justice leadership for a global world.* Charlotte, NC: IAP Publishers.

Covey, S. R. (1989). *The 7 habits of highly effective people.* New York, NY: Simon & Schuster.

Day, C. (2009). Capacity building through layered leadership: Sustaining the turnaround. In A. Harris (Ed.), *Distributed leadership. Studies in educational leadership* (pp. 121–137). Dordrecht, Netherlands: Springer.

Deal, T. E., & Peterson, K. D. (2009). *Shaping school culture: Pitfalls, paradoxes, and promises.* New York, NY: Wiley

Duke, D. (2015). *Leadership for low-performing schools: A step-by-step guide to the school turnaround process.* Lanham, MD: Rowman & Littlefield.

Epstein, J. L., & van Voorhis, F. L. (2010). School counselors' roles in developing partnerships with families and communities for student success. *Professional School Counseling, 14,* 1–14.

Glaser, B. G., & Strauss, A. L. (1967). *The discovery of grounded theory.* Hawthorn, NY: Aldine Publishing Company

Goldstein, J. (1999). Emergence as a construct: History and issues. *Complexity and Organization, 1*(1), 49–72.

Gredler, M.E. (2001). *Learning and instruction: Theory into practice.* Upper Saddle River, NJ: Prentice Hall.

Harris, A. (2008). *Distributed leadership in schools: Developing the leaders of tomorrow.* New York, NY: Routledge.

Hallinger, P., & Heck, R. H. (2010). Collaborative leadership and school improvement: Understanding the impact on school capacity and student learning, *School Leadership and Management, 30*(2), 95–110.

Heck, R. H., & Hallinger, P. (2009). Assessing the contribution of distributed leadership to school improvement and growth in math achievement. *American Educational Research Journal, 46*(3), 659–689.

Hipp, K. K., & Weber, P. (Ed.) (May, 2007). *Urban school leadership: Managing magnitude, urgency and complexity.* A Wallace Fellows project in cooperation with Cardinal Stritch University, Milwaukee, WI.

Lave, J., & Wenger, E. (1991). *Situated learning.* New York, NY: Cambridge

Leithwood, K., Harris, A., & Hopkins, D. (2008). Seven strong claims about successful school leadership. *School Leadership & Management, 28*(1), 27–42.

Leithwood, K., & Jantzi, P. (1999). The relative effects of principals and teacher sources of leadership on student engagement with schools. *Educational Administration Quarterly, 35*(5), 679–706.

Leithwood, K., Mascall, B., & Strauss, T. (2009). What we have learned and where we will go from here. In K. Leithwood, B. Mascall, & T. Strauss (Eds.), *Distributed leadership according to the evidence.* New York, NY: Routledge

Leithwood, K., Seashore Louis, K., Anderson, S., & Wahlstrom, K. (2004). *How leadership influences student learning.* New York, NY: Wallace Foundation.

Lipham, J. M. (1981). *Effective schools.* ERIC Document Number ED207131.

Michael, S., Dittus, P., & Epstein, J. (2007). Family and community involvement in schools: Results from the school health policies and programs study 2006. *Journal of School Health, 77*(8), 567–587. doi:10.1111/j.1746-1561.2007.00236.x

Miles, M. B., & Huberman, A.M. (1994). *Qualitative data analysis.* Thousand Oaks, CA: SAGE Publications

Milwaukee College Preparatory School (n.d.) *Accountability Report 2010–11.* Prepared for office of Charter Schools, University of Wisconsin–Milwaukee.

Milwaukee Public Schools. (n.d.). *Diversified community schools.* Retrieved from http://mps.milwaukee.k12.wi.us/en/District/About-MPS/School-Board/Office-of-Accountability-Efficiency/Public-Items-Emjay/District-Enrollment.htm

Muller, C., Katz, S. R., & Dance, L. J. (1999, Sept.). Investing in teaching and learning: Dynamics of the teacher-student relationship from each actor's perspective. *Urban Education, 34*(3), 292–337. ERIC Number: EJ594347

Mulvany, L. (2013, Nov. 8). *Black students near bottom in nation on benchmark math, reading test. 'Nation's report card' posts stagnant education scores in Wisconsin.* Retrieved from http://www.jsonline.com/news/education/states-black-students-rank-lowest-in-reading-math-scores-b99136626z1-230903121.html#ixzz30tx10kQ

National Alliance for Public Charter Schools. (n.d.). *What are public charter schools?* Retrieved from http://www.publiccharters.org/get-the-facts/public-charter-schools/

National Assessment of Educational Progress. (2013). *The Nation's Report Card 2013 Mathematics and Reading.* Retrieved from https://www.nationsreportcard. gov/reading_math_2013/#/

Noddings, N. (2002). *Starting at home: Caring and social policy.* Oakland, CA: University of California Press.

Ormrod, J. E. (2012). *Human learning* (6th ed.). Boston, MA: Pearson.

Petty, T., Fitchett, P., & O'Connor, K. (2012, Spring). Attracting and keeping teachers in high-need schools. *American Secondary Education, 40*(2), 67–88. ERIC Document Number: EJ986836.

Romell, R. (2013, April 20). *Milwaukee's deep racial, economic divisions are challenges to rebirth.* Retrieved from http://archive.jsonline.com/business/a-time-to-build-milwaukees-deep-racial-economic-divisions-are-challenges-to-rebirth-203641121.html/

Schools that Can. (2012). Retrieved from https://web.archive.org/web/20120331162835/http://stcmilwaukee.org:80/index.php/pathways-to-20000/

Sheldon, S. B. (2003). Linking school-family-community partnerships in urban elementary schools to student achievement on state tests. *Urban Review, 35,* 149–165.

Sheldon S. B., & Epstein J. L. (2002). Improving student behavior and discipline with family and community involvement. *Education in Urban Society, 35,* 4–26.

Spillane, J. P. (2006). *Distributed leadership.* San Francisco, CA: Jossey-Bass

Spillane, J. P., Hallett, T., & Diamond, J. B. (2003). Forms of capital and the construction of leadership in urban elementary schools. *Sociology of Education, 76*(1), 1–17. https://doi.org/10.2307/3090258

Strauss, A. L. (1987). *Qualitative analysis for social scientists.* Cambridge, UK: Cambridge Press

Youngs, P., & King, M. B. (2002). Principal leadership for professional development to build school capacity. *Educational Administration Quarterly, 38*(5), 643.

Walker, J. T., Shenker, S. S., & Hoover-Dempsey, K. V. (2010). Why do parents become involved in their children's education? Implications for school counselors. *Professional School Counseling, 14*(1), 27–41.

Waters, T. J., Marzano, R. J., & McNulty, B. A. (2003). *Balanced leadership: What 30 years of research tells us about the effect of leadership on student achievement.* Aurora, CO: Mid-continent Research for Education and Learning.

Wenger, E., McDermott, R., & Snyder, W.M. (2002). *Cultivating communities of practice.* Boston, MA: Harvard Business School Press.

WI Stat. (2012). §118.153.

Wisconsin Department of Public Instruction. (2014). *Promoting excellence for all.* Retrieved from https://dpi.wi.gov/sites/default/files/imce/excforall/exc4all-report.pdf

Wisconsin Department of Public Instruction. (2018). *School accountability report 2013–2014.* [Data file]. Retrieved from https:apps2.dpi.wi.gov/reportcards/home

PART III

SUCCESSFUL EDUCATIONAL LEADERSHIP PRACTICE

CHAPTER 7

LEADERSHIP IN HIGH-NEEDS/ HIGH PERFORMING SCHOOLS

Success Stories from an Urban School District

Jami Royal Berry, Sheryl Cowart Moss, and Peryenthia Gore

High-needs schools in the United States are characterized by their ethnically, linguistically, and economically diverse student populations, resulting in challenges that are interwoven with cultural and societal norms. This chapter presents characteristics of leadership that enable staff and student success in schools from one cluster of high-needs, high-performing schools in one large suburban, American school system, utilizing a case study methodology following the International School Leadership Development Network (ISLDN) research protocol. Literature reviewed highlights the context specific to high-needs schools, including leadership characteristics, instructional considerations, and implications for school culture. While the study employed a constructivist qualitative approach, a new theoretical framework, the High-needs School Leadership model, coupled with an overarching model of thematic analysis was used to drive the research design and for data analysis. Data were collected from personal interviews with educators including school leaders, assistant school leaders, and teachers at two schools within the identified cluster. These data and concurrent archival document analysis revealed the importance of several key themes: 1) Engagement, 2) Core Values, 3) Developing People, 4) Inclusion, 5) Equity, and 6) Persistence. As schools in the United States become increas-

Educational Leadership, Culture, and Success in High-Need Schools, pages 131–148.
Copyright © 2019 by Information Age Publishing

ingly diverse, the urgency to understand the contextual elements that lead to success grows. By considering the findings of this study, system and school leaders can enhance their awareness of factors with the greatest potential to significantly, and positively, impact educational settings for students in high-needs schools.

Keywords: high-needs schools, transformational leadership, social justice leadership, inclusion, equity, contextual understanding

INTRODUCTION

The International School Leadership Development Network (ISLDN) high-needs schools group research protocol was the primary document used to conduct this research and was appropriate as the goal of this study was to explore critical aspects of leadership in two high-needs schools (Baran & Berry, 2015). The purpose of the High-needs School Strand (HNS) of the ISLDN is to determine various qualities of leadership critical to leading high-needs schools focused on learning, leadership, and context. Therefore, the guiding research questions were:

- What fosters student learning in high-needs schools?
- How do school leaders enhance individual and organizational performance in high-needs schools?
- How do internal and external school contexts impact individual and organizational performance in high-needs schools?

LITERATURE REVIEW: HIGH-NEEDS SCHOOLS IN THE UNITED STATES

In the United States, formal education begins with early childhood education followed by primary (elementary), middle, and ultimately secondary (high) school (U.S. Department of Education, 2008). Across the United States, the National Center for Education Statistics (NCES) is responsible for collecting and analyzing data related to education, including measures related to high-needs schools, characterized primarily by the students they serve.

According to the Ready to Teach Act (2003), high-needs schools are those in which at least 25% of the student population lives below the poverty line. Additionally, schools serving large numbers of students who speak English as a second language, students with learning or emotional disabilities, or students not performing at grade-level in one or more subjects are also considered to be high-needs (Berry, 2008; Mid-Continent Research for Education and Learning, 2005; Silin, 2010). In the United States, any elementary or secondary school receiving federal financial assistance to help ensure that children from low-income families meet state academic standards is categorized as a Title 1 school (U.S. Department of Education, 2015); schools enrolling at least 40% of students from high poverty families are eligible to use Title I funds (U.S. Department of Education, 2015). The NCES reported that in school year 2013–2014, more than 69,000 schools across the country received Title I funds (Glander, 2015). In 2012–2013, approximately 23% of public schools were identified as high poverty (Kena, et al., 2015). Title 1 schools are often designated as high-needs.

Another measure for determining school poverty, and consequently high-needs status, is the number of students enrolled in the free and reduced lunch (FRPL) program. Researchers have recently identified three primary reasons that FRPL is commonly used for measuring school poverty: 1) FRPL is found consistently across survey collections, 2) FRPL has a strong correlation with district poverty, and 3) FRPL is correlated with measures of socioeconomic status reported at the student/household level. In high-needs schools, more than 75% of students are eligible for FRPL (Aud, et al., 2010; Kena et al., 2015).

The percentage of students identified as English language learners (ELLs) is also a factor in determining high-needs status. English language learners participate in language assistance programs, such as English as Second Language (ESOL), to help ensure that they acquire both Basic English Proficiency and high levels of academic English. The goal of ESOL programs is to provide support to ELLs so that they may master the same academic content and meet the same achievement standards as their peers. In the 2012–2013 academic year, 9.2% of public school students in the United States were English language learners (Kena et al., 2015).

Leadership Characteristics Necessary for High-needs Schools

An examination of literature related to leadership in high-performing, high-needs schools revealed that school leaders bring certain implied understandings leading to success for their students and teachers. Participants in Klar and Brewer's (2013) study of successful leadership in high-needs schools understood the importance of assessing the social, economic, psychological, and academic needs of their students before focusing on student achievement. Other scholars found leaders in these settings also understood the difference between decisive and shared leadership (Griffin & Green, 2013) and placed a greater value on leadership as a shared practice (Dodman, 2014; Griffin & Green, 2013; Johnson, Kraft, & Papay, 2012; Woods & Martin, 2016).

Leaders in high-performing, high-needs schools understood they were leading by example (Klar & Brewer, 2013; Medina, Martinez, Murakami, Rodriquez, & Hernandez 2014) and were the chief communicators of the asset view of students (Medina et al., 2014), regularly endorsing a belief in the value of the resources and knowledge students and families brought to bear (Ullucci & Howard, 2015). They communicated this by intentionally creating positive relationships with community members and behaving in ways that reinforced these relationships (Griffin & Green, 2013; Oylere & Fuentes, 2012; Woods & Martin, 2016).

Leaders in high-needs schools demonstrated a sense of caring for stakeholders' well-being (Griffin & Green, 2013) by listening (Klar & Brewer, 2013), responding to concerns (Dodman, 2014; Johnson et al., 2012; Klar & Brewer, 2013), and working to understand the nuances of their specific school contexts (Klar & Brewer, 2013). The practice of setting high expectations implied a belief in both the learning capacity of students (Griffin & Green, 2013; Oylere & Fuentes, 2012) and the capacity of teachers to assist students in meeting learning goals (Griffin & Green, 2013). The intentional selection, development, and support of teacher leaders also conveyed that the leader was adept at empowering teachers (Griffin & Green, 2013; Dodman, 2014). Lastly, the literature stressed that leaders must communicate a clear instructional direction aligned with what is best for students (Griffin & Green, 2013; Klar & Brewer, 2013).

Instructional Considerations of High-needs Schools

Students in high-needs schools exhibit wide diversity in school readiness, background knowledge, language proficiency, and culture (Oylere & Fuentes, 2012; Silin 2010). Consequently, instructional models must address a myriad of factors to increase students' chances for academic success (Barley & Beasley, 2007; Berry, 2008; Hazel, Pfaff, Albanes, & Gallagher, 2014; Mid-Continent Research for Education and Learning, 2005; Oylere & Fuentes, 2012; Silin, 2010). Many of these are considered best practices in any school setting, but in high-needs schools they are essential. One example is the need for culturally responsive curriculum. Because of differences in language, cultural assumptions, and values between teachers and students (Berry, 2008; Oylere & Fuentes, 2012), culturally responsive pedagogy aids in building trust and developing positive relationships with students from backgrounds underrepresented in traditional curricular materials (Silin, 2010).

The foundation of instruction in high-needs schools must be based on high expectations for all students (Barley & Beasley, 2007; Mid-Continent Research for Education and Learning, 2005; Medina et al., 2014; Oylere & Fuentes, 2012; Silin, 2010; Woods & Martin, 2015). High-needs schools often create strategic intervention systems to support students' attainment of rigorous learning goals (Hazel et al., 2014) ranging from a reliance on multi-tiered systems of support (MTSS) to after-school tutoring and remediation opportunities, to intentional differentiation of students grouping, to organizational structures (Barley & Beasley, 2007; Hazel et al., 2014; Oylere & Fuentes, 2012; Woods & Martin, 2015).

Implications for School Culture

Within the context of high-needs schools, school culture is defined as how the environment is characterized by factors including mutual trust, respect, and commitment to student achievement (Dodman, 2014; Griffin & Green, 2013; Johnson et al., 2012; Woods & Martin, 2015). Scholars have found that establishing a collaborative culture is essential for realizing gains in student learning (Griffin & Green, 2013; Johnson et al., 2012; Klar & Brewer, 2013). Johnson et al. (2012) noted the development of a culture based on trusting, collegial relationships consistently promoted by teachers and the principal can improve teachers' practice and ultimately student performance. In fact, the cultural factors that teachers valued most were social (Johnson et al., 2012).

Griffin and Green (2013) identified several positive outcomes when leaders in high-needs schools established a culture based on collaboration and high expectations including high faculty morale, low absenteeism, and increased job satisfaction. Students demonstrated an increased sense of student efficacy, more regular school attendance, fewer disciplinary infractions, greater engagement in school activities, interest in scholarship, and responsibility for learning. Dodman (2014) noted that within the context of high-needs schools, a data-driven culture had the potential to create "conditions of positive pressure, collective responsibility, and continuous problem posing" (p. 58). Ultimately, the culture defining a high-needs school should support effective teaching and learning for all students in all classrooms (Johnson et al., 2012).

CONCEPTUAL FRAMEWORK

Social justice must exist in the leadership repertoire in high-needs schools. Social justice leaders believe systems that provide separate programs effectively provide unequal levels of instruction, lead to the marginalization of particular students, and create situations where these students receive an inferior education (Theoharis, 2007). Social justice leaders work to create warm and welcoming school climates and set goals focused upon providing an equitable and inclusive education for all students (Theoharis, 2007). Furman (2012) characterized social justice leadership as action-oriented, persistent, and transformative; this characterization led to the inclusion of transformational leadership theory as part of the conceptual framework grounding this study.

Transformational leadership theory assumes a small number of leadership behaviors or practices increases the commitment and effort of organizational members toward achieving organizational goals (Leithwood & Sun, 2012). Leithwood and Sun (2012) identified these practices as setting directions, developing people, redesigning the organization, and improving the instructional program. Social justice leaders also value these practices.

School leaders are key to promoting social justice in schools, and leaders in high-needs schools must influence programs and actions within the school community (Theoharis, 2007). Leaders can accomplish this by providing the support for high levels of engagement and motivation to achieve goals associated with their values, as is typical of transformational leadership (Leithwood & Sun, 2012). For the purposes of this study, we offer a new model of leadership, the High-needs Schools Leadership model (see Figure 7.1).

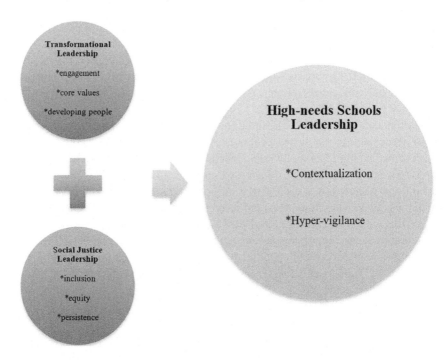

FIGURE 7.1. High-needs Schools Leadership

This model is more than combined principles from Transformational and Social Justice Leadership. Rather, it is a contextualization of the beliefs and behaviors of leaders in high-needs schools. Without an intentional desire to understand the context of their schools and communities, leaders in high-needs schools may persistently pursue equity and inclusion, but they may not understand the core values that encourage students and communities to engage. Without this understanding, leaders will struggle to develop faculty and staff who can authentically connect with their students and communities. We argue that an intentional, hyper-vigilant pursuit of the beliefs in our High-needs School Leadership model, with an understanding of the dissonance in definitions of success as perceived by district hierarchies and by high-needs communities anchor and focus leadership for high-needs schools.

METHODS

Qualitative case study methodology allows researchers to explore or describe phenomena in context using a variety of data sources (Baxter & Jack, 2008). Proponents of this methodology base their approaches on a constructivist paradigm, which claims that truth is relative and dependent upon individuals' perspectives (Baxter & Jack, 2008). Thematic analysis is useful as an analytic method because it works with a wide range of research questions, can be used to analyze different types of data, and can produce both data-driven and theory-driven analyses (Clarke & Braun, 2013).

This case presents data from one elementary and one middle school, within one cluster of schools in the Southeastern United States, utilizing thematic analysis through the lens of the High-needs Schools Leadership model. The schools were purposefully selected because they met the criteria for high-needs schools related to socioeconomic status and cultural diversity, and because the elementary school fed the middle school, providing a more robust picture of the overall educational context for the students served. Data collected from the two schools included interviews with over fifteen educators and concurrent document analysis. The case was bound by time and setting with all data collection taking place in the schools highlighted during the 2016–2017 academic year.

Sample

Thornton County. Thornton County is located in the southeast United States, in the northeast metro area of the state capital. With a total population of more than 800,000 residents, it is one of the most diverse counties in the country (53.3% White, 23.6% Black, 2.7% Korean, 3.1% two or more races; 20.1% Hispanic or Latino). The median household income in the county is above $60,000, and the per capita income is just above $25,000. Data from the 2010 census report revealed that 14% of the population was below the poverty line.

The county's public-school system is the largest in the state and has been ranked among the top 20 percent of school systems for percentage of low-income students performing at high achievement levels in core academic subjects like reading, math, and science. There are approximately 173,000 students in 136 schools (79 elementary, 28 middle, 21 high, and 8 alternative or nontraditional schools). Fifty-six percent of students qualify for free or reduced lunch.

Schools in Thornton are grouped into 19 geographic attendance clusters. A cluster contains three to six elementary schools that feed into the same middle school and then the same high school. The name of each cluster mirrors the name of the cluster's high school. This study offers a brief description of one elementary and one middle school within a cluster. There are a total of nine schools in the Mountainside Cluster, making it the largest cluster in the district.

Bubbling Brook Elementary School. Bubbling Brook Elementary School (BBES), one of 136 schools in the Thornton School District, has a long history. Fifty years ago, the school's original building opened with eleven classrooms. Three years ago, the school moved to its current site where it houses approximately 1,425 students in grades K–5. The staff includes 165 certified and classified educators including one principal and five assistant principals. It is located in an urban setting, where the movement of immigrants to the United States has resulted in extreme population growth.

The students at BBES come from diverse backgrounds: 74% of students are identified as second language speakers, the majority of whom are of Hispanic descent. The largest remaining subgroup is Black with a small percentage of White and other. The school has the highest free lunch rate in the school system with 96% of students qualifying. The school demographics have remained consistent over the last five years despite a high transience rate. Three years ago, the area underwent redistricting and lost several extended stay hotels to a neighboring school. However, it still serves several apartment complexes and maintains a high rate of mobility.

A proud graduate of the school district, the school principal has been at BBES for seven years. Prior to her appointment as principal, she served as a teacher and an assistant principal in the school system.

Robard Middle School. Robard Middle School is a study in symbolism, context, and change. The school is housed in a former newspaper production facility, and the New York Times financed its opening. It is named for a long tenured board member who is still active. At its opening, she declared that the school should be a lighthouse for the community. While the lighthouse symbol endures, its interpretation has changed, along with most other aspects of the school.

The school, like the system, was once a pastoral scene dotted with dairy farms. This gave way to small industries, such as the newspaper, and later to strip malls and small businesses. Pawnshops and quick cash loan businesses are now frequent sights. The administrative team at Robard includes the principal, six assistant principals, and a parent involvement coordinator.

As the economic landscape has changed, so has the demographic landscape. The population shifted from mostly White and middle class to 67% Hispanic or Latino, 24% Black, 5% Asian and 2% White, with 94% of the students receiving free or reduced lunch. The Hispanic population includes many unauthorized immigrants from Guatemala. Two redistricting initiatives decreased the school's population from 2,000 to 1,325 students.

FINDINGS

In the sections that follow, we reflect on how participants' responses reflect the key themes of engagement, core values, developing people, inclusion, equity, and persistence. A synthesis of each case revealed that participants recognized in their leaders' behaviors and actions that are commonly associated with Transformational and Social Justice Leadership. As was suggested in our High-needs School Leadership model, the prevalence of these behaviors and actions served to promote success for both students and staff. As we reviewed our data, we were able to recognize the constructs of contextualization, hyper-vigilance, and intentionality woven into participants' responses and the school communities that they create.

Case 1: Bubbling Brook Elementary School

Fostering Student Learning. At BBES, the school's mission is Nurture/Collaborate/Own. Interviewees provided examples of how this mission translates into action. They discussed the idea of nurturing students through initiatives such as coat drives and recognition for good behavior/academic performance, nurturing parents through the use of an active parent center that offers resources and support related to school and the community and nurturing new staff through mentorship and other initiatives. Regarding collaboration, interviewees highlighted planning and model lessons that offer teachers examples of how to enhance instructional approaches. Finally, they discussed working with students to build an understanding of the importance of owning their actions and the outcomes of those actions. Several interviewees cited the lack of discipline referrals and attributed this to the embodiment of the mission in everything done at the school.

Enhancing Performance. The interviewees highlighted enhancing individual performance by using Title I funds to employ four coaches who serve as teacher leaders for math and reading. Using funds in this manner allows coaches to deliver staff development to teachers, providing ongoing instructional support to teachers. Interviewees discussed the shift from a pull-out model of ESOL delivery to a push-in model. This shift enabled all students to receive stronger, more cohesive instruction, because they were all present for the regular instruction while being simultaneously supported by the ESOL teacher. In organizational performance, interviewees noted the structure of three days of professional development each week including grade level planning, data talks, and lesson modeling. This, in addition to regular walk throughs and ongoing feedback by administrators, was indicative of a school that was committed a culture of learning.

Impact of Internal and External School Contexts. The school's greatest challenge as echoed by teachers and administrators was transience of students and teachers, with staff transience being particularly problematic. Of the 165 staff members, only two lived within the school's attendance zone, and neither of those individuals was a certified staff member. Interviewees indicated that they commuted a minimum of 35 minutes to the school, and everyone mentioned this as a major contextual barrier to building and sustaining a long-term, stable staff. While interviewees highlighted the positive internal school culture around the ideal of Nurture/Collaborate/Own, the fact that none of the staff were members of the community was indicative of a contextual issue that permeates high-needs schools. The principal and assistant principals discussed the challenges associated with hiring and training over 25 new teachers annually; the teachers interviewed echoed this with several stating that if only the school could be moved closer to their homes, they would stay indefinitely.

Case 2: Robard Middle School

Fostering Student Learning. Changes to the local economic and demographic landscapes have required a shift in knowing and understanding for Robard's faculty. Faculty and staff face the harsh reality that most of their students will not come to school prepared to learn because they will be hungry. This must be addressed even if students arrive late, as they often do. Many students live with the stress of their parents' unauthorized immigration status, adding to the stress from hunger.

Enhancing Performance. While Robard's school population has decreased, the needs of the remaining students have drastically increased. This shift occurred in a climate of high stakes testing and intense accountability. The Thornton district's expectations have not changed to accommodate the shifts in population and faculty. On average, there are 67% of 6th graders who are below grade level, 67% of 7th graders are below grade level, and 50% of 8th graders are below grade level.

Impact of Internal and External School Contexts. In interviews with the principal and administrative team, several contextual themes emerged, including the need for hyper-vigilance and the reality of no "down-time" in their work. These leaders also emphasized the importance of meaningful symbols and rituals as ways to engage their communities. These contexts exist as counterpoints to the demands of district accountability measures and the realities of teacher quality and turnover, adding additional tensions to difficult work.

Synthesis of Participants' Perceptions

Engagement. One of the most prevalent elements highlighted at BBES was ongoing staff turnover and associated challenges. The longest tenured administrator stated, "In the ten years I have been here, the staff has completely turned over except myself and one other AP." She added that when the current leader came to the building, there was a good deal of pushback from teachers who did not want to work to address the ongoing academic challenges of the school: "Teachers retired or moved, but now teachers are here with high expectations for students, and those expectations are high regardless of whether a student is identified as gifted or as ESOL."

Similarly, given the challenges with Robard's population, its faculty, and district expectations, the many turnovers in the principalship are not surprising. The current principal has been at Robard for four years. The administrative team noted that her first meetings with faculty included data, with a "this is what we are facing" approach. She balanced this harsh reality with a call to action, letting the faculty know, "we need to be all in." She talked about "knowing why we are here." One of her signature phrases is, "*that* kid is every kid, and we are here for every kid." She resurrected the lighthouse as a symbol of the security and hope that the school represents. She emphasized that the school is more of a safe haven than it has ever been, and she extended the metaphor by noting that the weather conditions surrounding their lighthouse are more severe than ever.

Core Values. At BBES the data highlighted the idea of nurture/collaborate/ own being the cornerstone of the school's mission. One administrator articulated:

> We just foster a collaborative spirit of working with each other, and this means nurturing new teachers as well as the students. We have to make sure we support each other and collaborate on everything as an administrative team, so we eat lunch together every day and collaborate with the leadership team as well. Doing so means everyone owns the work we are doing here at school.

At Robard, the principal discussed the importance of shifting the mindset of her faculty from blaming families to highlighting possibilities. She referenced a community mindset that does not see very far into the future or understand the stepping-stones to long term goals. In her words:

> For many of our families, a 70 is not just a passing grade, it is something to be celebrated. These parents do love their children and they want good things for them, but their perception of good things is very limited. They need to be told that their children can go on to high school and to college, but they also need support to understand that it is not easy.

Developing People. The teachers at Bubbling Brook shared stories of how the leader facilitates leadership throughout the school. One stated, "I have chosen to stay in the classroom, because we are all looked at as leaders of our own classrooms. We are treated as part of the greater community and as leaders of our students." In creating a context of leadership throughout the building, BBES's leader has enabled the staff to continue to learn and grow. Another teacher shared, "Leaders are a part of the weekly planning meetings. Their classroom visits are not just to observe but to help build our teaching repertoire in authentic ways that improve our instruction."

After a contextualized call to action, Robard's principal began building her administrative and teaching teams by having difficult conversations with inherited members. It appears that she had district support in moving out those who did not support her vision. She noted that it takes teachers at least three years at Robard to "get it." In a typical year, at least twenty new teachers arrive, with several having no experience or having provisional contracts. Robard lost an entire 8th grade teaching team in one year, but the principal saw this as an opportunity to bring in teachers who embraced her vision.

Inclusion. At BBES, concepts related to inclusion were highlighted including a shift from a pull out to push in ESOL delivery model, sending home extra work in the students' first language to facilitate parental participation in the learning process, and a mindful hiring of employees who could better relate to students and families. One interviewee shared, "I'm bilingual and over attendance, so I sit down with the social worker and counselor. We give parents the opportunity to explain absences allowing us to bond with parents and students."

Every administrator at Robard shared stories of families experiencing deportation. Administrators shared incidents of Immigration and Customs Enforcement (ICE) raids at homes and at bus stops, noting that many of their students live with the real fear that their parents will not be home when they return from school.

Many children at Robard receive most of their meals at school. Administrators hear students say that they come to school mainly for the food. Several charitable organizations donate bags of food for students to take home over weekends and holidays.

The families with unauthorized status typically live with contacts who receive government assistance, but frequently two or three families live together, and only one family is eligible. Families that find employment often work in day laborer settings. Gangs are common and some offer protection from violence in exchange for money. These descriptions paint a vivid portrait of children who do not have the assurance of basic needs.

Robard's principal is seen as supportive, firm, forthright, willing to talk and listen, motivating, and positive. Administrators describe her as having a "we can do this" attitude:

> She checks on us. She wants to know that we are OK because she knows that we have a hard job to do. She also expects us to be all-in and to do whatever it takes to help our students succeed.

Equity. The operational structure of BBES is organized to address issues of equity. One interviewee highlighted:

> One big issue for our families is transportation. Many parents walk to conferences or events, so when we do offer things at the school, many people walk. We schedule things early enough so those parents can be home by dark.

Another shared that the parent center offered dual workshops during the day and night to accommodate families with varied work schedules.

At Robard, the longest tenured assistant principal has been in the school for 21 years. He believes that the climate of the school has improved dramatically under the current principal's leadership. He confirmed the demoralizing effects of the changes in how the district measures success. He echoed accounts from other administrative team members describing how the current principal came with a data-based approach, stressing that students must come first and that their success is not entirely measured by district standards.

Robard's principal agreed that she faced many challenges with her faculty coupled with increasing expectations from the district. Along with pressures from changes in metrics, she discussed the dissonance in the definitions of success:

The district has its expectations, but these don't allow for the challenges we face. You may think that multiple families in one apartment is appalling, but for these families it is light-years beyond what they had before they came here. Having a child to complete 8th grade is a dream fulfilled for many of these families. Having a child to actually graduate from high school is often seen as an unattainable goal. It is easy to say that these parents don't care, but they do care. They just define success differently. These folks need to hear that their children are capable, that college is a realistic goal. And they need to hear it over and over again.

Persistence. At BBES, the biggest issue is sustaining quality teachers. One administrator stated:

For a lot of our new teachers, this is their first job, and because of our demographics, teaching here is a harder job. When you couple this with traveling an extended distance to get to work plus a population of 74% ESOL and 96% Free and Reduced students, it is tough. In order to continue to strengthen our school, we have to keep doing what we are doing and come into the building everyday with an eye toward continuing to build and sustain a culture of learning.

At Robard, new teachers, most with no experience, have historically comprised the majority of the faculty, and they leave as soon as they are able to transfer elsewhere. With the change in district metrics for performance an acceptable rating, two years prior to this study, was unacceptable at the time of data collection. Assistant principals noted a strong tension in managing the urgent needs of the students and meeting district expectations. As one assistant principal observed,

Last year we were told that we were making impressive gains; we were told that we were great. Then the benchmarks changed and this year we are told that we are not making acceptable progress; this year we are a concern. If you look at our typical increases over three-year cycles, even though many of those students haven't been with us for all three years, I know that we are making a difference. It is very discouraging that a change in measurement makes our hard work seem inadequate.

Robard's principal deals with these tensions by persistently stating her expectations, sharing her agenda, and caring for her faculty. She has been unafraid to confront and remove faculty and administrators who do not buy into her vision.

To encourage persistence of her parents, the principal uses symbols and rituals. In addition to resurrecting the lighthouse symbol, she initiated rituals and ceremonies for 8th graders, not graduations, but transitions to the next level. These include special awards ceremonies recognizing achievement and celebrating steps that students have taken to earn high school credits.

With every step forward, there are new challenges. The principal shared a story of a father who was upset because his son was not recognized during an 8th grade ceremony, complaining that his son should "have a bigger piece of the pie." Seizing upon his word choice, the principal met with him and reviewed opportunities that his son ignored during the year. Noting that it was not too late for this student, she explained that he could not get a bigger piece of the pie "unless he chooses to pick up the fork and take a bite." Then she shared how the father, the faculty, and administration could work together if the student chose to take advantage of remaining opportunities. The principal was able to acknowledge the father's concerns, while emphasizing that the solution must include self-efficacy and persistence.

Robard's principal is proud that faculty turnover has decreased under her watch, stating:

> This year I did not renew contracts for five teachers. Two teachers are retiring. I have three resignations that I expected and four transfers. Next year, we will have the most continuity and stability since I came here. We can really build on what we know are our successes, regardless of how the district chooses to measure them.

DISCUSSION

In our model for High-needs Schools Leadership (HNSL), we argue that effective principals in high-needs schools utilize contextualization, hyper-vigilance, and intentionality as they navigate their unique school climates and communities. These leaders are constantly aware of the necessity to continually foster learning and enhance performance among their students *and* their faculties. They look for opportunities to increase engagement, align core values, and develop their people. HNS leaders intuitively create ways to increase inclusiveness for faculty, students, parents, and communities. They work tirelessly to create respect and interdependence among the faculty, students, parents, and the community outside their schools.

We saw that the constructs of HNSL were woven throughout our data, undergirding the dispositions most commonly associated with Transformational and Social Justice Leadership (see Figure 7.2). The principals in our study contextualized the core values in their schools and sought to hire faculty members who could authentically relate to their students and their parents.

We posit that there is often a dissonance in the ways school districts and communities define success. This is especially true in high-needs schools. As we noted in our findings, many immigrant families believe that any passing grade is a cause for celebration. For some, completing middle school is a great achievement, and thus, leaders in high-needs schools must both continuously work to articulate their visions for success and constantly strive to understand their families' definitions.

We further argue that the hyper-vigilance of HNS leaders causes them to challenge not only the dissonance in definitions of success but the variations in the metrics used to quantify it. The school district in this study raised the minimum scores on benchmark tests. This caused students who were "successful" one year to be "failing" the next year. When families have limited understandings of school success and when the school system's articulated definition varies from year to

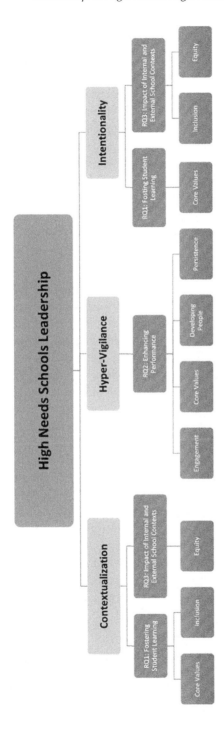

FIGURE 7.2. High-needs Schools Leadership Findings

year, the intricacies of high stakes accountability may not be viewed through the same lens of importance for all stakeholders.

The HNS leaders in this study believe that it is not enough to simply promote the standardized concepts of school and student success. Rather, they work to articulate and embrace a contextualized understanding of their school communities' core values, which are inclusive of definitions beyond the metrics typically used for measurement. Doing so helps them highlight the importance of growth over time in helping high-needs communities to commit to the persistence that is necessary for their children to achieve long term goals. HNS leaders intentionally organize their school programs to meet the needs of their communities and their students in every decision, from scheduling times for meetings, to honoring the world views of the families they serve, to designing recognition programs that encourage students to persistently strive for deferred dreams.

Conclusion

The major foci of our High-needs Schools Leadership model are contextualization, hyper-vigilance, and intentionality. While confirming the importance of these concepts, the findings of this study also point to the critical need for leaders to develop faculty and staff who understand the necessity of intentional strategies to promote authentic inclusion, equity, and persistence within the school setting. Students and parents in high-needs communities may not have innate understandings of these notions and their impacts on self-efficacy and achievement. Equally important is an understanding of the devastating consequences of what we see as a persistent dissonance in perceptions of success as defined by a high-needs school community and its school district. Parents who have limited perceptions of what success can be must be exposed to broader perspectives. This requires school leaders to facilitate intentional efforts that respect the dignity and life experiences of community members. District measurement plans must include contextualized understandings of their communities if they hope to provide meaningful assessments of student engagement and achievement. In the words of BBES's leader,

The kids have to know we believe in them. We have to push them more than anyone else because we live in a community where the parents are appreciative, but they don't know how to have high expectations for school. The push isn't always there from the parents, meaning we have to do more and to build the parameters for our teachers to do more as well.

Questions to Consider:

1. How might leaders in high-needs schools pursue equity and inclusion in ways that demonstrate an understanding of the core values that encourage their students and communities to engage?

2. What strategies might principals in HNS use to help ease the dissonance in definitions and measurements of success in their central offices and in their communities?

3. How should principals in HNS support their faculties and leadership teams to sustain the hyper-vigilance that HNSL demands?

REFERENCES

Aud, S., Hussar, W., Planty, M., Snyder, T., Bianco, K., Fox, M., Frohlich, L., Kemp, J., & Drake, L. (2010). *The condition of education 2010.* Washington, DC: National Center for Education Statistics, Institute of Education Science, U.S. Department of Education.

High-needHigh-needBarley, Z. A., & Beasley, A. D. (2007). Rural school success: What can we learn? *Journal of Research in Rural Education, 22*(1), 1–16.

Baxter, P., & Jack, S. (2008). Qualitative case study methodology: Study design and implementation for novice researchers. *The Qualitative Report, 13*(4), 544–559

Berry, B. (2008). Staffing high-need schools: Insights from the nation's best teachers. *Phi Delta Kappan, 89*(10), 766–771.

Baran, M. L., & Berry, J. R. (2015). *The international school leadership development network (ISLDN) high-needs schools group research protocol and members' guide.* Unpublished manuscript.

Clark, V., & Braun, V. (2013). Teaching thematic analysis. *Psychologist, 26*(2), 1201–123.

Dodman, S. (2014). A vivid illustration of leadership. *Journal of Staff Development, 35*(1), 56–62.

Furman, G. (2012). Social justice leadership as praxis: Developing capacities through preparation programs. *Educational Administration Quarterly, 48*(2), 191–229.

Glander, M. (2015). *Selected statistics from the public elementary and secondary education universe: School year 2013–2014.* Washington, DC: National Center for Education Statistics, Institute of Education Science, U.S. Department of Education.

Griffin, S. W., & Green, R. L. (2013). Transforming high poverty, underperforming schools: Practices, processes, and procedures. *National Forum of Applied Educational Research Journal, 26*(1–2), 77–93.

Hazel, C. E., Pfaff, K., Albanes, J., & Gallagher, J. (2014). Multi-level consultation with an urban school district to promote 9th grade supports for on-time graduation. *Psychology in the Schools, 51*(4), 395–420. https://doi.org/10.1002/pits.21752

Johnson, S. M., Kraft, M. A., & Papay, J.P. (2012). How context matters in high-needs schools: The effects of teachers' working conditions on their professional satisfaction and their students' achievement. *Teachers College Record, 114*(10), 1–39.

Kena, G., Musu-Gillete, L. Robinson, J., Wang, X., Rathbun, A., Zhang, J., Wilkinson-Flicker, S., Barner, A., & Dunlop Velez, E. (2015). *The condition of education 2015.* Washington, DC: National Center for Education Statistics, Institute of Education Science, U.S. Department of Education.

Klar, H. W., & Brewer, C. A. (2013). Successful leadership in high-needs schools: An examination of core leadership practices enacted in challenging contexts. *Educational Administration Quarterly, 49*(5), 768–808. https://doi.org/10.1177/0013161X13482577

Leithwood, K., & Sun, J. (2012). The nature and effects of transformational school leadership: A meta-analytic review of unpublished research. *Educational Administration Quarterly, 48*(3), 387–423.

Medina, V., Martinez, G., Murakami, E. T., Rodriguez, M., & Hernandez, F. (2014). Principals' perceptions from within: Leadership in high-needs schools in the USA. *British Educational Management and Administration Society, 28*(3), 91–96. https://doi.org 10.1177/0892020614537664

Mid-Continent Research for Education and Learning. (2005). Final report: high-needs schools—What does it take to beat the odds? *Mid-Continent Research for Education.* ERIC: ED486626

Oylere, C., & Fuentes, C. (2012). Leadership for rich learning in high-poverty schools. *Journal of Special Education Leadership, 25*(1), 5–14.

Ready to Teach Act of 2003, H.R. 2211, 108th Cong. (2003–2004). U.S. Department of Education. (n.d.). *Fast facts: Title I.* Retrieved from https://nces.ed.gov/ fastfacts/display.asp?id=158

Silin, J. (2010). *Introduction: High-needs Schools—Preparing teachers for today's world. Occasional paper series, 2011* (p. 25). Retrieved from https://educate.bankstreet.edu/occasional-paper-series/vol2011/iss25/1

Theoharis, G. (2007). Social justice educational leaders and resistance: Toward a theory of social justice leadership. *Educational Administration Quarterly, 43*(2), 221–258. https://doi.org/10.1177/0013161X06293717

United States Department of Education. (2008, February 20). *Organization of U.S. education: The school level.* Retrieved from https://www2.ed.gov/about/offices/ list/ous/international/usnei/us/edlite-org-us.html.

United States Department of Education. (2015, October 5). *Programs: Improving basic programs operated by local educational agencies (Title 1, Part A).* Retrieved from https://www2.ed.gov/programs/titleiparta/index.html.

Ullucci, K. & Howard, T. (2015). Pathologizing the poor: Implications for preparing teachers to work in high-poverty schools. *Urban Education, 50*(2), 170–193. https://doi.org 10.1177/0042085914543117

Woods, E. H. J., & Martin, B. N. (2016). What leadership behaviors were demonstrated by the principal in a high poverty, high achieving elementary school? *Cogent Education, 3*(1), 1–13. https://doi.org 10.1080/2331186X.2016.1172935

CHAPTER 8

SUSTAINING A CULTURE OF ACADEMIC SUCCESS AT A HIGH-NEEDS ELEMENTARY SCHOOL

Nathern S. Okilwa and Bruce Barnett

In the age of high-stake testing accountability systems, schools are under pressure to show improved student performance. Schools that achieve sustained academic success, particularly those in high-need contexts (i.e., high poverty, high student mobility, and limited resources), often attract the attention of stakeholders. One such case is Robbins Elementary School, the center of this investigation. The purpose of this study is to better understand the sustained high academic performance of Robbins for over 20 years despite several changes of principals. Our findings indicate that successive principals focused on establishing high expectations, distributed leadership, collective responsibility for student learning, and data-based decision making in their effort to maintain strong student performance.

Keywords: Principals, leadership, high performance, school improvement, high-need schools

INTRODUCTION

As public accountability for improved student performance has increased, principal turnover rates have risen while the number of individuals aspiring to become school leaders has decreased (Alvoid & Black, 2014). Consequently, principal succession is becoming increasingly important, especially in understanding how leadership sustainability affects school improvement and student achievement (Fink & Brayman, 2006; Hargreaves & Fink, 2006; Hargreaves, Moore, Fink, Brayman, & White, 2003). Although increased accountability mandates at the national, state, and local levels have influenced the number of applicants for principalship (Fuller & Young, 2009; Louis, Leithwood, Wahlstrom, & Anderson, 2010; Zepeda, Bengston, & Parylo, 2012), school policies and procedures also influence turnover. Some districts not only mandate principals rotate positions every few years (Louis et al, 2010), but also the lack of support from central office, job demands, and low compensation impact principal turnover (Fuller & Young, 2009).

Despite the challenges of raising student achievement and withstanding the potential detrimental effects of principal turnover, research indicates some high-need schools defy the odds by transforming their culture and improving academic performance (Duke, 2006, 2012; Jacobson, 2011). Therefore, the purpose of this chapter is to better understand the long-term performance of high-need schools by examining an elementary school that has maintained strong academic performance for over 20 years despite several changes of principals. After reviewing literature focusing on leadership turnover and succession, we describe the methodology of the study, which relied on semi-structured interviews with the four principals who lead the school from the early 1990s to the present time. Next, findings are reported regarding how principals enhanced the individual and organizational performance of the school and fostered student learning. The chapter concludes by comparing the findings with theoretical and empirical research on leadership turnover and succession.

LITERATURE REVIEW

To better understand principal turnover and succession, we examine several issues, including theoretical constructs of succession and the potential detrimental effects of principal turnover.

Theoretical Constructs of Succession

In studying leadership turnover and succession, scholars and researchers have relied on a variety of theoretical and conceptual frameworks to guide their investigations. Three prominent constructs influencing the field are: (1) job socialization, (2) stage theories of succession, and (3) change management and sustainability. *Socialization theory* examines the experiences of school leaders that shape their views about the job and its expectations (Bengston, Zepeda, & Parylo, 2010; Crow, 2006; Hart, 1991, 1993). Crow's (2006) typology of socialization includes:

(a) anticipatory socialization—school leaders' experience prior to beginning the job (e.g., as students and teachers), (b) professional socialization—the knowledge and skills learned about school leadership through formal preparation, (c) organizational socialization—the job duties and expectations experienced once hired as school leaders (e.g., induction experiences), and (d) personal socialization—changes in self-identify as new school leadership roles are learned.

Stage theories view leadership succession as a series of distinct phases. During the pre-succession stage (prior to taking the job), new leaders' expertise, experiences, and reputations are examined and judged by others in the organization (Fauske & Ogawa, 1987; Miskel & Cosgrove, 1985). Once leaders are on the job (referred to as post-succession), several stages occur. For instance, one depiction of leadership succession suggests leaders experience a series of predicable stages: initiation, implementation, consolidation, and refinement (Louis et al, 2010). In addition, Ogawa (1991) identifies three stages of post-succession: (1) enchantment (teachers' optimism about change), (2) disenchantment (teachers' disagreements with the principal's decisions), and (3) accommodation (teachers' isolation and views that change is ineffective).

Similar to stage theory, concepts associated with *change management and sustainability* view the innovations principals implement as a series of phases. Fullan (1991, 1993) depicts these phases as initiation, adoption, implementation, and institutionalization. Bryk, Sebring, Allensworth, Luppescu, and Easton (2011) conceive the change management process consists of initiation and sustaining phases. During initiation, the organization attempts to alter the status quo and introduce new reforms. These reforms are sustained as organizational members' roles and responsibilities become permanent and part of the expected routine. Similarly, Lewin's (1948) representation of change—unfreezing, moving to a new level, and refreezing—reflects another series of general phases or steps. Finally, Bullock and Batten's (1985) synthesis of change models reveals a four-phase process organization encounter when successfully implementing an innovation: (a) exploration, (b) planning, (c) action, and (d) integration.

Several conceptualizations of the change management process provide a more detailed analysis of the factors influencing how innovations are sustained and institutionalized. Kotter (1996), for instance, conceptualized that change occurs in eight sequential steps, nested in three distinct phases:

- Phase 1—creating a climate for change: (1) establish a sense of urgency, (2) create a guiding coalition, (3) develop a vision and strategy;
- Phase 2—engaging and enabling the organization: (4) communicate the change vision, (5) empower broad-based action, (6) generate short-term wins; and
- Phase 3—implementing and sustaining change: (7) consolidate gains and produce more change, and (8) anchor new approaches in the culture (Applebaum, Habashy, Malo, & Shafiq, 2012).

Because "turnover that occurs every two or three years makes it unlikely that a principal will get beyond the stages of initiation and early implementation" (Louis et al, 2010, p. 168), most stage and change management models indicate it takes five to seven years for principals to build a foundation of trust with teachers and community members to ensure changes are consolidated and become part of the culture (Gabarro, 1987).

Effects of Leadership Succession

Researchers have sought to understand the rationale, benefits, and detriments associated with leadership succession. Some of the earliest work in this area emerged from the business private sector, noting that effective leadership succession and management is an essential human resource strategy for companies to be competitive (Friedman, 1987) and to increase the talent pool of individuals who can contribute to the organization's strategic plan (Groves, 2003; Karaveli & Hall, 2003). Furthermore, the health care profession has emphasized the importance of thoughtful succession and management due to the projected attrition rates of leaders, which requires hiring clinicians and nurses in executive positions (Bolton & Roy, 2004; Zepeda et al, 2012).

These early attempts to understand leadership succession in business launched investigations in education, such as Carlson's (1962) study of school superintendents, which propelled additional studies of campus-level succession aimed at revealing the stages of pre- and post-succession, succession events, and preparation for subsequent succession. For example, a case study conducted by Jones and Webber (2001) revealed: (a) stages of succession (fear, detachment, expectation of change, enchantment, and disenchantment), (b) variables affecting succession (reason for the principal's departure, selection process for the successor, and reputation of the successor), (c) hierarchical power structures that decrease stakeholder groups' empowerment and efficacy, and (d) students' view of succession as an adult-controlled activity that ignores their input.

In addition, studies suggest principal turnover often occurs every three to four years (Fuller & Young, 2009; Louis et al, 2010); however, findings are inconsistent regarding the detrimental effects of principal turnover on schools and their communities. On one hand, some investigations indicate rapid principal turnover not only negatively affects school performance, school culture, and student achievement (Fink & Brayman, 2006; Louis et al, 2010), but also increases teacher cynicism and resistance to change (Reynolds, White, Brayman, & Moore, 2008). On the other hand, other studies reveal turnover has little or no impact on classroom content and instruction, student achievement, staff job satisfaction, communication, instruction, discipline, and school climate (Miskel & Owens, 1983; Noonan & Goldman, 1995; Louis et al, 2010).

Our investigation strives to build on these studies of leadership succession and sustaining change by capturing the perspectives of the four principals serving a high-need elementary school that has maintained strong academic performance for nearly 25 years. We describe the methodology of the study before reporting and discussing the findings.

METHODOLOGY

The current study examined how Robbins Elementary School (RES) sustained strong academic performance for two decades despite several changes in principals. To achieve this purpose, two questions guided our investigation: (a) How did principals enhance individual and organizational performance in the school? and (b) What fostered student learning in the school? To pursue this investigation, we utilized qualitative approaches to collect, analyze, and interpret data as well as report the findings.

Site

RES is nestled in an older neighborhood about five miles from the center of a major urban city in South Texas. The school was purposely selected because it fits the characteristics of a high-needs school, that is, high poverty and high student mobility, yet has sustained strong academic performance over the years. The school serves a predominately Hispanic student population, grades PreK–5.

Participants

Semi-structured interviews were conducted with the four principals who served RES from the early 1990s until the present. We interviewed Ms. Williams and Ms. Peterson together because their time and leadership at RES were interconnected. Here is a short profile of the four principals:

Ms. Williams is retired from education and still lives in the city where RES is located. She was the principal for five years at RES, from 1993/4 to 1997/98. She was hired by the district with a mandate to turn RES around. Prior to the appointment as RES principal, she served as an assistant principal for a year at an elementary school in the district. Williams held teaching positions in several states in the United States and abroad. Also, she formerly served as a teacher appraiser for the state of Texas. Williams stepped aside from the principalship in 1998 for family reasons.

Ms. Peterson is currently retired as well. She was principal for three years, from 1998/99 to 2000/1—she took over from Williams. She joined RES during the second year of Williams' principalship as a half time assistant principal at RES and at another elementary school. Eventually, she became fulltime at RES as the AP and curriculum and instruction coordinator (CIC). After three years as principal, she took a position at the district central office as the head in the Curriculum Department. Peterson is a native of the city and was raised in the district; however, she attended private schools. She started her teaching in the district, transferred to another district in the city, and then moved back to the AP position at RES.

Ms. Decker was the principal at RES for nine years, from 2001/2 to 2009/10. She is since retired; however, she is currently an independent education consultant, who contracts with school districts to provide coaching for sitting principals. She is a native of the city and was raised in a neighborhood close to RES. Decker taught in the district for many years, served as a CIC, and served one year as vice principal at an elementary school in the district.

Ms. Robinson is the current principal of RES since 2010. She has been with the district since 1990. Robinson started as a teacher at the elementary school. She served as a CIC, became AP, and principal for two years of another elementary school in the district before her appointment as the RES principal.

Veteran teachers. In addition to the four principals, we interviewed three veteran teachers (Ms. Beecham, Ms. Roberts, and Ms. Frio) who have taught at RES for over 25 years during the tenure of the four principals. We conducted a one-on-one session with Beecham and then one focus group session with all three teachers.

Instruments and Procedures

Interviews with participants lasted between 60 to 90 minutes per session. For the principals, the interviews were guided by six core questions, ranging from how they were selected for the job to their leadership style (see Appendix A). The teachers' interview protocol constituted three core questions with a number of subquestions exploring the transitions between the four principals and understanding how student achievement was sustained (see Appendix B). The interviews were then transcribed for our analysis. Also, the interviews with the current principal and the three veteran teachers were conducted at RES near the end of the school day.

Data Analysis

Both authors analyzed interview transcripts for emerging themes, guided by this study's research questions and theoretical underpinnings about sustaining school reform, even with the change of leadership. We each read the transcripts independently coding for themes. We compared and agreed on categories and themes using the process described by Saldaña (2013). This process yielded four main themes that addressed both research questions, which are: high expectations, distributed leadership, collective responsibility for student learning, and data-based decision making. In the next section that follows, we explicate these themes in detail using excerpts from the interviews with our participants.

FINDINGS

In this section, we report on the four themes (i.e., high expectations, distributed leadership, collective responsibility for student learning, and data-based decision making) that emerged from examining the data guided by the underlying question for this study (i.e., how principals enhanced the individual and organizational performance of the school and fostered student learning) and the theoretical constructs on sustaining reform in the midst of leadership changes.

High Expectations

The four principals emphasized the need for setting high expectations for everyone in the school, including teachers, students, parents, and support staff. Most importantly, they sought to set an example for everyone to follow, believing that high expectations started with them as leaders. Two of the principals reflected on their own upbringing as starting points for instilling the virtue of high expectations for themselves, which also shaped their professional lives as well. Williams noted:

> [My dad] would go to the PTA or when I brought my report card home it was never good enough. I might have four A's and a B and that was never good enough, so I learned from that experience throughout my school that he had high expectations for me, and I think that's another key to why [Robbins] achieved success.

Peterson reflected on her family experience:

> Because we were both products of that high expectation and we saw the key in succeeding in life if you had that tool. And my father, even though he had limited education, he believed in education…So our parents were a strong, I think, influence.

RES principals found it easier to require much from others when they themselves embodied high expectations. The high expectations had to be observable. The teachers, students, and parents had to see the principals' commitment to this ideal. According to Williams, using a positive approach and being highly visible set the tone for their expectations, "We were both highly visible…They never knew when [we would stop by their classroom]. We weren't looking for bad, we were looking for good… I believe in a positive approach in life and in school as well, and we had the best time." Williams and Peterson also talked about how they lead by example, modeling high expectations by the amount of time they invested in their duties and responsibilities. Williams noted:

> We did work and work and work and we stayed at school, especially before a big group meeting, school meeting, and we would stay until 2:00 in the morning. Then we'd come to the meeting and they thought we had been to the bar, but we were there preparing. And that was a great part of our success in my opinion, the preparation.

Decker also talked about how she worked long days including weekends: "I get here at about 6:00, and I leave about 6:00, and I work on Saturdays." For Robinson, modeling high expectations required total involvement—with instruction, teachers, students, and the community:

> You have to be involved in every aspect of curriculum, community. You have to be involved with the students, you have to be involved with the teachers on every grade level in order to keep that climate that we have established here of those high expectations. I feel like if I'm not a part of that, then those expectations are gonna decline.

Williams and Peterson were very clear about their efforts to never lose sight of their goal of increasing student achievement. Peterson noted, "I know for a fact we always kept the student success as our primary goal. That was the emphasis." They indeed achieved student success soon after their arrival. In referencing one of the programs they implemented, Peterson said, "That was one thing we took a hold of and it turned out to be highly successful. [We] raised our scores almost immediately in math and in reading." Also, they adapted a model of teaching and learning that impacted student outcomes as Peterson suggested, "We created a model that was resulting in the increase in student achievement and, from my point of view, in the increase of their [teachers'] proficiency as research-based teaching and learning."

The groundwork for high expectations that Williams and Peterson laid during their tenure was fundamental to the turnaround and future success of RES. Their successors built on it. For instance, Decker acknowledged the foundation for high expectations: "We had this reputation even before I got there that we were going to be great, and so it's tough to live up to that greatness year after year." Similarly, Robinson alluded to one of the potential challenges she faced as the new RES principal:

> I knew that I also had to maintain that success and those are big shoes to fill. I have a lot of respect for the principals that have been here in the past and those are huge shoes to fill so it was an opportunity, but it was also a challenge.

Defining high expectations or standards is often elusive; however, Decker offered her definition: "I don't care who you get in your room. The expectation is 90 percent or more of those kids will meet the expectations set by the state, or by the district, so every year the pressure was intense." She added, "It was definitely having high expectations." Robinson also provided a prescriptive example of high expectations directed toward parents: "Like our pre-Ks are reading 20 books, 100 books by the end of the year with their parent. That's our expectation, at the end of the year that they read 100 books with their pre-Ks."

Distributed Leadership

Most effective principals empower others or build capacity among teachers to partner in the arduous work of turning around schools. There is evidence throughout the tenure of the four RES principals that they all understood the importance of building capacity for the tedious work of reforming and maintaining a successful school. When teachers feel empowered, they go beyond the call of duty, as Peterson noted: "We had teachers who would stay there till 5:00, 6:00, and 7:00

sometimes just…preparing." They believed some teachers who were resistant to change could be influenced by the positive synergy, "So I learned real quick to give them the freedom to make the choices and decisions, and those who didn't want to, because there were some like Williams said, the synergy that was created brought them in" Peterson said. When Peterson left RES for a curriculum position at the district level, she was confident in the team of teachers she was leaving in charge, a team she and Williams had assembled over the past eight years. She felt most teachers were leaders already:

> I really, truly felt that I was leading leaders. In my mind I knew… I had that feeling that yes, they would be disappointed, that they would think the apple cart had been turned over and all that, but I had so much confidence in what they could do.

This demonstrates the investment in teachers' growth as leaders during the Williams and Peterson eras.

Decker devolved leadership responsibilities to what she referred to as a strong campus leadership team (CLT). She talked fondly about Beecham, a pre-K teacher at the time, whom she often left in charge if she (Decker) was out to a meeting, and other top individuals on the CLT (CIC and counselor) were off campus. Decker said, "I would go out to her room and I'd say, Okay Ms. Beecham, you're up. Everybody's gone. And she's like, "Okay, I can do it."" Also, when it came to new teachers, Decker included grade-level teachers on the interviewing committee and valued their input.

Robinson also acknowledged the trust, confidence, and empowering of teacher leadership: "I do grow my staff and once I put you in charge of something, I trust that you are going to do that important job that I entrusted in you." The investment in teachers seemed to bear fruit as Robinson bragged about her teachers:

> I have phenomenal teachers at this campus and they have a lot of great experience, they have a lot of great knowledge and they are the leaders, they know what the expectations are, they know where these kids have to go and they are the leaders.

However, Robinson cautioned, "I have to facilitate, I have to lead them in new initiatives…I have to lead." She recognized the importance of modeling for teachers. Under Robinson, every teacher was encouraged to lead and most oversaw some aspect of the school team or program, such as collaborative learning, campus leadership teams (CLT), and Positive Behavior Intervention and Support (PBIS).

One critical question to ask is how did these principals grow or empower their teachers? Most importantly, teachers were empowered as classroom instructors, experts, and leaders. Williams and Peterson constantly asked themselves how they could support teachers to deliver quality instruction. "I think we were there to support them, just to help and give support. I know that was a very strong tenet. I think, between the two of us, was how do we make their work easier and more effective?" said Peterson. One of the veteran teachers acknowledged the unwavering support of Williams: "She was a very big teacher advocate…I learned more from Williams and Peterson than any other principal." Also, Williams and Peterson provided professional development to promote best practices in the areas of reading and writing.

Besides providing professional support for teachers, principals recognized the emotional support teachers often require. Robinson, for instance, received accolades from teachers for promoting work-life balance. She clearly articulated her position for supporting her teachers:

> I really feel very strongly that there has to be a balance between work and life and I emphasize that with my teachers a lot. Teachers will never hear me say or get upset or whatever when a teacher comes in and says, "Mrs. Robinson, I have to leave, my baby is sick at daycare." Go, we'll figure it out. We'll take care of whatever we have to take care of here; you go take care of your sick baby. And I feel very strongly that I have to facilitate that and make that a priority for other teachers.

The different ways that principals demonstrated support for teachers, promoted a sense of empowerment enabling teachers to volunteer to take on various roles for the collective good of the school.

Collective Responsibility for Student Learning

Overall, our interviews revealed that the four principals expected teachers to take responsibility for all students' learning, not just those in their own classrooms. During Williams and Peterson's tenure, they built a sense of the collective by what Peterson described as, "Having a clear focus, a vision that everyone bought into. It was utilizing your resources effectively, and it was also celebrating, celebrating as a whole team." One of the veteran teachers recalled, "I did team teaching with another teacher, so we could bring the group size down, so she could be working with some students while I was working with some students... when they became strong and established they became the fifth grade." Williams and Peterson involved support staff as well: "Even our staff, our paraprofessional and our custodial staff, began to get involved with the students. I mean, it just became a happy place to learn" Peterson explained. When Peterson was leaving RES, she reflected on the effective teamwork: "At the time I loved what we were doing. As a team, it was really connected, and we were cohesive. Things were working really well."

Decker also strongly believed in teamwork and described their teamwork efforts in a positive manner: "It's about teamwork," "Teamwork was huge," "Our teamwork was extremely strong," "Teamwork was always big," and "We truly believe teamwork is the fuel in maintaining morale." In fact, Decker made "team is everything" a school slogan that was chanted every morning:

> For at least two, maybe three years...every single morning I got on the intercom, and at the end of it I shouted out, "Team is everything," and the entire office staff had

to do it, but that every classroom had to do it. So, you could hear down the hallway, you could hear them, "Team is everything," and then the day would start.

Williams and Peterson introduced a number of initiatives to advance collective responsibility for student learning, such as collective planning, a buddy system, pentathlon, and tutoring, which were sustained by the next two principals. Williams and Peterson supported collective planning by building a master schedule and creating a planning room which featured resources for teaching and learning. Peterson noted: "Every nine weeks we started off with one whole day of collaborative planning and that was one of the keys, the CIC and the grade level would meet for the whole day." Decker also ensured grade level teams met weekly to plan together and to support each other, "Making sure that the weakest link on [the] team was seeing the strongest link on [the] team on a weekly basis."

The buddy system, on the other hand, was aimed at supporting struggling students. Peterson noted, "[For] students who were still at risk, we came up with a plan to buddy them and the teachers were so receptive to everything." This concept allowed teachers to adopt students across the grades in order to provide extra support for reading, writing, and math. Robinson continued the buddy system by encouraging primary teachers (grades K–2) to support intermediate teachers and students (grades 3–5):

> Our teachers give up their conference time or they give up their music time in order to go into those other classrooms and they either take a small group or they monitor the kids while their teachers take a small group, so it is very much not just intermediate, but it's primary all the way through.

The buddy system, according to Robinson, ensured that "primary teachers have just as much of a stake as the intermediate teachers with STAAR results." In reference to the buddy system and mentoring of students, Decker said, "We kept it going because it was so powerful." Student collaboration was also promoted through the pentathlon concept, based on William E. Deming's (2000) principle of quality circles, whereby students would collaborate to problem solve in a variety of content areas. Peterson noted:

> [Students] would be at a table and there would be five problem solving questions in math, writing, reading, that they had to collaborate, work together so that every member of that team understood it and could articulate and explain the process of how they solved it.

With regard to tutoring, Robinson saw the need for all teachers to be involved: "Bringing our primary teachers to the after-school tutoring program so that one, they've had these kids before, they know these kids, but number two that no primary teacher is exempt from ever teaching a STAAR grade level." Decker also acknowledged that, "We did tutoring and everybody would volunteer to tutor and we didn't even pay out."

Data-Based Decision Making

All four principals emphasized the importance of data to guide instruction and overall school improvement decisions. For instance, Peterson said, "…It began real slow…the data, the data, the data…learning how to use the data to drive instruction." After several years of staff development on data use, comprehensive analysis of data became a common practice during the Williams and Peterson eras. Peterson noted:

> Well, at the beginning of the year, we all started with our teachers looking at the school data. You start off that way at the very first meeting before the school year begins as professional development, and then we had the grade levels break into groups and identify those areas there were strengths and weaknesses. And then we took it the next step. The next step was to have individual teachers look at their [student] population.

During Williams and Peterson's tenure, teachers realized the importance of examining data to improve student learning to the point that they gave up personal time, even during holidays, to collaboratively disaggregate data. One of the veteran teachers acknowledged that Williams and Peterson "taught [teachers] to look at data and hit those targets… focusing on [the] student and [making] sure you are teaching to their needs." Additionally, another one noted, "What made me realize with [Peterson] is I had never looked at data before like the way she taught me to look at data." Williams recalled their collective commitment to data, "We knew it was successful by the results from the TAKS test, but then when people are willing to give up their time at Christmas and willing to come to Peterson's house at spring break [because] they've bought in, and that's a sign of success to me." Williams and Peterson used both formative and summative data to inform instruction: "We had formative and summative data…so we studied the level of thinking required in the content areas [and] how they apply these concepts in the problem solving. So, we did a lot of examining of the depth that knowledge had to be taught."

The collective and grade-level use of data instituted by Williams and Peterson recurred in Decker and Robinson's tenure as well. The extensive and critical data analysis process was not meant to shame individual teachers, but rather to support each other and in turn support students. For instance, Decker noted:

> We were very open about our data. So, like if this was our data room, right here on the wall is going to be your name and your data. It's not to penalize you. So, when you push your data, then we as a group collectively can attack that problem.

Similarly, Robinson's view of data is for a collective purpose:

> I don't do data by teacher, I do data by grade level, because every grade level is responsible, I don't care what teacher it comes from, they're all responsible for it. I do care but…that whole grade level is responsible. If a teacher is maybe not as

successful as another teacher in an area, then we gotta figure out what we gotta do to help each other.

In summary, Williams and Peterson successors acknowledged the successful school they inherited, thus realizing the need to continue the school's practices for success:

We had this reputation even before I got there that we were going to be great, and so it's tough to live up to that greatness year after year. And so, the challenges over the nine years I was there was every year we would become either recognized or exemplary. The challenge is can you stay [at that level]. (Decker)

RES has had a reputation within the district of being a highly successful, I've even heard people say, like it's the golden school for [the district]. So, when I came over, I was kind of expecting it to just run by itself and no problems whatsoever. The community is great—however, it takes a very strong leader to run a highly successful school and keep it at that expectation. And so, we still have a very good reputation within the district as being a highly successful school. We have our concerns, we have our focus areas that we work on every single day, every single year. (Robinson)

Discussion

The work of reforming schools and sustaining a successful school culture takes time (Fullan 1991, 1993). During the five to seven years needed to turn around school performance, as some change management models suggest (Gabarro, 1987), trust is built, and changes must be given a chance to become institutionalized. Based on this premise, the length of principal tenure at RES may have worked in favor to consolidate the initial reform efforts instituted by Principals Williams and Peterson. Collectively, the two served RES for eight years. Williams served for five years as principal (during four of those years Peterson was CIC/AP) and when Williams left, Peterson took over as principal for the next three years. Given the kind of close-knit working relationship Williams and Peterson had, they were able to initiate and sustain the vision by incorporating a shared leadership philosophy and implementing a reform agenda for eight years. This was sufficient period of time to consolidate changes and enact a culture of success (Leithwood, 1994). Successive principals (Decker and Robinson) stepped into and acknowledged this culture of success, which they characterized as the *Robbins Way*. Their challenge and responsibility became to sustain the *Robbins Way*. Clearly, leadership stability (longevity in principal tenure beyond the five-year average for elementary principals) is a critical factor in supporting and sustaining reforms and a culture of success (Fuller & Young, 2009; Leithwood, 1994).

Additionally, Kotter's (1996) three-phase conceptualization of the change management process provides another lens to understand our findings regarding the sustained academic success in this high-need elementary school. Although Kotter's model suggests a series of sequential steps nested within the three distinct phases (phase one—creating a climate for change; phase two—engaging and enabling the organization; and phase three—implementing and sustaining change), our findings suggest a dynamic set of practices and processes, which do not necessarily adhere to a specific sequence. During phase one (creating a climate for change), Williams and Peterson laid the groundwork for change and school improvement. They were placed in a dysfunctional environment—low teacher and student morale, mistrust, leadership instability, low student performance—that needed to be revitalized. Williams was assigned to RES with a mandate from the district to change course at RES, especially to turn around student achievement. As Kotter (1996) suggests, creating a climate of change requires establishing a sense of urgency, which Williams and Peterson did by helping teachers analyze data to uncover areas of academic need that had been ignored in the past. By forcing teachers to examine data, they encouraged them to ask thoughtful questions about what students should know, how well they were performing, and what they should do to improve student achievement (Protheroe, 2001). The analysis of student performance data established the baseline for which they introduced a commitment to a new vision anchored in high expectations for themselves, teachers, students, and parents. Similarly, Louis and her colleagues (2010) suggest that building a shared vision, fostering acceptance of group goals, creating high performance expectations, and communicating the vision are key practices in setting a new direction for school reform.

Kotter's (1996) second phase (engaging and enabling the organization) was evidenced in how these principals coalesced the RES community—teaching and non-teaching staff, students, and parents—around the new vision of high expectations. During this phase, Williams and Peterson strived to establish a collective sense of responsibility for student learning by introducing team teaching, tutoring, and a buddy system, which were continued and expanded by Decker and Robinson. As Kotter (1996) notes, during this second phase, it is important to communicate the change vision, empower broad-based action, and generate short-term wins. As teachers began to see improvements in student performance fairly early in the Williams era, they began to understand the vision of high expectations could be accomplished. Data sharing and analysis became commonplace during all-staff and grade level meetings; data were explored not to "name and shame" but to collectively support each other toward achieving the common goal of making RES successful. Goals and strategies were communicated during the meetings to ensure everyone was in agreement. By creating a climate for shared accountability, these principals were establishing a "professional learning community culture," one that allowed teachers to take collective responsibility for student learning by sharing results publicly, engaging in critical conversations about improvement, and observing students achieve their high expectations (DuFour & Matthos, 2013).

Furthermore, by empowering teachers to take individual and collective action toward a shared vision for student learning and success, these school leaders were distributing leadership throughout the campus. Leithwood, Harris, and Hopkins (2008) note that, "School leadership has a greater influence on schools and students when it is widely distributed" (p. 26). Distributed leadership acknowledges that the work of reforming schools cannot be accomplished singlehandedly, allows teachers to take professional innovative risks, and finally builds capacity to collectively undertake the reform agenda. To build staff capacity, school leaders need to specifically provide individualized support, foster intellectual stimulation, and model appropriate values and behaviors (Leithwood et al., 2008), all of which were modeled by the four RES principals.

Finally, in phase three (implementing and sustaining change), the challenge for Williams and Peterson was how to sustain and institutionalize the *Robbins Way* by consolidating gains and anchoring new approaches within the school culture (Kotter, 1996). Evidence from our study indicates that by consistently engaging in four practices—high expectations, distributed leadership, collective responsibility, and data-based decision making—all four principals sustained RES as a model school. As Williams suggested, "Success breeds success," and both Decker and Robinson acknowledged the expectation to maintain the reputation of RES's success. As our study demonstrates, to sustain innovation or reform, effective practices must be continued and adapted (Duke, 2012; Jacobson, 2011; Jacobson, Johnson, Ylimaki, & Giles, 2009). Consequently, sustained reform eventually becomes part of the culture of the school, or in the case of our study, the *Robbins Way*.

Conclusion

Clearly, the principals serving RES have maintained some of the initial structures and expectations initiated by Williams and Peterson. When we began our investigation, we anticipated that there was an intentional succession planning process as each new principal began her tenure at the school. Surely, this happened when Peterson took over the principalship since she had served as the assistant principal with Williams for four years. However, when Decker took over for Peterson and then when Robinson succeeded Decker, there was no formal communication between them or any attempts to assist the new principal in understanding what was responsible for the success of the school. This was quite surprising to us, especially since those principals following Williams and Peterson maintained the underlying strengths of the school, namely high expectations, distributed leadership, a collective responsibility for student learning, and data-driven decision making.

In our conversations with Decker and Robinson, they had both worked in the district for several years and so they knew coming in that RES was a very successful school and felt the pressure to continue this reputation. While they each indicated there were aspects of the school they sought to improve (e.g., parental involvement), they also recognized the need to maintain the *Robbins Way*. They both understood the importance of keeping in place elements of the culture that were instrumental in the school's success. One critical factor in continuing the school's success was that very few teachers left the school, allowing the practices Williams and Peterson initiated to become institutionalized. As these new school leaders came on the scene, they were socialized to the *Robbins Way*. Rather than trying to implement a series of new changes, these principals were quite willing to continue strategies and approaches that staff were familiar with and had proven to be successful in improving student performance. Therefore, a key lesson to be learned from the RES story is that astute principals are able to quickly assess the positive aspects of the campus culture and are prepared to maintain and strengthen these elements (Duke, 2012; Peterson, 2002).

Chapter Questions

The ability to sustain success over time as principals and teachers leave has proven difficult in many schools, yet very little in-depth research examines how schools are able to maintain their success over time (Giles & Hargreaves, 2006). Although this investigation suggests the continuity of teachers may have contributed to the ongoing success of Robbins Elementary School, we did not solicit information about the teachers' role in mediating principal succession. Therefore, additional research can address questions dealing with principal succession:

1. When schools have a reputation for high student achievement, how do new principals assess the reasons for this success?
2. What role do teachers play in helping new principals understand the reasons for high student achievement?

APPENDIX A: PRINCIPAL PROTOCOL

- How were you selected for the principalship job?
- What opportunities and challenges have you encountered?
- Are there any programs/initiatives you have continued/changed?
- What sorts of accomplishments/results have you experienced thus far?
- To what do you attribute the accomplishments/results?
- How would you describe your leadership style?

APPENDIX B: TEACHER PROTOCOL

1. Transitions between principals (will explore the following questions for each of the four principals):
   a. Why did the principal leave and was replaced?
   b. What was the selection process for the new principal?
   c. What contact and/or communication did the new principal have with the staff before beginning the job?
   d. What were the initial feelings of the staff about the new principal?
   e. What did the principal do in the first year?

        f.   What initiatives were implemented after the first year?

        g.   What was the role of the AP and did it change over time?

        h.   What did the principal do that was similar or different than their predecessor (new, changed, same, and altered)?

2.   Examples of themes (will explore the following questions for each of the four principals):

        a.   In what ways did the principal emphasize high expectations for staff, students, and parents?

        b.   In what ways was leadership shared on the campus?

        c.   In what ways did teachers share responsibility for the learning of all students?

        d.   What ways were data used in making decisions?

3.   Why has the school been able to sustain high student performance over time with different school leaders?

4.   Do you have any other comments or thoughts about the various principals you have worked for at Robbins?

REFERENCES

Alvoid, L., & Black, W. L. (2014). *The changing role of the principal.* Washington, DC: Center for American Progress.

Applebaum, S. H., Habashy, S., Malo, J-L., & Shafiq, H. (2012). Back to the future: Revisiting Kotter's 1996 change model. *Journal of Management Development, 31*(8), 764–782.

Bengston, E., Zepeda, S. J., & Parylo, O. (2010). *School systems' practices of controlling socialization during principal succession: An organizational socialization theory.* Paper presented at the annual meeting of the American Educational Research Association, Denver, CO.

Bolton, J., & Roy, W. (2004). Succession planning: Securing the future. *Journal of Nursing Administration, 34*(12), 589–593.

Bryk, A. S., Sebring, P. B., Allensworth, E., Luppescu, S., & Easton, J. Q. (2011). *Organizing schools for improvement: Lessons from Chicago,* University of Chicago Press, Chicago, IL.

Bullock, R. J., & Batten, D. (1985). It's just a phase we're going through: A review and synthesis of OD phase analysis. *Group and Organization Studies, 10,* 383–412.

Carlson, R. O. (1962). *Executive succession and organizational change.* Chicago, IL: University of Chicago, Midwestern Administration Center.

Crow, G. M. (2006). Complexity and the beginning principal in the United States: Perspectives on socialization. *Journal of Educational Administration, 44*(4), 310–325.

Deming, W. E. (2000). *The new economics for industry, government, and education* (2nd ed.). Cambridge, MA: MIT Press.

DuFour, R., & Mattos, M. (2013). How do principals really improve schools? *Educational Leadership, 70*(7), 34–40.

Duke, D. L. (2006). Keys to sustaining successful school turnarounds. *ERS Spectrum, 24*(4), 21–25.

Duke, D. L. (2012). *"Raising test scores was the easy part": A case study of the third year of school turnaround.* Paper presented at the annual convention of the University Council for Educational Administration, Denver, CO.

Fauske, J. R., & Ogawa, R. T. (1987). Detachment, fear, and expectation: A faculty's response to the impending succession of its principal. *Educational Administration Quarterly, 23*(2), 23–44.

Fink, D., & Brayman, C. (2006). School leadership succession and the challenges of change. *Educational Administration Quarterly, 42*(1), 62–89.

Friedman, S. D. (1987). *Leadership succession.* New Brunswick, NJ: Transaction.

Fullan, M. (1991). *Leading in a culture of change.* San Francisco, CA: Jossey-Bass.

Fullan, M. (1993). *Change forces: Probing the depth of educational reform.* London, UK & New York, NY: Falmer.

Fuller, E., & Young, M. (2009). *Tenure and retention of newly hired principals in Texas.* Austin, TX: University Council for Educational Administration. Retrieved from https://www.casciac.org/ pdfs/ucea_tenure_and_retention_report_10_8_09.pdf

Gabarro, J. J. (1987). *The dynamics of taking charge.* Boston, MA: Harvard Business School Press.

Giles, C., & Hargreaves, A. (2006). The sustainability of innovative schools as learning organizations and profession learning communities during standardized reform. *Educational Administration Quarterly, 42*(1), 124–156.

Groves, K. S. (2003). Integrating leadership development and succession planning best practices. *Journal of Management Development, 26*(3), 239–260.

Hargreaves, A., & Fink, D. (2006). *Sustainable leadership.* San Francisco, CA: Jossey-Bass.

Hargreaves, A., Moore, S., Fink, D., Brayman, C., & White, R. (2003). *Succeeding leaders? A study of principal succession and sustainability.* Boston, MA: Boston College.

Hart, A. W. (1991). Leader succession and socialization: A synthesis. *Review of Educational Research, 61*(4), 451–474.

Hart, A. W. (1993). *Principal succession: Establishing leadership in schools.* Albany, NY: State University of New York Press.

Jacobson, S. (2011). Leadership effects on student achievement and sustained school success. *International Journal of Educational Management, 25*(1), 33–44.

Jacobson, S. L., Johnson, L., Ylimaki, R., & Giles, C. (2009), Sustaining success in an American school: A case for governance change, *Journal of Educational Administration, 47*(6), 753–764.

Jones J. C., & Webber, C. F. (2001). *Principal succession: A case study.* Paper presented at the annual meeting of the American Educational Research Association, Seattle, WA.

Karaveli, A., & Hall, D. T. (2003). Growing leaders for turbulent times: Is succession planning up to the challenge? *Organizational Dynamics, 32*(1), 62–79.

Kotter, J. P. (1996). *Leading change.* Boston, MA: Harvard Business School Press.

Leithwood, K. (1994). Leadership for school restructuring. *Educational Administration Quarterly, 30*(4), 498–518.

Leithwood, K., Harris, A., & Hopkins, D. (2008). Seven strong claims about successful school leadership. *School Leadership & Management, 28*(1), 27–42.

Lewin, K. (1948). Frontiers in group dynamics. In D. Cartwright (Ed.), *Field theory in social science.* London, UK: Social Science Paperbacks.

Louis, K. S., Leithwood, K., Wahlstrom, K. L., & Anderson, S. E. (2010). *Learning from leadership: Investigating the links to improved student learning.* Minneapolis, MN: University of Minnesota.

Miskel, C., & Cosgrove, D. (1985). Leader succession in school settings. *Review of Educational Research, 55*(1), 87–105.

Miskel, C., & Owens, M. (1983). *Principal succession and changes in school coupling and effectiveness.* Paper presented at the annual meeting of the American Educational Research Association, Montreal, Quebec.

Noonan, W., & Goldman, P. (1995). *Principal succession and elementary school climate. One year's experience in an urban school division.* Retrieved November 3, 2016 from: ERIC (No. ED396426).

Ogawa, R. T. (1991). Enchantment, disenchantment, and accommodation: How a faculty made sense of the succession of its principal. *Educational Administration Quarterly, 27*(1), 30–60.

Peterson, K. D. (2002). Positive or negative. *Journal of Staff Development, 23*(3), 10–15.

Protheroe, N. (2001). *Improving teaching and learning with data-based decisions. Asking the right questions and acting on the answers.* Retrieved from: www.ers.org/spectrum/sum01a.htm

Reynolds, C., White, R., Brayman, C., & Moore, S. (2008). Women and secondary school principal rotation/succession: A study of the beliefs of decision makers in four provinces. *Canadian Journal of Education, 31*(1) 32–54.

Saldaña, J. (2013). *The coding manual for qualitative researchers* (2nd ed.). London, UK: Sage Publications.

Zepeda, S. J., Bengston, E., & Parylo, O. (2012). Examining the planning and management of principal succession. *Journal of Educational Administration, 50*(2), 136–158.

CHAPTER 9

SCHOOL LEADERSHIP PRACTICES IN EARLY CHILDHOOD EDUCATION

Three Case Studies from New Zealand

Ross Notman and Stephen Jacobson

This study was guided by two key issues: (1) a renewed interest in quality early childhood education (ECE) producing higher rates of economic return than similar investments at the primary, secondary or tertiary levels, especially for children living in poverty, and (2) a dearth of studies addressing leadership practices in ECE. We examined leadership practices in three quality ECE settings in New Zealand serving high-needs communities and found evidence supportive of three core practices deemed necessary for successful school leadership by Leithwood and Riehl (2005): (1) setting direction, (2) developing people, and (3) redesigning the organization. Our most noteworthy finding was the positive, nurturing relationships developed by all three ECE leaders that were helping young parents learn how to parent.

Keywords: Early Childhood Education (ECE) leadership, Teacher leadership, Successful leadership in high needs schools.

Educational Leadership, Culture, and Success in High-Need Schools, pages 169–184.

INTRODUCTION

There is renewed interest in nations around the world about making greater investments in the quality of early childhood education (ECE), because ECE is seen as the most efficient approach to providing children with the types of non-cognitive abilities (e.g., motivation, trustworthiness, self-discipline, perseverance, and dependability) essential for later school and career success (Heckman & Krueger, 2005; Schweinhart, et al., 2005). This human capital argument contends that ECE investments produce higher rates of economic return than similar investments at the primary, secondary or tertiary levels, especially for children living in poverty (Reardon, 2011). Yet, with the possible exception of Thornton's work in New Zealand (Thornton, 2010; Thornton 2011; Thornton & Wansbrough, 2012), there is a dearth of studies addressing school leadership practices in ECE (Bush, 2013). Therefore, while this study does not report the long-term effects of ECE, it does add to the literature on school leadership practices in quality ECE settings, particularly those serving high-needs communities.

LITERATURE REVIEW

As noted, the value of ECE programs serving children from economically disadvantaged communities has been gaining support. This has been especially the case in the USA since the release of findings from the Perry Pre-school study (Schweinhart et al., 2005). This study followed 123 African-American children ages 3–4 from high poverty families living in Michigan from 1962 until 1967. The youngsters were randomly divided into either a group that received a high-quality ECE program or a comparison group that received no preschool. Forty years later, 97% of the study's still living participants were interviewed about their educational, social service, and criminal records. The data revealed that those involved in a high-quality ECE program had higher earnings, were more likely to hold a job, had committed fewer crimes, and were more likely to have graduated from high school than those who did not.

More specifically with regard to their subsequent education, there were three key findings:

1. More of the group who received a quality ECE graduated from high school than the non-program group (65% vs. 45%), particularly females (84% vs. 32%).
2. Fewer females who received a quality ECE required treatment for mental impairment (8% vs. 36%) or had to repeat a grade (21% vs. 41%).
3. The group that received a quality ECE outperformed, on average, the non-program group on various intellectual and language tests during their early childhood years, on school achievement tests between ages 9 and 14, and on literacy tests at ages 19 and 27.

With regard to their subsequent economic status, more of those who received a quality ECE were employed at age 40 (76% vs. 62%); had higher median annual earnings ($20,800 vs. $15,300); owned their own homes; and, had a savings account (76% vs. 50%) than the non-program group.

Finally, with regard to their criminal record, the group who received a quality ECE had significantly fewer arrests (36% vs. 55% arrested five times or more); significantly fewer arrests for violent crimes (32% vs. 48%), property crimes (36% vs. 58%), or drug crimes (14% vs. 34%). In bottom line terms, every dollar invested in ECE produced a societal return of more than $16.

Although agreement about the magnitude and sustainability of student gains from ECE is not universal (Lipsey, et al. 2015), it is hard to imagine that no benefit would accrue to a child who experienced a quality ECE, particularly as compared to one who has not. However, what accounts for a quality ECE and how does a school leader help create such an environment? Currently there is consensus that far too little empirical research has attended to the work of school leaders in ECE. For example, the International Successful School Principalship Project (ISSPP) has conducted more than 120 case studies in 25 nations over the past 15 years, yet only one case has been of an ECE center (www.uv.uio.no/ils/english/research/projects/isspp/). Empirically measurable metrics, such as standardized test scores, enable ISSPP researchers to identify 'successful' schools, whereas guidelines for ECE 'quality' rest more on subjective assessments, such as those undertaken by New Zealand's Education Review Office (ERO) to rate an ECE center's ability to promote and sustain positive learning outcomes for children. Nevertheless, this study used ERO ratings to identify three "well-placed" or quality ECE programs serving high-needs communities, to serve as our case sites to study the work of their educational leaders.

CONCEPTUAL FRAMEWORK, METHODS AND RESEARCH OBJECTIVES

The conceptual framework used for this study is based upon a comprehensive review of empirical research conducted by Leithwood & Riehl (2005) that identified three core practices deemed necessary, but insufficient, for successful school leadership: (1) setting direction, (2) developing people, and (3) redesigning the organization. This same framework undergirds the work of the ISSPP and subsequently that of the High-Needs Schools (HNS) group of the International School Leadership Development Network (ISLDN) project.[1] Consequently, the study used a case study methodology and semi-structured interview protocol initially developed for the ISSPP (Jacobson & Day, 2007) and then further refined by the ISLDN.

---

[1] It is important to note that none of the studies reviewed by Leithwood and Riehl (2005) included ECE settings.

Using interview responses from the center's leader, other center teachers and parents of children currently in the center, we examined the beliefs and practices of the teacher leaders (all women) in three ECE centers deemed by the ERO to be a "well placed" service to promote and sustain positive learning outcomes for children. This is the third best of four ERO scores a center can receive. In addition to the interviews, secondary data was obtained from government and school documents and ethnographic notes made during the site visits. Two of the sites serve students primarily from culturally diverse and high-need communities, while the third serves a diverse tertiary student body, where the associated level of need is not as great.

Our primary study objectives, similar to those of the other ISLDN cases, were to determine whether key participants—teachers, parents and the leaders themselves—believe the leader played a key role in the center's success and, if so, how. We recognize that the small size of the study's sample limits the robustness and generalizability of the findings to a wider population. Nevertheless, given the dearth of research about ECE leadership, we feel this small study is an important first step in filling this gap in the literature.

THE CONTEXT

There are different types of early childhood services available in New Zealand. They may differ in terms of ownership (government organizations, private individuals, cooperatives or trusts); home-based or center-based services; structural differences such as sessional or whole-day programs; and a range of philosophies such as playcenter, kindergarten, Montessori, or Rudolph Steiner programs. In addition, kōhanga reo offer children total immersion learning in the Māori language (te reo) and culture (tikanga Māori).

New Zealand was selected for study because it has a long history of ECE provision (May, 2007), an on-going national assessment of ECE quality, and a unique national curriculum. Additionally, New Zealand also utilizes *Te Whāriki Bahariki* (a Māori concept of society as a fabric of interwoven values) that shapes policy, pedagogy and practice (May & Carr, 2013), and an educational policy context that is highly decentralized, giving educational leaders considerable autonomy (Notman, 2011). New Zealand's ECE programs are also likely to have teacher and parent leaders (Thornton, 2011), further expanding our understanding of educational leadership beyond the work of primary and secondary school principals. Finally, like many countries around the world dealing with waves of immigrants and displaced populations, New Zealand is desirous of using ECE to promote cultural pluralism amongst its Māori, immigrant Asian, and long-entrenched European populations, known as Pakeha.

The Māori are the indigenous Polynesian people of New Zealand. They make up approximately 15% of New Zealand's population, making them the nation's second largest ethnic group behind New Zealand's Pakeha (New Zealand Government, 2013). The Māori, on average, run greater risks of negative economic and social outcomes with over 50% living in New Zealand's top 30% of deprivation, as compared to 24% of the rest of the population. Moreover, they make up almost 50% of the nation's prison population. Māori also have higher unemployment-rates and numbers of suicides than non-Māori. Moreover, while New Zealand rates high on PISA rankings, a disaggregation of the data reveals that Pakeha students rank second in the world, Māori children 34th. Māori suffer higher levels of alcohol and drug abuse, smoking, and obesity and Māori women and children are more likely to experience domestic violence than any other ethnic group in New Zealand. Though increasing, life expectancy rates for Māori still lag behind those of Pakeha. In 2013, the comparisons were 73 years for Māori men and 77 years for women, as compared to 80 years for non-Māori men and 84 years for women—7 years less by gender on average.

Māori culture and tradition also provide a unique perspective to the nation's education: *Te Whāriki,* an ECE curriculum that emphasizes language and culture intended to enable children (and their families) to learn and grow through self-determination (Smith & May, 2006). Metaphorically, the curriculum is based on the Māori woven mat (*whāriki*) upon which all can stand. It is the tapestry for a life built upon cultural values, and beliefs, that weave the disparate elements of a society into a unified pattern (May & Carr, 2013). Within the concept of *Te Whāriki,* teachers construct a curriculum with their children and families, through a process of talk, reflection, planning, evaluation and assessment that weaves five key strands: wellbeing, belonging, contribution, communication and explora-tion, with four key principles: holistic development, empowerment, relationships, and family and community (May, 2014). Then all learning is built upon this *Te Whāriki* curriculum.

FINDINGS

We examined three ECE sites, collecting data about each center's social context and key aspects, its success factors and the role of the head teacher. Next, we re-view each of the sites, using pseudonyms to maintain confidentiality:

Case 1—Aurora ECE Center

The center provides services for babies and children up to 5-years. The Aurora community is socio-economically diverse, yet families at the center are in the lower income range. There is a high rate of unemployed parents and diverse fam-ily structures, including single parent households and shared care of children. The center has a broad ethnic mix of Pakeha, Māori and Pacific Island children and a strong sense of community, which acts as a magnet for young families. Teacher respondents identified high levels of parental involvement in activities such as family social events, and meeting children's individual needs e.g. a community member taught teachers and children how to use rudimentary sign language to help a deaf child. As a result, Aurora has attained a high level of visibility within the community it serves, both in support of children's learning and in support of parents learning how to become better parents—perhaps our most unexpected finding across sites.

The work of teachers at Aurora focuses on three key tasks: (1) cultivating children's interests and building on their skills and knowledge base; (2) not engaging in deficit thinking due to perceived disadvantages in the community; "because, as a teacher, you are just working with the child in that moment." Teachers are adamant about maintaining a positive perspective when dealing with children and families; and (3) developing nurturing relationships between themselves and parents/caregivers built around the notion that Aurora is the community's hub. The head teacher told us about an ERO reviewer's observation during a center inspection visit: "The ERO lady said this is the only center she's ever been to that she felt that there was this whole community feel and that parents were really engaging in children's learning and what was happening for them." Teachers also believe that Aurora gives parents a forum for developing social networks among themselves where, "if you don't have a lot of money and you don't have a job, then your network's going to be a whole lot smaller. So maybe that's why we're important to them" (Jane, teacher).

Aurora Center was not without problems related to children and parents. Children were presenting challenging behaviors such as anger management, verbal abuse of others, and a lack of self-control. For severe behavioral dysfunction or for special needs children, teachers sought help from government social welfare agencies. At the time of this study, some 30% of children were being assisted with external agency support. Another challenge was enrollment fluctuations caused by children moving away, leaving for primary school at age five, and children who were visiting New Zealand for a short period of time. In one two-week period, Aurora lost 10 children—45% of its enrollment, which put stress on funding to pay teachers' salaries.

A third challenge was assisting parents who lacked important life and/or parenting skills. Teachers worked alongside such parents to develop consistency of behavioral expectations between home and Center by, for example, establishing a joint behavior management plan. On occasions, teachers had to address parents' denial that their child was in need of help to self-regulate their behaviors:

> One child transitioned to school last year—probably a real success story for us. But it took two years of backtracking, going back [to the parent]. Then the parent at the end said "Thank you. My child is who he is today because of you." But there were lots of denial and tears and anger. But we had to keep saying that it's not about you as a parent—it's about your child and we want the best for your child (Sylvia, Head Teacher).

The Head Teacher's response exemplifies three key factors behind Aurora's success in this community of high need: child-centeredness, teaching, and families. The Center's leader and teachers are always child-focused in their planning, teaching activities and program evaluation. They are especially competent in identifying the learning needs of each individual, whether a special needs child or gifted and talented. The quality of teaching and its different facets are paramount to Aurora's success, including: growing teachers' professional capacity and preparing for leadership succession; encouraging teachers in their risk taking; shared decision making among the staff; and working to maximize each teacher's pedagogical strengths and interests. The outcomes of successful teaching practice are mirrored in another parent comment about support for the holistic development of her child:

> I think that social intelligence is just as important as education. You can be the most intelligent person in the world but if you can't communicate with people, it makes life hard for you as a person... It's not just about educating her; it's also about giving her a really good environment to learn from (Mary, parent).

Its strong connections with families enables Aurora to build cooperation and trust with parents. The open-door policy at Aurora that allows parents to feel comfortable sharing their thoughts, feelings and concerns about their children is well summarized by the Head Teacher:

> For some parents it's a big decision to put their children into early childhood education... So, we take our time with our parents, we do a meet sheet, so we get to know the child really well and what's happening for them at home. We also do amazing social events for our parents—we'll have shared kai [food] together. At our last one, we unveiled our philosophy with our parents, so they actually contributed that... it's their place, they're contributing to their child's wellbeing.

In addition to the educative process for children, Center teachers go out of their way to meet the needs of parents. For example, for parents who do not have access to a computer, the Center has a computer specifically set up for them to access their child's learning profile online. They also produce hard copies of the child's learning book (a record of learning in which the child, teacher and parents make comment) that can be given to separated parents or, on one occasion, taken on a prison visit to maintain that learning link between child and both parents. Aurora, via the Head Teacher, also supports families by accessing human services and social welfare agencies on their behalf. As the Head Teacher pointed out, people such as a public health nurse are vital assets given their knowledge about the community and the extent of its human needs.

ROLE OF THE HEAD TEACHER IN AURORA'S SUCCESS

It is important to note the centrality of Sylvia, Aurora's Head Teacher, to its success. Sylvia has been at Aurora for 10 years. Raised in an underprivileged community within the same city, she has personal empathy for children and families who live in disadvantaged urban areas. Her ECE teaching experience in New Zealand has been supplemented by international experiences as a pre-kindergarten teacher in Australia, a nanny in England, and as the head teacher of a London pre-school. Without any mentoring assistance, Sylvia rose through the teaching ranks to her present leadership position at Aurora.

She is a vehement advocate for children and families in her community, as evidenced by her unrelenting pursuit of external help from social agencies to support the learning of pre-school children and the stability of family environments. Teachers and parents alike attribute her success to her ability to communicate on a personal level and to show total respect for children and families, all of which is underlined by a deeply held conviction that human relationships matter.

The range of Sylvia's leadership skills have also contributed to the Center's success. Commonly identified features include managerial strengths in planning; understanding and implementing systems processes such as teacher appraisals and organizational self-review; an ability to have honest and respectful conversations about challenging issues; an open-door policy in which she makes herself available to all; a willingness to lead by example and role model good behavior management practices to younger teachers, e.g. how to intervene effectively in children's altercations. Her educational philosophy makes it clear that she wants ECE to be about community, and her leadership direction emanates from this simple philosophical underpinning. At a personal level, the driving force behind her leadership is her capability to reflect on and problem solve challenging situations, and her self-belief that she can make a difference for children:

> I think every day I'm challenged with something different… If I'm challenged in that way and I learn from it, and I reflect and share it with my team, that's got to be great. I definitely think I can make a change.

Case 2: Winton Kindergarten

Winton Kindergarten differs from an ECE center in that it offers sessional, similar-aged groupings of children, wherein 3–5-year olds attend in the morning and the younger 2–4 year olds in the afternoon. Winton draws on a diverse community, including families with extreme wealth to a majority of families from lower income levels. There is considerable financial pressure on single parents, first home and rental home families, and transient families. Despite this, teachers regard the kindergarten's community as close-knit, with 95% of its children continuing on to the local primary school.

Winton's diversity is also reflected in its ethnic mix including children whose background is European, Pacific Island, Māori, Korean and Indian. They range from gifted children who excel at literacy and numeracy, to children who have little language, to those with physical disabilities, autism, cerebral palsy, and some whose special needs remain undiagnosed. Of particular concern to teachers has been an increasing number of children presenting anxiety issues, which teachers attribute to parent insecurities and inconsistencies of expectations and routines due to having a variety of caregivers (grandparents, other day care centers). Rebecca, the Head Teacher, cites examples where anxious children may be "stuck for two hours at the play dough table and don't feel comfortable to walk three steps to somewhere else, and need a teacher to support them to move."

Teachers and parents identified four strengths at Winton. First, like Aurora, there are strong symbiotic relationships built around trust and mutual respect between parents and teachers, and thus parents are keenly involved in their child's education. Second, having teachers who are experienced, approachable and willing to recognize a child's strengths and interests, and then set behavioral boundaries so that children "know where they stand." As a result, parents generally take pride in their child's learning experiences and the documentation of those experiences in the child's profile book. A third strength was the holistic help provided to parents in need. This might come in the form of clothing, food, and/or gaining access to specialist medical and psychological personnel. Parents felt comfortable talking to teachers about domestic issues and, in particular, childrearing practices. It was, as two teachers said, "a case of parenting some of the parents, as well as their children." Fourth, and finally, parents were unanimous in their acknowledgement of the teachers' ability to support special needs children, and to identify individual issues of learning and behavior. In this respect, they acknowledged the pivotal role of the Head Teacher and her special needs training in leading this teaching emphasis.

Winton also faced a number of key challenges. Teachers pointed to the busyness of life for families across the social spectrum creating a challenge for parents to give quality attention and time to their children. From Rebecca's perspective, some of these challenges were about seemingly simple everyday task of parenting: "For some families, how to put my child to bed and get a routine..., is actually really difficult." Another challenge came in the form of children's anxiety disorders, often manifested in a lack of language development and an inability to understand and process words. In one cohort of 3-year olds, five little boys had single-word vocabularies, with adverse implications for their ability to communicate with teachers in the event of accident or personal concerns. In such cases, teachers worked hard to address barriers to meeting the well-being as well as educational needs of children. Often, this meant additional time spent in accessing the assistance of medical, psychological and/or social agency specialists to support the child's learning and development: "So we're often talking to families about getting ears checked, eyes checked... referrals for speech... phone numbers of places to go... because some families just don't have that confidence" (Meredith, senior teacher).

Another challenge centered on helping children and their families make the transition from kindergarten to primary school at age 5. For some parents, their memories of schooling and educational outcomes are distinctly negative. Consequently, they lack self-confidence helping their child make the transition, and frequently ask teachers to help them through the process. Not that the transition is an easy one for the kindergarten teachers either because, at a professional level, primary teachers have a particular focus on literacy and numeracy in order to meet national standards for student achievement. This academic emphasis stands in contrast to Winton's focus on the child's holistic development:

> So, we're wanting to protect the child, I guess… that nurturing and looking at their personality and social competency, independence, all those sorts of skills, as well as the academic… so that information is supported when they start school. (Rebecca, Head Teacher)

Winton's success lies in the quality of its teaching team; its interlinked relationship building; its sessional approach to learning; and in giving credence to children's voice. The teaching team consists of a very stable, experienced group of ECE educators. Their experience helps Winton maintain a critical focus on the needs of children and families. Respondents all acknowledged the positive relationship the school enjoys with its parent community. The team maintains open communication with each other about what is happening with each child, which leads to the positivity of its linked personal and professional relationships: Child—Family—Community—Teachers. A safe, trusting climate has been created, parents appreciate, and act on teachers' suggested strategies for addressing a child's challenging behaviors at home.

The sessional approach to learning, that groups similarly aged children, is viewed by both parents and teachers as a success factor, together with an emphasis on children learning the skills of social competency. A senior teacher explains:

> We do a lot of work around social play, social grouping, social interactions, social skills and strategies, how to work with each other. And as we've said, they are life-long skills, and to be able to learn how to live in society. We believe that's really important, and we work a lot with children on it—And we've had that [positive] feedback from lots of people too. (Meredith, senior teacher)

A final success factor is the attention paid to children's input into their learning activities. It is part of Winton's child-centered philosophy of creating independent thinkers, and underlines the concept of a partnership in learning between teacher and child:

> We've discussed things with children that it all provokes their learning, what they want… and we've asked them about what they want to see or where they want to hide, all those kinds of things… That it is an environment not just built by an adult and staged by an adult, because that doesn't work. So the children have a big say in what goes on here (Karen, senior teacher)

Role of the Head Teacher in Winton's Success

Rebecca has been Winton's Head Teacher for 11 years, culminating a career that began as an ECE foundational teacher in a rural region. With the arrival of her own family, she moved to the city and worked part-time for a local kindergarten. She did not receive any professional development that prepared her for leadership in ECE.

Rebecca's array of personal qualities include her inclusiveness of staff, parents and children; her capacity to be approachable, actively listen and engage in open communication; an ability to relate to a wide range of people from gang members to doctors and lawyers in a non-hierarchical way. Parental feedback indicated she was not seen as patronizing or judgmental, but rather showed complete respect and support for these parents' "parenting."

Teacher respondents appreciated her willingness to allow them to take risks in their teaching programs, even though she claimed not to be a risk taker herself. Rebecca's collaborative skills were demonstrated by the way she encouraged shared decision making and distributed leadership roles to teachers e.g. curriculum development.

A universally identified factor in her contribution to Winton's success lay in her training and work with special needs children. Some years previously, she had undertaken extra professional development in the form of a two-year course of study in teaching special needs children. As a result, Rebecca is deeply committed to early identification of special needs:

> So as much as we may not get support for a [special needs] child, or we may not get a diagnosis or everything may be fine, we've started that ball rolling. If later in life they look at their medical records, they can see that actually somebody did try or somebody did acknowledge something wasn't right.

This training and commitment enabled her to support early intervention for teaching children with special needs, and to share such issues honestly with affected parents. In one instance, a parent commented that Rebecca had patiently helped her deal with her young child's anxiety levels. She appreciated Rebecca's role modeling when working with her child and gained confidence from that: "She helped me to feel more confident as a mum and just to confirm that, whereas I was kind of hearing those voices and things going 'You're doing it wrong.'"

Case 3: Smithfield Early Childcare Center

Smithfield Early Childhood Center has a total of 28 children. It is a mixed-age setting with a maximum of 10 children up to two years of age. In contrast to the other cases, Smithfield draws from a community associated with tertiary institutions. Its parents are predominantly students or lecturers who comprise two-parent families. They are well educated and come from mostly affluent backgrounds. The Center also has a high proportion of families who come from other countries such as France, Australia, Germany, China, Ireland, Canada, Nepal and the Caribbean.

Children at Smithfield present few behavioral issues, although there are instances of anger management or delayed language development. According to the Head Teacher, Smithfield attracts a considerable number of gifted children that requires teacher who can recognize and act on individual learning styles and interests.

Respondents identified four areas of strength, starting with the Smithfield's mixed-age groupings, whereby older children were able to role model learning and behavior for the younger ones, sometimes in a simple form of peer tutoring. A second area was family support for Center activities, particularly social events e.g. 60 people representing 28 families attended the most recent Christmas party. It was noted that social events produced more attendance than educational information evenings designed to share curriculum developments and teaching strategies.

Teacher capability was another highly regarded strength. The teaching staff has been stable for some time and acknowledged by parents as being experienced, constructive and calm in their dealings with children. Parents appreciated teachers' ability to build social competencies within each child e.g. how to resolve conflicts with others, while teachers recognized children's individual learning styles and allowed them to develop independent strengths and interests at their own pace:

> They let the children set their own challenges and reach them on their own timescale, but not intervene. They don't help them to do something they just let them work and work and work away at it until they do it on their own (Maisey, parent)

Finally, parents expressed gratitude for the manner in which teachers built positive interpersonal relationships with them. They appreciated open conversations about their child's progress and, importantly, teachers' personal support in the absence of extended families in New Zealand. Parental help from teachers came in the form of strategies for coping with examination study stress, being active listeners to parents' private concerns, and providing advice and guidance in parenting skills. As Jane, a parent, commented:

> I will probably burst into tears right now because, without them, without the guidance, without the ability to come in and not feel as though you were being judged, and judged in a negative way ... I don't know how we would have survived this darned thing [parenting].

There were few challenges for Smithfield in terms of children's behavioral dysfunction or anxiety issues. However, one teacher pointed to a general situation wherein the lack of family back up in the community led some parents to rely on the teachers for their main form of support:

> We'll often let families change their days or do different hours to support them when there aren't other family members who can look after the children. Or just offering them guidance and even emotional support when things are happening in their lives. (Emily, teacher)

Success factors at Smithfield were similar to those of the other cases in regard to relationships; quality of teaching staff; shared leadership strategies; and a philosophical focus on child-centered learning. All respondents identified personal and professional relationships among children, parents and teachers as fundamental to success. Head Teacher Andrea saw these interpersonal relationships as the means by which she could empower teachers to try new teaching strategies and take risks in the way they interacted with the children. Quality teaching was paramount and reinforced by Andrea's emphasis on teamwork and professional development. For example, all of the teachers except one had committed to a one-year course in Māori language acquisition.

In addition, all respondents viewed Andrea's insistence on shared leadership among teachers as a contributory factor in Smithfield's success. Leadership strategies included shared decision making and working towards a shared vision. This vision for child-centered learning is well encapsulated by one teacher's description of an internal change process, which promoted collaborative leadership and reflective practice built around holistic child development:

> We did a social competency self-review and we looked at children entering groups, so we tried to focus it down. Through that, we really got reflective on what we were doing and worked together to find strategies for helping children to initiate play—and that was really good. (Emily, teacher)

Role of the Head Teacher in Smithfield's Success

Teachers and parents describe Andrea as an energetic and enthusiastic leader. She is very organized and uses her knowledge of policies and procedures to benefit Smithfield. She demonstrates an ability to plan ahead and to make things happen in her advocacy for families, particularly in her pursuit of resources for the children.

Andrea's leadership style is quiet and unassuming style, which as noted earlier, builds on her sharing leadership with the staff. She shows respect for teachers' skills and recognizes the individual strengths they bring to the team. She gives teachers clear directions and helps them to be consistent in teaching children who may require extra support. She is open to change and new ideas, whether they come from teachers or parents. Andrea is especially supportive of helping parents better understanding their child's learning and their own parenting skills. She is passionate about children's learning and this is clearly seen in her drive for early identification of children's learning styles. This is the impetus behind her push for continuing professional development for her staff on learning styles and supporting learning opportunities for all children, whether they are struggling with language development or requiring extension activities in the case of gifted and talented children.

A sign on the bathroom wall at Smithfield epitomizes Andrea's and her staff's focus on the individuality of each child: *Your child is not in the process of becoming someone. Your child IS someone.*

DISCUSSION AND CONCLUSIONS

Since these cases are based on protocols developed for ISSPP, and subsequently adapted for high-need case studies by ISLDN, we presented our results in a fashion similar to those earlier studies, i.e., we reported findings about both the center's and leader's demographics, leadership preparation, experience, etc. We also implicitly considered the leaders' work in relation to the core practices for successful school leadership; setting direction, developing people and redesigning the organization (Leithwood & Reihl, 2005). Next, we plan to draw analogies between the practices of the three ECE leaders studied and those of leaders in primary and secondary education. As noted earlier, we did not track children longitudinally therefore, we cannot confirm or refute the economic productivity arguments presented at the beginning of the paper. However, the study can provide initial insights of what high-quality ECE looks like in a high-needs setting. The study also addresses a noted gap in the literature namely, how teacher leaders work with parents to make this happen

At all three ECE sites, we found that teacher leaders had a fundamental interest in cultivating their children's unique and collective interests, as well as building their skills and knowledge in a highly child-centered environment that aligned with the precepts of *Te Whāriki*. This approach clearly aligns with the core practice of 'setting direction.'" These leaders explicitly refrained from engaging in any form of deficit thinking based on stereotypic perceptions of the disadvantages of their community, "because, as a teacher, you are just working with the child in that moment." There were also constant references across all three sites to the symbiotic relationship that can emerge between teachers and parents/caregivers when teachers go out of their way to meet the material and emotional needs of parents while supporting the holistic development of their children. In other words, these leaders were "developing people." In studies of primary and secondary schools, "developing people" typically focuses on the continuing professional development of teachers, but for the ECE leaders studied, while developing teachers was important, it was no more so than the development of the child's primary teachers—their parents.

Moreover, these ECE leaders were constantly "redesigning the organization" to help meet the needs of children and their families. As a result, strong connections developed with families that built cooperation and trust, and the comfort parents felt with teachers and teacher leaders (and vice versa) was obvious at all three sites. These positive, nurturing relationships revealed what we believe is our most noteworthy finding, i.e., the extent to which these three ECE leaders were helping young parents learn how to parent. Social disruptions, whether caused by economic factors such as job loss or relocation, or more catastrophic upheavals such as war and natural disaster have wreaked havoc on the composition of extended families in New Zealand (and elsewhere) and, as a consequence, on the traditional childrearing practices of many. For an increasing number of young parents, they are having to work and parent without the support of an extended family. For many, especially for first-time parents, it is the child's teachers, teaching them how to raise their child, which may be the 'make or break' factor in that child's future success. While we can only speculate as to the long-term effects of these quality ECE centers on the life chances of the youngsters in their care, we have to believe that the positive impact of the teachers and teacher leaders on parenting skills will have a beneficial effect both in the short and long term. This is clearly an area in need of further examination.

Questions to consider

1. How do we best support early childhood head teachers who lead in a high-needs environment?
2. To what extent should early childhood teachers and leaders be expected to meet the holistic needs of parents as well as the educative needs of children?

REFERENCES

Bush, T. (2013). Leadership in early childhood education. *Educational Management Administration Leadership, 41*(1), 3–4.

Heckman, J., & Krueger, A. (2005). *Inequality in America: What role for human capital policies?* Cambridge, MA: MIT Press.

Jacobson, S., & Day, C. (2007). The International Successful School Principalship Project (ISSPP): An overview of the project, the case studies and their contexts, *International Studies in Educational Administration, 35*(3), 3–10.

Leithwood, K., & Reihl, C. (2005). What we know about successful school leadership. In W. Firestone & C. Reihl (Eds.) *A new agenda: Directions for research on educational leadership.* New York, NY: Teachers College Press.

Lipsey, M., Weiland, C., Yoshikawa, H., Wilson, S., & Hofer, K. (2015). Prekindergarten age-cutoff regression-discontinuity design: Methodological issues and implications for application. *Educational Evaluation and Policy Analysis, 37,* 296–313. https://doi.org/10.3102/0162373714547266

May H. (2007). 'Minding,' 'working,' 'teaching': Childcare in Aotearoa/New Zealand, 1940s—2000s. *Contemporary Issues in Early Childhood, 8*(2), 133–143

May, H. (2014). New Zealand: A narrative of shifting policy directions for early childhood education and care. In L. Gambaro, K. Stewart, & J. Waldfogel (Eds.), *An equal start? Providing quality early education and care for disadvantaged children* (pp. 147–170). Bristol, UK: Policy Press.

May H., & Carr M (2013). *Te Whāriki:* A uniquely woven curriculum shaping policy, pedagogy and practice in Aotearoa New Zealand. In T. David, K. Goouch, & S. Powell (Eds.), *The Routledge international handbook of philosophies and theories of early childhood education and care* (pp. 316–326). London, UK: Routledge, Taylor & Francis Group.

New Zealand Government. (2013). *The census of population and dwellings.* Retrieved from https://www.stats.govt.nz/topics/census

Notman, R. (2011). Building leadership success in a New Zealand education context. In R. Notman (Ed.), *Successful school leadership in New Zealand: Case studies of schools and an early childhood center.* (pp. 135–152). Wellington, NZ: NZCER Press.

Reardon, S. (2011). The widening academic achievement gap between the rich and the poor: New evidence and possible explanations. In G. Duncan & R. Murnane, (Eds.), *Whither opportunity: Rising inequality, schools, and children's life chances* (pp. 91–116). New York, NY: Russell Sage Foundation.

Schweinhart, L., Montie, J., Xiang, Z., Barnett, W. S., Belfield, C. R., & Nores, M. (2005). *Lifetime effects: The HighScope Perry Preschool study through age 40.* (Monographs of the HighScope Educational Research Foundation, 14). Ypsilanti, MI: HighScope Press.

Smith, A., & May, H. (2006). Early childhood care and education in Aotearoa-New Zealand. In E. Melhuish & K. Petrogiannis (Eds.), *Early childhood care and education: International perspectives.* (pp. 95–114). Oxon, UK: Routledge.

Thornton, K. (2010). School leadership and student outcomes: The best evidence synthesis iteration: Relevance for early childhood education and implications for leadership practice. *Journal of Educational Leadership, Policy and Practice, 25*(1), 30–40.

Thornton, K. (2011). Whanau leadership in early childhood. In R. Notman (Ed.), *Successful educational leadership in New Zealand* (pp. 99–109). Wellington, NZ: NZCER.

Thornton, K., & Wansbrough, D. (2012). Professional learning communities in early childhood education. *Journal of Educational Leadership, Policy and Practice, 27*(2), 51–64.

EPILOGUE

MAKING WORLD CONNECTIONS

Educational Leadership in High-need Schools

David Gurr, Elizabeth Murakami, and Ross Notman

The improvement of schools has been a continuous concern within countries, states, district or municipalities, with their school leaders closely monitoring ways in which students can succeed. Monitoring is based on learning expectations—often set not only within the country, but also in comparison with other countries. To this end, mechanisms to control the quality of educational delivery, is controlled by a variety of supervisory benchmarks, funding formulas, and processes for interventions. Nonetheless, the performance of schools continues to vary. Despite interventions and assessments, we find schools in need of much improvement in order to provide equitable opportunities for students.

School principals and local administrators are working hard to improve strategies, but forces external to this system are also needed to be considered. In this volume we confirm that external forces impacting schools are much harder to control—such as social issues, poverty, war and other disasters, location and environment, unequal funding, teacher retention, or specific needs from student and families, just to name a few. Therefore, we purposefully included high-need areas and high-need schools as sites for school leadership improvement, as a means to

Educational Leadership, Culture, and Success in High-Need Schools, pages 185–194.
Copyright © 2019 by Information Age Publishing
All rights of reproduction in any form reserved.

understand the impact of variables that still challenge the quality of experiences students need to succeed in schools.

Of concern is the number of countries demonstrating a need to improve the educational experiences of students. In the U.S., for example, The Every Student Success Act (ESSA) (U.S. Department of Education, 2018) specifically includes provisions needed to address the education of disadvantaged and high-need students. Such policy language recognizes that a problem exists and demonstrates a need for social justice measures that are beyond the instrumental control set by accountability systems. It is in this intersection that the school principal becomes the most important advocate at a local, state, and national levels, reporting on the need of students, families and communities, as well as the one empowered with a vision to adapt and modify structures and processes, and represent these communities in order to effectively generate change that can positively impact student learning.

This book has brought together nine studies that represent school leadership research from five countries—Australia, Belize, Brazil, New Zealand, and five studies in the United States of America with the purpose of exploring leadership in high-need schools through the ISLDN framework (Baran & Berry, 2015). This consists of three areas as shown in Figure 10.1.

Across the nine studies, there were 19 schools involved covering all stages from early years through to high school and involving interviews with 23 princi-

FIGURE 10.1. The International School Leadership Development Network Framework for the study of high-needs schools (adapted from Baran & Berry, 2015).

pals. Of the 23 principals, six were male. In keeping with the collaborative and evolving nature of the ISLDN project, each research group used the ISLDN protocols depending on focus needed for their research (some research projects included only principals, while others included teachers and other stakeholders). In each case, sufficient description of methodology allows the reader to judge the integrity and trustworthiness. The case of a school in Belize was the study that most closely adhered to the ISLDN protocols, but it did not include parent interviews. The New Zealand study also used ISLDN protocols but was focused on early childhood settings (which the ISLDN was not designed to explore). The study from Australia used ISSPP protocols, which the ISLDN are based upon; the Australian study was the most complex in that included all the required interview categories (governors, principal, other leaders, teachers, students and parents), as well as observation of practice and document collection. All other studies have allegiance to the ISLDN protocols, but all use some modification, typically restricting the extent of the research by not incorporating the full suite of perspectives: studies by Murakami/Kearney, and Alford interviewed principals only, whilst de Oliveira/de Carvalho, Baran/Van Harpen, and Berry/Cowart Moss interviewed principals and teachers. Okilwa and Barnett interviewed principals and teachers in a study that was longitudinal in nature through interviewing four principals that led the one school over a 20-year period. Table 10.1 provides a summary of key aspects of each study in the chapters:

Whilst all the research presented in this book is part of the ISLDN high-needs research group, it is difficult to provide a synthesis chapter, as there is considerable richness and diversity across countries that can be lost by trying to simplify common findings, or merely highlighting general aspects. In many ways, it is best for the reader to read and reflect on each of the nine chapters. To this end, each chapter ends with reflective questions. Some of the insights also link to Gurr and Drysdale's (2018) synthesis of the companion special issue, in the *International Studies in Educational Administration* journal, launched in 2018, volume 46, issue 1. The companion journal issue reports on seven articles, covering some of the cases in this volume and presenting additional cases completed after this volume. Cases from Mexico (Torres-Arcadia, Rodríguez-Uribe & Mora, 2018), an additional case from South Texas (Murakami, Kearney, Scott & Alfaro, 2018), different conceptualizations of cases from Australia (Gurr, Drysdale, Longmuir & McCrohan, 2018), Belize (Waight, Chisolm & Jacobson, 2018), New Zealand (Jacobson & Notman, 2018) and South Texas (Okilwa & Barnett, 2018) further inform a focus on high-needs schools.

The chapters in this book were divided into sections that represent important themes in the consideration of leadership in high-need schools. Here, it is also important to recognize a larger number of scholars who are contributing to the improvement of schools that relate to this topic. For each section of this book, new and concurrently work can be found. For example, within our first thematic area of **contextually-responsive leadership**, it is also important to observe the work

TABLE 10.1 Key Features of the Nine Studies

Author(s)	Location	Number of Sites	School Type	Gender	ISLDN Protocol
Murakami & Kearney	South Texas, USA	4	2 public elementary 1 charter middle 1 magnet high school	2 female 2 male	Interviews with principals and observation of practices.
Gurr, Drysdale, Longmuir &McCrohan	Melbourne, Australia	3	3 public secondary schools (years 7–12)	1 female 2 male	Adapted version for interview questions. Interviews with school governors, principals, senior teachers, teachers, students and parents, and observation of practices.
Oliveira & Carvalho	Rio de Janeiro, Brazil	2	Elementary (years 1–9)	1 female 1 male	Interviews with principals and teachers and observation of practices.
Chisolm, Waight, &Jacobson	Blue Cove Caye, Belize	1	Secondary (years 8–11)	2 female co-principals	Interviews with principals and teachers and observation of practices.
Alford	Southern California, USA	2	Public elementary	2 Female	Interviews with principals and observation of practices.
Baran &Van Harpen	Milwaukee, USA	1	Charter elementary	1 Male	Interviews with principal and senior leadership
Berry & Cowart Moss	Southeast, USA	2	1 elementary 1 middle school	2 Female	Interviews with principals and teachers, and document analysis.
Okilwa &Barnett	South Texas, USA	1 school with 4 principals over a 20-year period	Public elementary	4 female	Interviews with principals and veteran teachers
Notman &Jacobson	New Zealand	3	Early childhood centers	3 Female	Interviews in non-school settings

of Bredeson, Klar, and Johannson, (2011), the recent work of Hallinger (2018), and also Morrison (2017).

When focusing on **leadership for learning**, especially in a social justice context, a new volume edited by Angelle (2017) with scholars from the ISLDN social justice focus is available. In addition, the work of Bogotch and Shields (2013), who compiled a handbook on social justice, and Leithwood and Mascall's (2008) consideration of the effect of leadership in student achievement, merit further review and consideration. Finally, with a focus on **successful educational leadership practices**, Day and Gurr (2014) provide an edited collection of ISSPP cases focused on leadership for school success. Klar and Brewer's (2013) ISSPP cases are more specific on successful leadership in high-need schools, and Notman (2011) similarly observes successful schools and also includes early childhood centers. This community of scholars bring together important findings about how to improve schools. This volume then adds to the research within this community of scholars. In the following section, we provide comments and observations that might help readers gain more insight about this work of high-needs school leadership and school improvement. We reflect on each of the three themes drawing across the nine chapters.

Contextually Responsive Leadership

One of the most striking aspects across the cases is how the school leaders adapted their interventions or practices to suit the context; Okilwa and Barnett described this as contextual acuity. In the school from Belize, Chisolm, Waight and Jacobson described how the two principals at the school connected the curriculum closely with current interest in STEM education and the local industries that were likely to be sources of employment for students. In the New Zealand cases described by Notman and Jacobson, the three early childhood leaders of course focused on developing teachers, but, more importantly for their context, they focused on developing parents, helping young parents to become better parents (also see Jacobson & Notman, 2018). In Australia, the principals had different approaches to change (Gurr, Drysdale, Longmuir & McCrohan, 2018). One principal, in a school that was close to being closed, tried anything that would work to get a more student focused learning environment. The principal was searching for 'next practice' ideas and assembling these into a coherent program. The other principals led 'best practice' environments where the schools operated using ideas that were known to be good approaches to learning. One of these principals also searched for 'next practice' ideas but did so in a carefully considered way so that these were a good fit with the already established school direction. Across the three schools change was driven quickly by the principals in the two schools that had more dire contexts whilst in the more established school change was slower. Moving to the history of four principals at the one school (Okilwa & Barnett, 2018), it was shown how each principal was able to adapt to their context and build on the foundations laid by previous principals. This is a wonderful story of how thoughtful leaders were able to read their immediate and past school contexts and continue to nurture school success.

The case studies help us to better understand leadership in context. They confirm that leadership and context have a reciprocal influence process. As Doherty (2008) observed in her ISSPP study, principal leadership can influence a school, but the school can equally influence the leadership of a principal. While the leaders in high-needs school reported in this book were often faced with what seemed to be insurmountable obstacles, they were not captured or made inert by context. Instead, they were typically optimistic about a better future. They were contextually sensitive and responded positively with strategic interventions that promoted school success. The principals appeared to adapt to changing circumstances. Whilst systemic, school and community contexts may change, the school leaders were able to navigate these changes and to do so over extended periods. In the ISSPP, there are cases of principals who have led the one school successfully for over two decades (e.g. Drysdale, Goode & Gurr, 2011). Finally, the case study principals showed personal leadership that helped bring people together in a common purpose of providing quality education for students.

Leadership for Learning

Leaders developing appropriate school cultures featured in many of the studies. Baran and Van Harpen's paper focused on one turnaround school and how this school developed a culture of learning. They described how the school focused on organizational leadership (attendance, character development, academic excellence, staff selection, shared goals), distributed leadership, academic achievement and behavior (monitoring student learning, focus on academic excellence, celebrating success), character building and celebrating student efforts through daily assemblies, relationship and emotional connections through believing in and valuing people, fostering relationships with external partners, and targeted resourcing (such as forgoing student transport so a teacher assistant can be employed in many classrooms). In Alford's study of two schools, culture also featured, and developing a positive school culture was key to the success of the schools. To facilitate this trust, respect and integrity based on sound ethical and moral principles were all important. The principals described their leadership in servant leader terms, demonstrating authentic, culturally responsive, and present behavior. The principals were described as focusing on critical thinking, engagement and high expectations to promote learning, engaging with parents as partners, sharing leadership and creating structures to facilitate collaboration, and developing staff through professional learning. Chisolm, Waight and Jacobson's study of a small secondary school in Belize showed how a school could be constructed that was targeted tightly to the needs of a community but utilized contemporary curriculum ideas (in the case a STEM curriculum). Learning in this context was not measured by traditional assessments alone, but also by the extent to which students were able to secure positive futures in work or further schooling.

Whilst these studies, and others in the book, described leadership that impacted on teaching and learning, none provided a model for leadership for learning in the way that, for example, the Leadership for Learning (LfL) project has. LfL (www. educ.cam.ac.uk/networks/lfl) set out from its beginnings in 2001 to construct a model that would explain how leadership influences student learning (MacBeath. Dempster, Frost, Johnson, & Swaffield, 2018). Some of the studies in this book have used conceptual/theoretical or leadership models to frame learning (e.g. Berry, & Cowart Moss; Oliveira & de Carvalho; Murakami & Kearney), and had confirmation of their model through the case studies. These studies did not necessarily provide a view of leadership for learning that arises from this collection—as yet.

Successful Educational Leadership Practice

What is also striking is how common views of leadership work well to describe the work of these principals. For example, the core practices of setting directions, developing people, redesigning the organization and improving teaching and learning, championed by Leithwood and colleagues (e.g. Leithwood, Day, Sammons, Harris & Hopkins, 2006) and found in the literature on successful school leadership (Gurr & Day, 2014), were also evident in the cases. In the Australian cases (Gurr, Drysdale, Longmuir & McCrohan, 2018) all three principals had clear direction, two were focused on developing staff (Robyn and Peter). They were all able to redesign their schools, and there was a clear focus on improving teaching and learning. Therefore, contexts do matter but not so much in terms of the core leadership practices that lead to success, but rather in the way these practices are employed. The early childhood head teachers (Notman & Jacobson) were shown to exhibit the first three characteristics and, in Jacobson and Notman (2018) it was further shown how these head teachers emphasized the creation of positive school/family relationships. At Robbins Elementary School (Okilwa & Barnett, 2018) there was a four-principal history of setting a clear improvement direction, supporting teachers to improve, altering school conditions, a relentless yet supportive focus on improving teaching and learning, and, fostering significant parent and community engagement. In Alford's study the two principals were described as improving teaching and learning through focusing on critical think, engagement and high expectations, creating a culture of collaboration through engaging with parents as partners, sharing leadership and creating structures to facilitate staff collaboration, and developing staff through professional learning.

The two cases described by Berry and Cowart Moss uncovered themes related to engagement, values, developing people, inclusion, equity and persistence and these were said to support a view of leadership for high-needs schools that includes responding to context, intentional behavior and hypervigilance. Overall, this paper supported a leadership focus on developing people (student and staff) and producing a conducive and supportive school climate that engaged all. It also had much to say about the leadership qualities that are important for this such as having a social justice orientation and being persistent and vigilant in the pursuit of this. Murakami and Kearney's adoption of advocacy leadership view has similar orientations in terms of developing a high expectation, yet in an inclusive and welcoming learning community, with genuine student voice and family engagement, and teacher development. Murakami, Kearney, Scott and Alfaro (2018) described an additional ISLDN case that showed significant developments in staff retention, curriculum, student behavior and attendance, parent involvement, and student learning outcomes. The authors noted that this was dependent on the principal establishing a collaborative school vision, creating a culture of learning, and implementing incremental change across the areas of discipline, attendance, training and curriculum implementation.

Comparative to other international studies such as the ISSPP, leadership does not just rest solely with the principal or headteacher (see Gurr & Day, 2014 for discussion of this from the ISSPP perspective). Baran and Van Harpen's case describes a leadership partnership between the principal, two deans and chief academic officer, with clear responsibilities, but also a sense of collective effort. Similarly, Alford's paper describes how the two principals not only shared leadership, but changed structures so that teachers could better work together.

CONCLUSION

We are grateful to the group of ISLDN scholars in this book for their contributions, and we believe that all those involved with the improvement of education can benefit from the studies reported in these chapters. Lessons provided by the scholars in relation to context-responsive leadership included attention to contextual acuity, with leadership that both informed and capitalized on the strengths and knowledge of school principals and on strategies promoting positive interventions. They maintained high optimism in the most challenging contexts. When focusing on leadership for learning, the leaders and teachers demonstrated that high-need schools require leadership that is not limited by traditional assessments, but dependent on an elaborate and focused strategy that included relationships that can secure collaborations with external partners, targeted resourcing, and a focus on building professional learning among adults. Promoting contemporary curricular ideas, these principals facilitated trust and respect, bringing the leadership for social justice to the fore, and lead with ethical and moral principles.

We conclude by recognizing that successful educational leadership practices in high-need schools is continuously threatened by external forces, many times out of the school principal's control, but directly affecting people's experiences and outcomes. Hence the importance of principals with a social justice orientation, who are both persistent and vigilant in order to generate strong foundations for learning in the most challenging contexts. These principals guide with an optimistic vision, and establish collaborative engagements with internal and external stakeholders, working towards a culture of learning, with professional learning opportunities for teachers, and support for parents and community members. These principals are relentless in their intentionality and hypervigilance for the needs of their students. To them, we dedicate this book, acknowledging their special talents and courage to advocate for their respective school communities around the world.

REFERENCES

Angelle, P. S. (Ed.). (2017). *A global perspective of social justice leadership for school principals.* Charlotte, NC: Information Age Publishing.

Baran, M. L., & Berry, J. R. (2015). *The international school leadership development network (ISLDN) High-needs schools group research protocol and members' guide.* Washington, DC: ISLDN and UCEA/BELMAS.

Bredeson, P. V., Klar, H. W., & Johannson, O. (2011). Context responsive leadership: Examining superintendent leadership in context. *Education Policy Analysis Archives, 19*(18), 1–24.

Bogotch, I., & Shields, C. M. (Eds.). (2013). *Educational handbook of educational leadership and social (in)justice.* Dordrecht, The Netherlands: Springer.

Day, C., & Gurr, D. (Eds.). (2014). *Leading schools successfully: Stories from the field.* London, UK: Routledge.

Doherty, J. (2008) *Successful leadership in an independent school in Victoria, Australia.* Doctor of Education thesis, The University of Melbourne.

Drysdale, L., Goode, H., & Gurr, D. (2011). Sustaining school and leadership success in two Australian schools. In L. Moos, O. Johansson, & C. Day (Eds.), *How school principals sustain success over time: International perspectives* (pp. 25–38). Netherlands: Springer-Kluwer.

Gurr, D., & Day, C. (2014). Thinking about leading schools. In C. Day & D. Gurr (Eds.), *Leading schools successfully: Stories from the field* (pp. 194–208). London, UK: Routledge.

Gurr, D., & Drysdale, L. (2018). Leading high need schools: Findings from the International School Leadership Development Network, *International Studies in Educational Administration, 46*(1), 147–156.

Gurr, D., Drysdale, L., Longmuir, F., & McCrohan, K. (2018). Leading the improvement of schools in challenging circumstances, *International Studies in Educational Administration, 46*(1), 22–44.

Hallinger, P. (2018). Bringing context out of the shadow, *Educational Management Administration & Leadership, 46*(1), 5–24.

Jacobson, S., & Notman, R. (2018). Leadership in early childhood education: Implications for parental involvement and student success from New Zealand, *International Studies in Educational Administration, 46*(1), 86–101.

Klar, H. W., & Brewer, C. A. (2013). Successful leadership in high-needs schools: An examination of core leadership practices enacted in challenging contexts. *Educational Administration Quarterly, 20*(10), 1–41.

Leithwood, K., Day, C., Sammons, P., Harris, A., & Hopkins, D. (2006). *Seven strong claims about successful school leadership.* Nottingham, UK: National College of School Leadership.

Leithwood, K., & Mascall, B. (2008). Collective leadership effects on student achievement. *Education Administration Quarterly, 44*, 529–561.

MacBeath, J., Dempster, N., Frost, D., Johnson, G., & Swaffield, S. (Eds.). (2018). *Strengthening the connections between leadership and learning.* London, UK: Routledge.

Morrison, M. (2017). Conceiving context: The origins and development of the conceptual framework. In P. Angelle (Ed.), *A global perspective of social justice leadership for school principals* (pp. 43–64). Charlotte, NC: Information Age Publishing.

Murakami, E. T., Kearney, W. S., Scott, L., & Alfaro, P. (2018) Leadership for the improvement of a high-poverty/high minority school. *International Studies in Educational Administration, 46*(1), 2–21.

Notman, R. (Ed.) (2011). *Successful educational leadership in New Zealand: Case studies of schools and an early childhood center.* Wellington, NZ: NZCER Press.

Okilwa, N. S., & Barnett, B. G. (2018). Four successive school leaders' response to a high needs urban elementary school context, *International Studies in Educational Administration, 46*(1), 45–85.

Torres-Arcadia, C., Rodríguez-Uribe, C., & Mora, G. (2018). How principals lead high needs schools in Mexico, *International Studies in Educational Administration, 46*(1), 123–146.

U.S. Department of Education (2018). *Every Student Succeeds Act (ESSA).* Accessed July 10, 2018 at https://www.ed.gov/essa?src=rn.

Waight, N., Chisolm, L., & Jacobson, S. (2018). School leadership and STEM enactment in a high needs secondary school in Belize. *International Studies in Educational Administration, 46*(1), 102–122.

BIOGRAPHIES

EDITORS

Elizabeth T. Murakami is a professor and Mike Moses Endowed Chair in Educational Leadership at the University of North Texas. She earned her master's in Curriculum and Teaching and Doctor of Philosophy degree in Educational Administration at Michigan State University. Before becoming a professor, she worked in American international schools in Latin America for 14 years. She is the co-editor of the *Journal of School Leadership*, and IAP book series *International Research on School Leadership* and *Hispanics in Education and Administration*. Her research includes publications in prestigious journals such as *Academe, Journal of Studies in Higher Education; the International Journal of Qualitative Studies in Education; Journal of School Leadership; Educational Management Administration and Leadership (EMAL); Journal of School Administration and Supervision*; and the books *Beyond marginality: Understanding the intersection of race, ethnicity, gender, and difference in educational leadership research, Abriendo puertas, cerrando heridas (Opening doors, closing wounds): Latinas/os finding work-life balance in academia, Brown-Eyed Leaders of the Sun: A Portrait of Latina/o Educational Leaders & Educational Leaders* encouraging the intellectual and professional capacity of others.

Educational Leadership, Culture, and Success in High-Need Schools, pages 195–202.

David Gurr is an Associate Professor in educational leadership within the Melbourne Graduate School of Education at the University of Melbourne. He teaches in the areas of educational leadership, strategic leadership, and school effectiveness and improvement. He is a founding member of the International Successful School Principalship Project, and the International School Leadership Development Network, which is a joint partnership between UCEA and BELMAS. He has more than 160 publications and has more than 170 presentations at major conferences. David has been the Vice-president of the Australian Council for Educational Leaders and past Editor of Hot Topics, Monograph and the academic journal, Leading and Managing. David is currently co-editor of the CCEAM journal International Studies in Educational Administration and co-editor of the IAP book series International Research on School Leadership. He has received several honors from ACEL including being awarded the National Presidential Citation in 2004, a national fellowship in 2006, the Hedley Beare Educator of the Year award in 2012, and the Gold Medal in 2014.

Ross Notman is Professor in Education at the University of Otago, New Zealand, and director of the Centre for Educational Leadership and Administration. He is the New Zealand project director of an international research study, across 20 countries, into the leadership practices of successful school principals, and the ISLDN study of leadership in high-needs schools and centers. Ross's major research interests focus on teacher and school principal development, particularly in the field of the personal dimensions of the principalship. He became Dean of the College of Education in April 2017.

AUTHORS

Betty Alford a professor and Doctoral Program Co-Director of the Educational Leadership Doctoral Program at California Poly technic State University, Pomona and professor emerita from Stephen F. Austin State University (SFA), completed her Ph.D. from The University of Texas in Austin. Her professional experiences at SFA included teaching in the doctoral and the principal preparation programs, serving as coordinator of the doctoral program and as department chair, and serving as lead or co-writer for educational partnership school-university-community grants that totaled over 20 million dollars. Her honors included receiving the SFA Foundation Faculty Achievement Award for Research and the James Vornberg Texas Council of Professors of Educational Administration Living Legend Award. Alford is a member of the International School Leadership Development Network. Her research agenda has focused on strengthening a college-going culture through school-university-community collaboration, school leadership for equity and excellence in high-need settings, and educational leadership program improvement processes and practices.

Mette L. Baran completed her Ed.D. in Administrative Leadership and Supervision from DePaul University. She obtained an M.B.A. in International Business and a baccalaureate degree in Marketing from DePaul University. Dr. Baran is a tenured assistant professor in the School of Leadership-Doctoral Studies Department within the College of Education and Leadership at Cardinal Stritch University and teaches Leadership, learning, Higher Education, and Research Methodology courses. Her background includes being a faculty member and senior executive at Robert Morris University in Chicago including the positions as campus director, director of education, and director of development. She is an international consultant preparing U.S. professional for their overseas assignments. Dr. Baran's research interests and expertise include looping, student attitudes and achievement, charter schools, middle school education, higher education administration and access, and international family policy. She is the author of two books and is a national and international speaker at conferences. She is a member of the Board of Trustees to Robert Morris University. In addition, she is a Board member of several not-for-profit organizations.

Bruce Barnett is a Professor in the Educational Leadership and Policy Studies Department at the University of Texas at San Antonio. His scholarly interests include educational leadership preparation programs, novice school administrators, mentoring and coaching, and reflective practice. He engages in international research and program development, co-authoring books, researching mentoring/coaching programs, and presenting workshops in different countries. He co-directs the International School Leadership Development Network, which examines leadership for social justice and in high-need schools in different cultural contexts.

Jami Royal Berry is a clinical assistant professor at the University of Georgia and co-director of the UCEA Center for the International Study of Educational Leadership. Her research interests include leadership in high needs schools, leadership certification, the performance-based leadership model, and principals' perceptions. She has presented on these topics at conferences throughout the world. Berry has received grants to continue her work with professional learning communities and the study of leadership for high needs schools in international settings. She has also developed numerous educational leadership programs and served as a dissertation chairperson or committee member for over twenty doctoral students. Her graduates include local school leaders, system level leaders, and superintendents throughout the United States. Prior to her university service, Berry was a music teacher and elementary school administrator. She remains active in K–12 education through volunteering in schools and serving as a board member for several education organizations.

Lorenda Chisolm is a Central Office School Administrator in a large urban school district in Western New York with 15 years of experience in education. Dr.

Chisolm earned her Ed.D. in Educational Administration from the Department of Educational Leadership and Policy from the State University of New York at Buffalo. Dr. Chisolm's research examines successful school leadership practices, high needs schooling, social justice school leadership, and leadership decision-making around STEM curricula and implementation; contextualized from both a local and international setting.

Dr. Chisolm is a UCEA 2014–2016 Dr. Barbara L. Jackson Scholar, as well as the recipient of the Paul A. and Margaret E. Bacon Scholarship and the Gregory J. Dimitriadis Dean's Excellence Fund from the Graduate School of Education—State University of New York at Buffalo. She has also been named to Buffalo Business First 40 Under 40.

Sheryl Cowart Moss is a Clinical Associate Professor at Georgia State University where she directs Advanced Programs in Educational Leadership. She is a former high school principal and she has teaching experience in general and special education at all levels of P–12 schools. Dr. Cowart Moss is President of the Georgia Educational Leadership Faculty Association (GELFA), President Elect of the Council of Professors of Instructional Supervision (COPIS) and a site visitor for the Georgia Professional Standards Commission. She is also a Technical Assistance Consultant for the CEEDAR Center, a national grant project of the US-DOE's Office of Special Education Programs and a participant in the Council of Chief State School Officer's National Collaborative on Inclusive Principal Leadership. Her research interests include the aesthetics of leadership, particularly as they impact marginalized populations.

Lawrie Drysdale is an associate professor in Educational Leadership at the Melbourne Graduate School of Education, The University of Melbourne, and coordinator of the Master of Education (Educational Management). He has an extensive career in teaching, human resource development, lecturing and research career spans over forty years. His professional development activities include development, design and implementation of leadership programs for school administrators. Lawrie teaches in leadership, human resource management, marketing, school effectiveness and improvement, and learning communities. His research interests are in marketing in education (market orientation and brand management), and successful school leadership.

Lawrie has a long history of international collaboration where he has been engaged a several successful international projects. Currently he is a member of the International Successful School Principalship Project (ISSPP) and the International School Leadership Development Network (ILSDN). Both organisations include teams of international researchers who are investigating successful school leadership in a range of contexts in over 18 countries. This research has produced important findings on school leadership in different contexts and created models of successful school leadership. Lawrie is involved in consultancy work in the

Victorian school system including conducting government school reviews and independent school inspections, and involvement in a wide range of professional learning programs. He has published extensively in international and local journals.

Peryenthia L. Gore is a veteran educator originally from Chattanooga, Tennessee. She began her career in education as a high school English teacher and has served in multiple roles, most recently as an Assistant Principal. Peryenthia received her Doctorate of Education in Educational Leadership from Georgia State University. She is the proud mom of one son, Miles Kilpatrick. She currently shares her talents with students, teachers, and staff at a high school in the Atlanta Area.

Stephen L. Jacobson is a Distinguished Professor in the Graduate School of Education (GSE) at the University at Buffalo / State University of New York. He has served as the GSE's Associate Dean for Academic Affairs, Chair of the Department of Educational Leadership and Policy and Coordinator of Educational Administration programs.

His research interests include the reform of school leadership preparation and practice, and successful leadership in high poverty schools, most recently in New Zealand and Belize. In addition to numerous publications in some of the leading journals in the field, he has given invited keynote presentations around the world. He is a past President of the University Council for Educational Administration (UCEA) and the Association for Education Finance and Policy (AEFP). He is the lead editor of *Leadership and Policy in Schools* and was recently awarded a Fulbright Scholarship to teach Educational Leadership and Administration in Albania in spring 2019.

Wowek Sean Kearney is Associate Professor of Educational Leadership and Interim Dean of the College of Education and Human Development at Texas A&M University-San Antonio. As such, he oversees educational programming for aspiring educators, kinesiology majors, counselors, principals, and superintendents. Dr. Kearney has conducted training sessions for school board members, served as a regional director for principal certification, and led consortiums of central office administrators from across Texas. He has research interests in principal influence, change orientations, school culture and climate, and the confluence of administration, ethics, and emotionally intelligent leadership.

Fiona Longmuir (PhD) is a Lecturer in Educational Leadership at Monash University. Her doctoral research was completed at the University of Melbourne in 2017 and investigated principal leadership in two Victorian secondary schools that used innovative, student-centred approaches to transform their schools. Current research projects are investigating leadership for social cohesion and improving school systems. Fiona worked for over 15 years in Victorian government primary schools and held leadership positions for much of this time. For the past nine years, she has also worked as Senior Consulting Researcher – Director of Research in Innovative Professional Practice at Educational Transformations in Melbourne, Victoria. This role saw her lead and contribute to research projects that have investigated education systems, school effectiveness and school leadership across Australia and around the world.

Her research interests include school leadership, school culture, contextual influences (particularly concerning advantage differences and equity) and innovative approaches to student engagement. She has presented at Australian and international conferences and co-authored journal papers and book chapters.

Kieran McCrohan is a PhD candidate at The University of Melbourne studying educational leadership. Kieran's background is in primary education, completing a Bachelor of Education and Master of Education. Throughout his career, Kieran has held numerous leadership positions. These have included curriculum and pastoral leadership roles and he is currently the Head of Junior School at one of Melbourne's leading independent schools, Wesley College, Elsternwick. Kieran's educational philosophy seeks to develop active and compassionate learners who model empathy and open-mindedness to accept the perspective of others. He believes a holistic education offers students the greatest foundation for lifelong learning.

Nathern S. Okilwa is an Assistant Professor in the Department of Educational Leadership and Policy Studies at the University of Texas San Antonio. His research interests include educational and life outcomes of disadvantaged, underserved, or marginalized students (e.g., low SES, culturally and linguistically diverse, racial/ethnic minorities, refugees, and special education), school leadership in diverse school contexts, and educational policy. He is also engaged with consortiums of international school leadership researchers—International Successful School Principal Project and International School Leadership Development Network. Additionally, he is involved in local school district partnerships where he co-coordinates one of the master's level leadership cohort programs. He teaches and advises students in the master's and doctoral programs.

Cynthia Paes de Carvalho is an Assistant Professor at Catholic University of Rio de Janeiro (PUC-Rio) since 2008. PhD in Education concluded at Catholic University of Rio de Janeiro, PUC-Rio, Brazil (2004). Master's Degree in Education concluded at Getúlio Vargas Foundation at Rio de Janeiro, Brazil (1992). Extensive professional experience in the social area, particularly in education, worked as a research, project evaluation and public policies consultant for public and private social institutions. Since 2010 coordinates the research group GESQ—Management and Quality of Education. Advisor for masters and doctors in the area of educational and school management, sociology and education policy. Collaborates as a reviewer with several qualified journals in the area and for educational research project evaluation of Brazilian Research Agencies.

Ana Cristina Prado de Oliveira is an Adjunct Professor at Federal University of the State of Rio de Janeiro (UNIRIO). PhD in Education concluded at Catholic University of Rio de Janeiro, PUC-Rio (2015)—her thesis was awarded with Honor Mention in the 2016 Prize CAPES (National Center for Academic Research). Master's Degree concluded at Catholic University of Rio de Janeiro, PUC-Rio (2012). Graduated in Pedagogy at Federal University of Minas Gerais (2000) and had a specialization course in Piaget Theory and Practice at University of Campinas, Unicamp (2001). Worked in Basic Education for 17 years, as teacher, teachers' coordinator and tutor in Courses for teachers. Actually, is part of interinstitutional research groups (at UNIRIO, PUC—Rio and UFRJ) developing different projects about school leadership and educational policies. Her research in educational area involves the following topics: school leadership, management, school climate, assessment, student learning and public policies, having articles and book chapters published. The author also finished recently (2016) a Post-Doctoral Project (PDJ, CNPq).

Glady Van Harpen completed her Ph.D. in Leadership for Learning and the Advancement of Service through Cardinal Stritch University, in Milwaukee, Wisconsin. She earned a M.A.E. in secondary school administration from Northern Michigan University in Marquette, Michigan. She received a B.S. in natural resource management and secondary education teaching certification at the University of Wisconsin Stevens Point. Dr. Van Harpen is an Assistant Professor in the Department of Educational Leadership and Policy at the University of Wisconsin Oshkosh. Shas been involved in education and leadership for more than 25 years. Her experience includes work with early adolescents through adults in the public educational system. She has specialized teaching experiences in the juvenile corrections system, alternative high schools, and outdoor education. Additionally, she has assisted high school principals across the US, with leadership development, through a national non-profit corporation.

Noemi Waight is an Associate Professor of Science Education in the Department of Learning and Instruction in the Graduate School of Education at the University at Buffalo. Her research examines the design, development, implementation, adoption, and enactment of technological tools (e.g., computer-based models, bioinformatics tools, databases) in the context of central, reform-based, K–12 science teaching approaches. Two complimentary perspectives guide this research: First, she examines the enactment of technological tools by documenting the full cycle from design and development to actual implementation in science classrooms. Second, to fully understand the implications of the above cycle, her research seeks to elucidate the theoretical underpinnings of the Nature of Technology (NoT) as it pertains to K–12 science education, and empirically examine the factors, conditions, and agencies that impact and mediate enactment of technology in science education. More recently, Dr. Waight's work has evolved to examine the role of school leadership and STEM implementation in high needs schools locally and internationally, collaborating on research in Belize and Japan. Dr. Waight has served as Co-PI of a National Science Foundation grant: *Connected Chemistry as Formative Assessment*. She currently serves as an Associate Editor for *Journal of Research in Science Teaching*.

Made in the USA
Coppell, TX
10 September 2021

62138702R00122